RE-PRESENTING THE PAST

Re-Presenting the Past

Archaeology Through Text and Image

edited by

Sheila Bonde and Stephen Houston

Oxbow Books
Oxford and Oakville

Joukowsky Institute Publication 2

General series editor: Prof. John F. Cherry
Joukowsky Institute for Archaeology and the Ancient World
Brown University, Box 1837/60 George Street, Providence, RI 02912, USA

ISBN 978-1-78297-231-0

A catalogue record for this book is available from the British Library

Library of Congress Cataloging-in-Publication Data

Re-presenting the past : archaeology through text and image / edited by Sheila Bonde and
Stephen Houston.
    pages cm. -- (Joukowsky Institute publication ; 2)
  Includes bibliographical references and index.
  ISBN 978-1-78297-231-0
  1. Archaeology and history--Case studies. 2. Semiotics and archaeology--Case studies.
3. Archaeology and art--Case studies. I. Bonde, Sheila, author, editor of compilation. II.
Houston, Stephen D., author, editor of compilation. III. Title: Representing the past.
  CC77.H5R425 2013
  930.1--dc23
                                                   2013015071

This book is available direct from
Oxbow Books, Oxford, UK
(Phone: 01865-241249; Fax: 01865-794449)
and
The David Brown Book Company
PO Box 511, Oakville, CT 06779, USA
(Phone: 860-945-9329; Fax: 860-945-9468)

www.oxbowbooks.com

Index by Richard Bartholomew

Typeset by Queenston Publishing, Hamilton, Canada
Printed and bound in Great Britain by
Berforts Information Press

Contents

List of Figures

Notes on Contributors

Sheila Bonde is professor of History of Art and Architecture and professor of Archaeology at Brown University. Her research focuses on ritual and function in medieval architecture and archaeology, and issues of visual representation. Much of her research has been devoted to excavation and study of the monasteries of Saint-Jean-des-Vignes in Soissons and Notre Dame d'Ourscamp, and the charterhouse at Bourgfontaine (France). She has published *Fortress-Churches of Languedoc* and, with Clark Maines, *Saint-Jean-des-Vignes in Soissons: Approaches to its Architecture, Archaeology and History.*

Thomas Devaney, Assistant Professor of History at the University of Rochester, studies the late-medieval and early modern Mediterranean World, with particular interests in urban culture, frontier studies, and interfaith relations. He received his Ph.D. from Brown University and has published on the history of Castile, Venice, and Cyprus. He is currently completing a monograph entitled *No One Shall Wear Mourning: Urban Spectacle and the End of the Spanish Frontier.* His other ongoing research projects include articles on medieval concepts of race, memories of Crusade, and sixteenth-century pageants in Spain's North African outposts.

Barbara W. Fash is Director of the Corpus of Maya Hieroglyphic Inscriptions Program at the Peabody Museum, Harvard University and the Gordon R. Willey Laboratory for Mesoamerican Studies. An artist and museum professional, she has worked on sculpture documentation and conservation at the Maya site of Copan, Honduras since 1977, directed and co-directed several archaeology and cultural heritage projects, and curated exhibitions at the Peabody Museum and the Copan Sculpture Museum. Her academic interests and publications include Maya iconography, Precolumbian water management, archaeological illustration, plaster casts, heritage conservation, and 3-D scanning. She was awarded the Hoja de Laurel de Oro by Honduras (2008).

Diane Favro is a Professor of Architecture and Urban Design at UCLA. Professor Favro's research focuses on the urbanism of ancient Rome, archaeological historiography, women in architecture, and architectural history methodologies. Her publications include *Streets: Critical Perspectives on Public Space* (University of California Press, 1994; revised in Turkish 2007), *The Urban Image of Augustan Rome* (Cambridge University Press, 1996), award-winning websites such as the Digital Roman Forum, Digital Karnak, and Digital National Archive, as well as articles on Roman construction traffic, architectural laws and administration, and urban experience. She is Director of the UCLA Experiential Technologies Center and served as President of the national Society of Architectural Historians.

Stephen Houston teaches at Brown University, where he serves as Dupee Family Professor of Social Sciences. Holder of many grants and fellowships, including the MacArthur and Guggenheim, Houston is active in fieldwork and publishing projects, including continuing research on Maya aesthetics, urbanism, texts, and imagery.

Clark Maines is Kenan Professor of the Humanities and Professor of History of Art and Archaeology at Wesleyan University. His research examines medieval archaeology and ritual; water management; and history of construction practice. His work has engaged with excavation and study of the monasteries of Saint-Jean-des-Vignes in Soissons, Bourgfontaine and Notre Dame d'Ourscamp (France). He has published T*he Western Portal of Saint-Loup-de-Naud* and, with Shcila Bonde, *Saint-Jean-des-Vignes in Soissons: Approaches to its Architecture, Archaeology and History.*

Cassandra Mesick holds a Ph.D. in anthropological archaeology from Brown University. A museum specialist, she now serves as Curator of Global Indigenous Art at the Spencer Museum of Art, University of Kansas. Her doctoral research concerned architectural practices and building technologies of the ancient Maya.

Michael Shanks teaches at Stanford University, where he holds the Omar and Althea Dwyer Hoskins chair in Classical Archaeology. Prior teaching includes a Readership in archaeology at the University of Wales, Lampeter. His training was principally at the University of Cambridge, where he took his Ph.D. in 1992, his MA in 1983, and a BA in 1980. He also holds a Docentur position at the University of Göteborg. Founder of the Stanford Strategy Studio and former director of the Stanford Humanities Lab, Shanks has explored the first Greek cities in the Mediterranean, as well as early farming societies and their monuments in Wessex and Sweden. Other interests range from new models and stories of early agriculture to the first cities and empires, longterm social and cultural trends, and how much the modern world has in common with antiquity. A longstanding research focus is in the Roman borders of the north of England and Scotland. His books investigate debates about the character of the archaeological past, as explored in *ReConstructing Archaeology* (1987), *Social Theory and Archaeology* (1987), *Experiencing the Past* (1992), *Art and the Early Greek State* (1999) and *Theatre/Archaeology* (2001).

Sam Smiles is Programme Director for Art History and Visual Culture at the University of Exeter and Emeritus Professor of Art History at the University of Plymouth. He is an art historian who has written widely on British art from the eighteenth century to the present. His publications on art and antiquarianism include *The Image of Antiquity: Ancient Britain and the Romantic Imagination* (Yale University Press, 1994) and *Envisioning the Past: Archaeology and the Image* (Blackwell, 2005). He is currently a member of the Visualisation in Archaeology research project at the University of Southampton.

Timothy Webmoor works at the interface of Science and Technology Studies (STS) and archaeology. He researches how instruments, technologies and media impact the translation and assemblage of the past into evidence. He is a founding member of the Metamedia Lab at Stanford University, and has excavated in the western United States, Alaska, Britain, Sicily, and Teotihuacan, Mexico, where he conducted a long-term project on heritage sustainability. Currently, Tim is an Assistant Professor adjunct in Anthropology at the University of Colorado, Boulder.

Christopher Witmore is Associate Professor of Archaeology in the Department of Classical and Modern Languages and Literatures at Texas Tech University. He has worked on issues of landscape and time in Peloponnesus, Greece, and crafted new approaches to media and things in archaeology. Articles dealing with these concerns have appeared in *Archaeologies, Archaeological Dialogues, Visual Anthropology Review, Norwegian Archaeology Review, The Journal of Material Culture*, and *World Archaeology*.

Contributor Addresses

Sheila Bonde
Department of History of Art and Architecture
Brown University
Providence, RI 02912
sheila_bonde@brown.edu

Stephen Houston
Department of Anthropology
Brown University, Box 1921
Providence, RI 02912
Stephen_Houston@brown.edu

Thomas Devaney
Department of History
364 Rush Rhees Library
University of Rochester
Rochester, NY 14627
Devaney@iusb.edu

Barbara W. Fash
Director, Corpus of Maya Hieroglyphic Inscriptions and Gordon R. Willey
Laboratory for Mesoamerican Studies
Peabody Museum of Archaeology and Ethnology
Harvard University, 11 Divinity Avenue
Cambridge, MA 02138
bfash@fas.harvard.edu

Diane Favro
UCLA's Experiential Technologies Center
Office of Information Technology/Academic Technology Services
5308 Math Sciences Building
Box 951557, Mail Code 155705
Los Angeles, CA 90095-1557
dfavro@ucla.edu

Clark Maines
Department of Art History
Wesleyan University
Middletown, CT 06457
cmaines@wesleyan.edu

Cassandra Mesick
Spencer Museum of Art
University of Kansas
1301 Mississippi Street
Lawrence, KS 66045-7595
cmesick@ku.edu

Michael Shanks
Department of Classics
450 Serra Mall, Building 110
Stanford University
Stanford CA 94305-2145
Email: mshanks@stanford.edu
Website: http://michaelshanks.org, http://metamedia.stanford.edu/

Sam Smiles
University of Plymouth
Room 105, 6 Portland Villas, Drake Circus
Plymouth, Devon, PL4 8AA
ssmiles@plymouth.ac.uk

Timothy Webmoor
Department of Anthropology
University of Colorado
Campus Box 233 UCB
Boulder, CO 80309-0233
timothy.webmoor@colorado.edu

Christopher Witmore
Department of Classical and Modern Languages and Literatures
Foreign Languages Building
Texas Tech University
2910 18th
Lubbock, TX 79409-2071
christopher.witmore@ttu.edu

Re-Presenting Archaeology

Sheila Bonde and Stephen Houston

The archaeological past exists for us through intermediaries that vary widely in form and nature. Some are written works, the stories or descriptions about what the past was like, often to bold claims of truth or validity (Hodder and Hutson 2003). Others are visual, if frequently combined with writing. These consist of the drawings, paintings, photographs, powerpoints, or computer visualizations. As tools, these devices allow scholar and general audience alike to access past forms of human existence. At a more ambitious level, they purport to capture and revivify past realities through written or visual reconstructions of past ways of life. The essays in this book explore the means by which the archaeological past comes to us. All periods and geographic areas fall within the purview of this book, which examines various strategies through which material culture is digested and re-presented.

Representation in archaeology, either written or graphic, is a matter of choice and thus inherently subject to the times in which they exist (Molyneux 1997; Moser 1998; Jameson et al. 2003; Smiles and Moser 2005). A representation will accord with the background of the person creating that image, or the audience for which the image was intended. In this respect, archaeology is a discipline that can be studied much as Bruno Latour's work on the conduct and practice of "hard science" (Latour 1987): much that appears to be "self-evident" or "logical" is not; his more recent engagement with Actor-Network Theory suggests alternative ways of looking at interactions between things, people, and their representations (e.g., http://www.lancs.ac.uk/fass/centres/css/ant/antres.htm).

The topic of visual representation is rich, although with a history that varies greatly by region or specialty. Prominent archaeologists with training in drafting were among the first to explore the subject, as in Stuart Piggott's *Antiquity Depicted* (1978), who drew on the inspiration of Heywood Sumner's *Ancient*

Earthworks of Cranborne Chase (Cunliffe 1985). The nature of reconstruction as a means of displaying buildings goes back even further, to the interventions of Viollet-le-Duc (Viollet-le-Duc 1867–1870; Murphy 2000) and, earlier still, to engravings by Giovanni Piranesi. Textbooks of archaeological and forensic illustration are themselves charged with unwitting cultural and historical statements (Addington 1986; Adkins and Adkins 1989; Di Grazia 1991; Dillon 1985; Steiner 2005; Taylor 2000). Such images arise in part from contact with other modes of scientific illustration, which grapple with similar problems of aesthetics, clarity, and claims to veracity (Baigrie 1997; Blumenfeld-Kosinski 1990; Cazort et al. 1997; Dickenson 1998; Lynch and Woolgar 1990; Roberts and Tomlinson 1992).

The physical reproduction of the past at places like Williamsburg and, in Europe, "Heritage sites," involves decisions of comparable complexity (Handler and Gable 1997; Lowenthal 1996). Images of hominid evolution are among the most thoroughly canvassed, often from a feminist perspective, for what they reveal of attitudes about past and modern humans (Moser 1998; Wiber 1997). Finally, each region has its own, growing literature on archaeological representation, but, as yet, with relatively little, mutual contact (Baudez 1993). The sole exceptions are two, recent edited volumes. One is on archaeology and the humanities, with essays that span a far broader reach than visual representation (Jameson et al. 2003). The other is pioneering, but heavily focused on Europe and, in particular, the United Kingdom (Smiles and Moser 2005). The VIA workshops at the University of Southampton have engaged with a cross-regional investigation of visualization in archaeology (http://www.viarch.org.uk/).

Much of archaeology concerns itself with visual representation, the translation into images of what is viewed or understood in the field. Written representation—the preparation of monographs, marshalling of argument, jotting of field notes—forms its own category of study, susceptible to literary categorization by genre, plot, coherent narrative or trope, and to political and philosophical judgments about the varying weight of "authority" or "objectivity" (e.g., Bradley 2006; Hodder 1989, 1994, 1998, 2003; Joyce 2002; Pluciennik 1999). For both written and rendered materials, however, it is safe to say that prior views favoring "objectivity" as a detached, morally valid way of doing research (Daston and Galison 1992) have been replaced by an opposed set of dogmas: that subjectivity and ever-shifting interpretation lie at the heart of archaeology, that it is plainly wrong to impose one view or voice over others, especially as part of a past controlled by the academy, and that the subjective experience of archaeological sites is of comparable weight to clearly framed questions about them (Hodder 1989:269, 272, 2003:65–66).

The problem with such notions, which have genuine merit as goads to ethical reflection and well-honed study, is that they perceive, not so much additions to knowledge, as changes that are neither better nor worse than what came before. Through overstatement, they do not recognize improvements in representation as these have been influenced by evolving questions asked of evidence; they tend also to imply that all people interpreting or representing the past enjoy the same level of information, skill, talent, and insight (Bradley 2003:155). Any story or image is as good as another because of its value to the person proposing it. In their most extreme form, ideas of this sort are unpalatable to archaeologists who believe in excavating with control, taking and supervising advanced degrees in archaeology or discerning in current scholarship a store of greater knowledge than was available a century ago—namely, the perspective of any creditable professional. Ian Hodder (2003:60), the principal importer of post-modern theory in archaeology, himself admits that "it is not possible for large numbers of unskilled people to be involved in excavation itself."

In all likelihood, the divide between "objectivity" and "subjectivity" is specious on a cognitive level. It reflects an over-simplified dichotomy between the conscious and unconscious complexities of brain processing, that is, how the mind apprehends external objects, only to form its own identity through consideration of such objects. For archaeologists, the real issues are how claims are made and how they are to be evaluated. A further point is that a useful emphasis on subjectivity in archaeology—the positioning of the viewer and image-maker with respect to an external world—becomes disquieting when taken too far as a posture towards evidence. Strictly speaking, no past exists outside of the present. The present-day, subjective brain forges impressions of what a lost past might have been like. No dead person continues to think about these matters, and impressions of antiquity mutate over time, as they are reshaped in different minds: in the jargon of our age, "[o]ur knowledge of the Other is always mediated by many factors, not the least the conceptual language we use and apply to other cultures…[and o]ur brush with alterity may inform or even transform us" (Nelson 2000:3). This means that there can be no one past but, rather, a plurality of them.

Yet one provocative book suggests that, since no real past exists, or rather, no past removed from constant reinvention, the preservation or maintenance of archaeological sites is a wrong-headed pursuit (Holtorf 2005:130–135). It also asserts that popular concepts of prehistory lie on equal footing with appraisals by scholars. Perhaps the inadvertent value of such statements, irresponsible and anti-intellectual as they may be, is that they take archaeologists to the edge of a cliff from which few will jump. Ultimately, most of us—other than those discouraging conservation or choosing to focus academically on the Maya pyramid at Epcot Center in Florida—affirm that what is said or depicted should derive from reasoned evidence and argument and that, if rightly presented, these two elements reveal more about the past than was known before, as conditioned by the questions to which representations respond (Fagan and Feder 2007).

Still, there are benefits to grasping traditions of, in this case, visual representation as the sum of decisions and practices over time, sometimes with considered goals in mind, more often as a conduit for unconscious or indefensible attitudes. Whatever their intent, these practices attempt to impose order and draw conclusions from observations that are seldom uniform. They also pertain directly to how archaeologists learn their craft and react to precedent through small acts of rebellion or innovation (Bradley 1997; Dillon 1985:4–5). Such a history is worth studying, implying as it does continual change and development, and reflecting in broader scope a set of varied intellectual trends and political needs (e.g., Dietler 1994:599; Moser 1998:6–7; Piggott 1978:7), some nefarious or conflicted (Halle 2005:100–101).

The present volume began as a seminar "Re-Presenting the Past: Archaeology through Image and Text," co-taught by the editors, Sheila Bonde and Stephen Houston. With twelve undergraduate and graduate students, we explored a range of issues, including the notions of objectivity and subjectivity, the particular challenges of "writing archaeology" as well as the ethical responsibilities involved in recording and in representing human groups. We examined the imaging of nations and ethnic groups, as well as the strategies for recording sites and landscapes. We compared fixed and streamed images of photography and video, approaches to representing buildings and objects, the problems and potential of Virtual Reality, avatars and simulations, and, in our last class, the opportunities for historical re-presentation at historic sites in a session entitled, "Archaeology as Tourism and Theme Park." Our students produced research papers and graphic representations. We encouraged professional writing by telling them that the two best papers, if acceptable, would be published as part of the conference volume. Casey Mesick's essay on Piedras Negras and Tom Devaney's study of festival routes in Jaén are the result of this incentive.

Most of the other essays in this volume are the result of a symposium organized in conjunction with the seminar. That symposium (which took place during an epic ice storm in mid-March) hosted scholars from a wide range of disciplines and backgrounds, united in their expertise in various aspects of archaeological representation. Three papers from the symposium have not been included in the present volume. Larry Coben demonstrated how recent developments in architectural software provide new ways to analyze the construction, site layout, access, and movement through prehistoric sites and buildings. He used digital and virtual reality reconstructions to investigate the monumental Inka site of Incallajta, Bolivia. Hsin-Mei Agnes Hsu examined a set of wall paintings found in a Buddhist grotto in northwestern Xinjiang, modern Chinese Central Asia. By treating the images as ethnographic documents, Agnes re-presented a lost culture that once flourished along the Silk Road. Brad Johnson of Second Story presented the visually engaging Theban Mapping Project. Since 1978, the project has been working to prepare a comprehensive archaeological database of the Valley of the Kings and the entire Theban Necropolis. With its robust content management tools for the nearly 5,000 photographs and illustrations, maps, and bibliographic resources, glossaries and timelines, the site aims to serve researchers as a repository for active fieldwork, and as a dynamic publication system for academic and general audiences. Our keynote speaker, David Macaulay, also gave an entertaining look at the representational strategies behind his popular books where the castle, cathedral and other buildings and objects have been creatively represented.

The present volume, then, brings together nine papers, six of which were presented at the symposium (Bonde and Maines, Fash, Favro, Houston, Smiles and Witmore), two of which were student papers from the seminar (Devaney and Mesick), and one of which was invited afterward (Shanks and Webmoor). Two papers explore the classical past: Witmore on Greek maps and Favro on representations of ancient Rome. Two engage with medieval visualizations: Bonde and Maines on medieval monasteries and Devaney on the festivals of medieval Jaén. Three treat the Maya: Houston's paper on Mayan iconographies, Mesick on Piedras Negras, and Fash on the Copan hieroglyphic stairway. Smiles' paper treats the imaging by eighteenth-century antiquarians of British history, from ancient to early modern, and Shanks and Webmoor use a variety of examples, including the antiquarian and the Mayan.

The first three papers take on issues of visualization and self-imaging. Sam Smiles looks at the infancy of attempts to represent the past, especially those images produced in the eighteenth and nineteenth centuries. Rather than see these early illustrations as awkward first steps in the development of archaeological illustration, he restores to them something of the complex milieu that brought them into being. Debates about the value of illustration within the antiquarian community show that scholars were keenly aware of the utility of images. This desire, in turn, needs to be seen within broader understandings of the relationship between images and the dissemination of scientific knowledge and the quest for objectivity in notation. In complete contrast, contemporary art theory emphasized the place of the imagination when painting history. As a result, competent artists could find themselves torn between these two competing understandings of how the past should be approached. Smile's paper explores a variety of case studies in which artists illustrated Britain's past, from the time of Stonehenge to the high middle ages. Sheila Bonde and Clark Maines explore the ways in which medieval monasteries have been represented in modern scholarship and the ways in which those communities represented themselves through written texts and material presentations such as seals and plans. Rather than trace an historical survey in this article, they propose two genres of monastic representation: the *panoptic*—that is, an image or a text that aims at a comprehensive view of the monastery or of monastic life, and the *synecdochal*—one in which a portion of the monastery (like the church) stands for the whole. To date there has been little consideration of how scholars, artists, architects, and the public see and reproduce the ancient Maya of Mexico and Central America through fixed and fluid imagery. Stephen Houston's paper examines several dimensions of such evolving practices, including the reductive depiction of objects, buildings, and archaeological deposits, the population of images with human narrative, and reconstructions and consolidations that create telegenic images for tourists. These images conform to overt models of "acceptable" professional practice yet often derive from unconscious decisions by previous generations: what is seen replicates that which others have seen, in a regress of vision that needs correction and reworking.

The next two papers engage with issues of recording. Barbara Fash's paper uses the Copan Hieroglyphic Stairway project as a starting point for a discussion of the ways in which photographs from nineteenth-century excavations can aid in the reconstruction of a Mayan inscription. The process has also engaged the contemporary local community to reflect on their past. Cassandra Mesick's paper describes the process of mapping the Classic period Maya site of Piedras Negras through ArcGIS and computer animation software. She then describes efforts to use geospatial data to reconstruct elite and non-elite social spaces.

The four final essays raise questions about the function of representations in current archaeological practice. Michael Shanks and Timothy Webmoor shift emphasis away from the representational function of visual media to consider its "political economy." For them, the process of archaeology is that of crafting the material remains of the past into mediations intelligible to present-day work. Thomas Devaney takes the textual account of Christmas, 1492 festivals in the Spanish town of Jaén. By mapping the festival routes, Devaney directs our attention to the active role played by the architecture of the town. He argues for a spatially-sensitive reading of the ways in which medieval pageants and processions were viewed and experienced. Christopher Witmore explores the inherent tension between maps as flat projections of the material world and necessary modes of archaeological documentation and visualization. He compares and contrasts the creation and use of mapping, from those created by antiquarians to those compiled by nineteenth-century military geographers to maps in the hands of contemporary survey archaeologists. Diane Favro's essay, "To Be or Not To Be in Past Spaces" focuses attention on the potential for environmental experiences such as Second Life. As modern designers seek to create ever more realistic artificial, alternative worlds, archaeologists are appropriating their tools and expressing greater interest in experiential research. Explorations of "being in past spaces" rely not only on physical models, drawn reconstructions, and dioramas, but increasingly on immersive virtual-reality simulations replete with sounds and movement. Her essay engages with both the established field of experimental archaeology, as well as newer archaeologies of corporality, anthropology of the senses, and other exploratory categories.

The field of archaeological representation is a rich one, and this volume, of course, is not—and does not pretend to be—comprehensive. Some of the topics explored in the seminar and symposium are not touched, or are only examined in a summary way. The ethics of representation is treated briefly by several authors in this volume, but merits further study. As archaeologists, inevitably, we destroy the context of our study as we excavate. Recording is thus an ethical imperative. Another seminar, another symposium may be necessary.

— 2 —

Imaging British History: Patriotism, Professional Arts Practice, and the Quest for Precision

Sam Smiles

This paper engages with the reflexivity of archaeological image-making, its sensitivity to modes of representing the past and its critical self-awareness. It does so, however, not by examining contemporary practice in archaeological representation but by considering the self-consciousness within the antiquarian project of the eighteenth and early nineteenth centuries. This may appear paradoxical, for so deep-seated is the knock-down image of the antiquary— the credulous snapper-up of unconsidered trifles, lacking both the wit and the learning to write elegant prose or contribute to serious historical study— that any attribution to such a figure of a self-conscious concern about the imaging of the past seems misplaced. Yet sensitivity to the problematics of the image contributed to the work that some notable antiquaries undertook and, on this basis, we should be cautious about simple progressivist accounts that would only include antiquarian illustration as the hesitant and faltering first steps leading to the deployment of archaeological imagery today. Instead, it is more productive to review antiquarian use of the image in terms of the debates that animated it. The antiquaries' engagement with modes of depiction was marked by many of the concerns that still preoccupy archaeological illustration: How shall the past be known? What are the limits of illustrative accuracy? What would constitute an unmediated visual presentation of data? How should text relate to image? Can knowledge be crystallized in graphic representation?

Antiquarian illustration in Britain from about 1750 to 1850 developed a rich array of imaging procedures: scale models, engravings, watercolors, and oil paintings. However, rather than provide a chronological survey, with an implicit evolutionary narrative, the account that follows is ordered around four key concepts whose concerns may be regarded as constants in archaeological illustration: making and disseminating the image; modes of illustration; cultural expectations and the reception of the image; aesthetics versus scholarship. Together, these considerations underline the extent to which every attempt at the disinterested production of the image is in fact compromised by its position within a complex web of technical and academic possibilities.

As a starting point it is worth recalling that the eighteenth century should take the credit for a major epistemic shift in historiographical method: the use of images to investigate antiquity. In one sense we may regard this as contributing to a Baconian enterprise, substituting for textual authority a careful working though of material data. For the enterprise to succeed the extant remains of antiquity had to be accurately recorded, allowing scholars to assess any conclusions drawn from them. Images were therefore mobilized as evidence at one remove; they functioned as portable data banks aiding and abetting antiquarian scholarship. In Britain, at least, this antiquarian turn to the image owed an intellectual debt to the sciences. The Royal Society had long supported the idea of accurate recording as a means of disseminating knowledge, including prints in its *Philosophical Transactions*, while individual publications such as Robert Hooke's *Micrographia* (1665) had helped demonstrate the value of the illustrated account. It should be noted that Hooke and others in the Royal Society collected engravings and were interested in devising improved reprographic techniques.

Formally re-established in 1718, the Society of Antiquaries promoted visual records as a contribution to scholarship and specified the importance of producing engravings of antiquities to disseminate antiquarian research via high-quality images. (Evans 1956:58–60; Myrone 2007:99–121; Nurse 2007:199–225). In much the same way as the Royal Society prioritized the collecting of accurate empirical data from which valid scientific inferences could be drawn, so the Society of Antiquaries undertook to illustrate scrupulously the objects and monuments within its remit. William Stukeley, the Society's first Secretary, wrote that, "without drawing and designing the study of Antiquities ... is lame and imperfect."[1] Many antiquaries could draw, some of them very well indeed, a few enjoyed fruitful relations with professional artists and one, James Douglas, was an active picture-dealer as well (Jessup 1975). Of course, an interest in the arts was expected of a gentleman and drawing was a social accomplishment; but those antiquaries who argued for the research potential of images were thinking about the utility of representation in ways that no amateur would have promoted.

---

1. Society of Antiquaries of London, SAL MS 268, p. 2. This is Stukeley's comment in his copy of the minutes and was inserted some time after 1726.

The Society of Antiquaries published *Vetusta Monumenta* from 1747 and *Archaeologia* from 1770, both of which used engravings to impart reliable empirical information. As with their scientific colleagues, the antiquaries were interested in the distinctive imaging possibilities of different engraving techniques and they made conscious use of the options available to them. Line engraving was a skilled art, best handled by a trained professional engraver. The Society first employed George Vertue for that purpose and after his death in 1756 turned to James Basire and his sons. The illustrations provided by line engraving were not only easily legible but, in the circumstances of the later eighteenth century, were seen as conferring on any monument so illustrated the same prestige associated with classical remains. The line engravings published in these articles, and especially those produced in the 1790s for the Society's large-scale individual volumes dedicated to English cathedrals, used what we might call the rhetoric of the incised line to assert the importance of what they depicted.

Etching, on the other hand, was a technique that any competent draughtsman could master: using an etching needle on the wax coating of the plate was very similar to the practice of drawing. Etching was the technique routinely adopted by John Carter, the Society of Antiquaries' first official draughtsman, in his own publications (e.g., *Views of Ancient Buildings* [1786–1793]). His colleague, James Douglas, also etched but chose also to make use of the relatively new technique of aquatint for the illustrations in his account of Saxon graves, *Nenia Britannica* (1793), introducing a more textured effect closer to watercolor wash.

Thought was also given to how images should be presented. In 1786 the Director of the Society of Antiquaries, Richard Gough had written with some passion of the lost years in which the fabric of mediaeval England had been allowed to crumble away unrecorded: "Had the remains of ancient buildings been more attended to, we should before now have seen a system of Gothic architecture in its various æras: we should have all its parts reduced to rules; their variations and their dates fixed together" (Gough 1768:xx). In 1794 Gough wrote to John Carter with reference to the latter's *Ancient Sculpture and Painting* (1780–1786) and noted that, "you seem to be making a Dictionary of Gothic Architecture, instead of a System which you should do in chronological order" (Crook 1995:67). Carter's next publication, *Ancient Architecture of England* (1795:Vol. I), used its engravings to group architectural parts and ornamental features together to show typologies of form. This use of composite plates, a technique borrowed ultimately from illustrated works of natural history, produced an understanding of stylistic evolution that could not otherwise have been achieved (Smiles 2000).

In the eighteenth century the relationship of image to data had become a particularly hot topic in medical illustration, as a sequence of anatomical atlases demonstrated different possibilities of what might constitute a "truthful" likeness: for example, whether to illustrate one individual cadaver as it existed uniquely on the dissecting table or to show instead the typical body, as a synthesis of multiple dissections. And beyond this, debate ensued as to how the "grammar" of the engraved line could be made to signify both bone and soft tissue or whether other engraving methods (mezzotint, for example, which was a less linear technique) were better suited to the human body. What these examples indicate is that those who commissioned or used images were acutely aware of their mediating function and how knowledge was encoded by different techniques. The engraver associated with many of these medical atlases was Jan van Rymsdyk (or John Rymsdyk as he anglicized his name). In 1778 he published *Museum Britannicum*, an illustrated guide to the collections in the British Museum, which contained a lengthy disquisition on the relationship between knowledge and illustration, concluding thus:

> ...as this Work is to consist Chiefly of Figures, there is no need I think of a great deal of Writing. Engraved Figures accompanied with a few Words, are preferable to those bulky Works of Authors, where there are but a few bad Figures, or perhaps none, for a description of a Figure, in writing, will never depict so strong an Idea on the Mind, as a true Representation of an Object in Drawing...(Rymsdyk and Rymsdyk 1778:xi).

Rymsdyk's belief in the engraving as a communicative device was widely shared. Interest in the image and its relationship to knowledge circulated easily in a small world of social and intellectual contacts. From the 1780s the Royal Society, the Royal Academy of Arts, and the Society of Antiquaries were all housed in Somerset House on the north bank of the Thames. It was possible, like the anatomist William Hunter, to belong to all three societies and to work proficiently, as he did, to advance the study of Greek and Saxon coins as well as researching anatomy. He was elected to Fellowship of the Royal Society in 1767, to the Society of Antiquaries in 1768 and was made Professor of Anatomy at the Royal Academy the same year. Precisely because intellectual inquiry was broadly based, developments in reprographic techniques were not restricted to separate disciplines.

This self-consciousness about the recording of data and the power of images to constitute a form of knowledge allowed the antiquaries to treat illustration as a form of research. James Douglas referred to the detail recorded in his aquatinted plates as "the facts here established" (Douglas 1793:94–95). John Carter likewise insisted that his drawings had resisted the stylistic mannerism of contemporary artists. In an essay published in 1803 he declared that his drawings were designed "not alone to please the eye...but to give information to the rising generation of Antiquaries and Architectural Professors." (Carter 1803:106–107). He was fastidious about recording exactly what he saw, including mutilations and losses, and refusing to deviate from the record.

But, of course, images also possess the power not simply to record but to invent and, as such, to attempt the retrieval of cultures that have vanished. We accept that contemporary imaging techniques offer a multitude of possibilities, as new technical advances allow the researcher to devise fresh approaches to the problem of visualizing the past. Drawing inferences from the surviving material record, structures can be rebuilt, spaces repopulated, individuals dressed and ornamented in a bid to simulate the appearance of a vanished world. What possibilities were on offer in the eighteenth and early nineteenth centuries and how were they deployed? In what follows I will restrict myself to a consideration of images that attempted to envisage the early history of Britain. The main thrust of my remarks will be to show that all attempts to represent the past in this period, irrespective of any desire to found them on sound archaeological knowledge, were always and inevitably caught up in wider contexts, chief among them being contemporary considerations about national identity.

Initially, however, it is important to remember that the very possibility of bringing the past to life in the eighteenth century was frustrated by contemporary art theory. Sir Joshua Reynolds, the President of the Royal Academy, intent on dignifying the painter's profession as a cultivated pursuit, insisted that artistic representation was always more than mere technical skill. Imitation was always, therefore, subservient to invention. Anyone could be taught to make an accurate copy; what mattered in a work of art was intellectual awareness and creative imagination. In his Fourth Discourse of 1771, Reynolds explicitly recommended the artist to avoid "minuteness and particularity" and insisted that the history painter should "deviate from vulgar and strict historic truth" (quoted in Wark 1975:59).

To understand what this meant in practice for the historicist imaging of antiquity, we can compare two paintings, both exhibited in 1787. They represent two opposed solutions to the problem of recreating the past and so throw light on the ways in which academic thinking influenced the representation of vanished epochs. In James Barry's *King Lear weeping over the Dead Body of Cordelia*, (Figure 2.1) Reynolds' requirements are very much in play. Barry's painting was produced for the new commercial venture known as the Shakespeare Gallery, which was established by the alderman and entrepreneur John Boydell in London in 1786. Boydell commissioned the best contemporary artists to memorialize Shakespeare's achievement in paintings, exhibited in the eponymous gallery from 1789 and also reproduced as engravings to be sold to subscribers from 1791 to 1802. Barry's picture was not therefore

Figure 2.1   James Barry, King Lear weeping over the Dead Body of Cordelia (1786–1787), oil
on canvas, 269.2 x 367 cm, Tate.

intended as any direct contribution to British history *sensu stricto*, but Shakespeare's rather hazily indicated chronological period of remote antiquity did
require a plausible mise-en-scène for Lear and the other dramatis personae.
Barry places the protagonists in front of a megalithic landscape (the enclo-
sures on the hill behind and on the promontory in the distance), drawing on
the image of a restored Stonehenge circulating in contemporary antiquarian
accounts. As recommended by academic precept, this is an approximation to
a past epoch with the trilithons in the background deployed merely to signify
Britain's earliest history. By Reynolds' standards Barry correctly avoids any
attempt to give his figures anything "particular" connected to the knowledge
he might have derived from classical accounts of the Britons. Had he done so,
"vulgar and strict historical truth" would have infected his painting.

    In contrast, Benjamin West's *Institution of the Order of the Garter* (Figure
2.2) flaunts its research into minute particulars. West had already crossed
swords with Reynolds about the provision of accurate details in paintings
and offered a radical alternative to the older artist's notions of what history
painting might be. Here, rather than Barry's vague gesturing at antiquity,
West attempts to conjure up a precise historical moment. This picture is one
of eight large canvases West painted for George III's Audience Chamber in

Windsor Castle depicting the reign of Edward III and the establishment of the Order of the Garter. In this picture West went to considerable trouble to make use of medieval manuscript illuminations and he studied armor and accoutrements in the royal collections to recreate the world of Edward III (Greenhouse 1985:178–191). It is very probably the most diligent historicizing picture of the whole eighteenth century and nothing like it was to be seen again until the 1820s.

From our point of view, looking back to this moment in the 1780s, Barry's confection, although in line with contemporary art theory, is not to be taken seriously as a recreation of the past. Yet West's, in its explicit rejection of what Reynolds promoted, seems prophetic of our modern attempts to use archaeological evidence to reconstruct a lost culture. Certainly, West's picture could be seen at the time as attempting an antiquarian approach, although John Carter, the Society of Antiquaries' former draughtsman, viciously attacked it, some twenty years later, for not being accurate enough (Smiles 2000:47–49).

While much divides these two pictures, what unites them is also noteworthy, for it reminds us that the circumstances in which the past is recuperated are important, too. Both of these paintings were, in fact, produced as

Figure 2.2   Benjamin West, *The Institution of the Order of the Garter* (1787), oil on canvas, 287 x 448.3 cm, The Royal collections © Her Majesty Queen Elizabeth II.

emblems of national pride at a critical moment in English history when British imperial ambitions had just received a massive check. Nine years before these pictures were painted, and reflecting on the worsening situation in America, Horace Walpole had written: "Our empire is falling to pieces; we are relapsing to a little island. In that state, men are apt to imagine how great their ancestors have been…the few, that are studious, look into the memorials of past time; nations, like private persons, seek lustre from their progenitors" (Lewis 1937:117). George III's patronage of Benjamin West can be readily understood in this light as a reassertion of the British monarchy, with Edward III, as its shining exemplar, in the wake of the loss of the American colonies. All educated visitors to Windsor would know that Edward III had conquered Britain's oldest enemy, France, and had successfully defeated rebellious tendencies among his subjects. The Shakespeare Gallery, too, where Barry's picture was exhibited, was explicitly designed as a patriotic venture through which the national school of painting would be encouraged. Its concentration on Shakespeare necessarily spoke to notions of English identity as vested in the nation's greatest playwright.

It might seem that this class of historical re-enactments should be sharply distinguished from the more scholarly use of illustrations I discussed in the first part of this paper. Yet, for all their apparent differences I think it would be helpful to think of the distinction between these two classes of image as one of degree not kind. John Carter, for instance, for all his rectitude in seeking to make only the most scrupulous and accurate records of mediaeval England was a zealous promoter of its pre-eminence in the middle ages, especially under Edward III whose achievements represented a high water mark of European civilization. Carter's project was thus to use graphic accuracy as a means of waking up his contemporaries to the glories of their cultural patrimony: it was only through a precise understanding that the cultural achievement of medieval England could make its proper impact. More generally, the Society of Antiquaries treated research into the past as a sort of patriotic duty, which would clarify the course of British history, so helping the public towards a better-founded conception of the origins of British society and the nature of national identity. What I am suggesting, therefore, is that no image could provide an unmediated encounter with the past but inevitably carried with it the traces of the wider epistemic contexts in which it operated.

The image of British antiquity promoted in Samuel Rush Meyrick and Charles Hamilton Smith's *Costume of the Original Inhabitants of the British Islands* (Figure 2.3) provides a final example (Meyrick and Smith 1815). In approach, it occupies the middle ground between the publications of the Society of Antiquaries and individual paintings exhibited at the Royal Academy. Both authors were antiquaries, specializing in research into arms and

Figure 2.3   Robert Havell, after Charles Hamilton Smith, "A Briton of the Interior," aquatint
engraving, in Samuel Rush Meyrick and Charles Hamilton Smith, *The Costume of
the Original Inhabitants of the British Islands* (1815). Yale Center for British Art,
Paul Mellon Collection.

armor, but this publication was a deliberate attempt to reach out beyond the
scholarly world. To place their findings before a wide audience they opted
to use hand-colored aquatint and they employed a specialist artist, Robert
Havell, to produce these appealing images. Costume books were in vogue in

the 1810s, and aquatint was the technique of choice for them: it simulated the look of watercolors and was relatively straightforward to hand-color. The resulting volume could therefore combine a learned letterpress with images that were very easy on the eye. Meyrick and Smith's book ranges from the tribes inhabiting Britain at the coming of the Romans through the barbarian invasions to the early medieval period. Although modern archaeologists may wince at their errors in dating or their bringing together of objects from different eras in one image, in a sense this is not the point. Instead, we should pay attention to the way that the image takes the fragmentary archaeological knowledge in the book's letterpress and makes a convincing whole from it. The doubts, contestations, and contradictions of antiquarian debate are replaced by an image that allows the past to become tangible, because its representation offers such a convincing simulacrum. Where possible the authors guarantee the verisimilitude of the presentation by demonstrating the relationship of this represented past to actual excavated data, taking material from different sites and uniting them in one pictorial presentation. Again, whether or not the relationship as shown is accurate, judged by today's understanding, as a method this is similar to today's imaging procedures when building up a picture of the past, piecing together archaeological finds to reconstitute a culture.

Here, however, it behooves us to pay attention to the semiotic register of the image. The deployment of archaeological data in representations may be considered to exemplify what Roland Barthes called the "effect of the real" (Barthes 1986:141–148). Here what is fundamentally a rhetorical presentation—in other words a form of persuasion—is made convincing by its exploitation of details. For Barthes, these concrete details—in this instance representations of archaeological finds—are presented as though they had escaped the normal semiotic function of the image, whose signifying function we usually accept as a species of artifice. With these concrete details the gap between sign and object is closed down because the sign ceases to be read *as* a sign. As a result these details seem to anchor the representation in verifiable contexts, and thus to offer unmediated meaning. Yet their ultimate purpose is still rhetorical; through their very concreteness they signify to the spectator "this is reality" and thus secure the validity of the image as a whole. Detail, in other words, has a role to play as a rhetorical device within the narrative structure, and it is conditioned by it.

If Barthes is correct, until we understand the aims of the reconstruction as a whole, or think about its ideological context, we are missing the organizational matrix within which these details do their work. When reviewing a work like Hamilton and Smith's, geared to a wide readership, that matrix must include the authors' ambitions, their intellectual preconceptions, the standing of archaeological knowledge at the time within society, and wider considerations about the literate public's attitude towards antiquity and the presumed relationship, if any, between ancient and modern culture. On turning these pages in the 1810s one would find that early Britain was no degraded episode in the national history but an epoch of some refinement in agriculture and metal work, peopled by what we could call the British noble savage. Appearing at the moment the endgame in the Napoleonic wars reached its climax, British cultural, economic, and military superiority may have seemed to possess deeper roots than was previously imaginable (Smiles 1994).

The transition from antiquarian practices in the eighteenth and nineteenth centuries to the emergence of archaeology proper coincided with the rise of photography and the mechanical reproduction of images. Many of the graphic media hitherto used to record finds or locations (etching, engraving, aquatint) were replaced with others. That said, the importance of making drawings on site remained uncontested as part of excavation procedure, while diagrammatic illustration in excavation reports and other publications could direct attention to specific features that were difficult to articulate via photographic means. By comparison with their antiquarian predecessors, these newer practices of graphic representation seem more accurate, insofar as the mode of presentation is often a rigorously applied schematic notation. But, of course, as Stuart Piggott insisted, all representational systems employ a grammar of marks, lines, symbolic conventions and the like, relying for communication on a shared language which is fundamentally artificial (Piggott 1965:165–176). The benefit of reviewing antiquarian imaging practices is that they offer a clear testing ground for Piggott's hypothesis, precisely because subsequent changes in representational modes have made the artificiality of past representation immediately apparent.

How then should we assess the graphic languages that have replaced older imaging regimes? If all systems of representation are reliant on a shared understanding of visualization, one immediate task is to attempt a rigorous self-scrutiny of the methods used to represent archaeological discovery today. For example, most reconstructions attempt to present the appearance of a site in its heyday and operate in ways that all painters working since the Renaissance would understand. One-point vanishing perspective privileges the individual observer and organizes the visual field into one experiential moment. Yet, with the advent of new digital technology, the possibility exists to supplement or replace these perspectival techniques with multiple vantage points, a mobile gaze and transitions in scale. The customary resolved image, offering the best interpretation of what the material record contains, can be replaced by a visual array whose presentation allows the gaps in that record to signify, makes a virtue of indeterminacy and encourages continual amendment and revision. The resultant image could thus become a field of possibilities, a fractured site, capable of putting conflicting interpretations of data into visual dialogue.

The second element of encoding, the wider epistemic structures that may contain archaeological research, are inevitably easier to detect in hindsight, when the emphases and orientations of representation are placed within this larger frame. As I have indicated, in the eighteenth and early nineteenth centuries the place of the past in the life of the nation was a key consideration for any representative practice, whether in antiquarian or fine art contexts. While these concerns are themselves historically specific, we should not assume that the relationship between archaeology and its imaging processes today is innocent of similar constraints. Irrespective of its scholarly underpinning, what is chosen for representation and how it is represented can never be entirely disinterested decisions. Likewise, the image's power to tidy up the past and to offer a coherent picture of antiquity has an ideological potential. The intriguing question that this raises is whether or not the contexts for our more recent representational practices can be acknowledged and accommodated within the operation of the image itself.

— 3 —

Re-Presenting the Monastery:
From Ordo to Google Earth

SHEILA BONDE AND CLARK MAINES

Monastic life and the architectural frame that contained and shaped that life have long been objects of study for archaeologists, historians, and art historians. It is therefore surprising that very little attention has been paid to the various modes of representing monasteries. The present article is a preliminary investigation into the ways in which monks and nuns have sought to represent themselves—to themselves and to others—and the ways in which modern scholarship has in turn represented the monastic past.

Rather than trace an historical survey in this article, we will instead examine two genres of monastic representation: the *panoptic*—that is, an image or a text that aims at a comprehensive view of the monastery or of monastic life, and the *synecdochal*—one in which a portion of the monastery (like the church) stands for the whole.

One of the most common panoptic representations of the monastery is the site plan. Such plans normally present a record of buildings on the site, either the entirety of surviving buildings, or those that existed at a specific moment. A comparison of two site plans from our excavation project at Saint-Jean-des-Vignes in Soissons, France, can illustrate the two alternatives. The first (Figure 3.1a) records the extant portions of all remaining structures on the site regardless of their date of construction. The next (Figure 3.1b) interprets those extant buildings to represent what we believe to have been the state of the monastery as it was in 1375, at the close of its rebuilding during the Gothic period.

Monastic site plans like those for Saint-Jean are two-dimensional abstractions that must inevitably distort the reality of lived experience on any

monastic site. Figure 3.1a represents the monastery in a state that no monk
ever saw. All site plans necessarily flatten varied circulation levels onto a single horizontal plane and reshape the natural topography as well as the cultural landscape. Site plans like Figure 3.1b present an interpretative record
of a state of a particular site as seen through the mind(s) of the recorder(s).
This one presents our hypothesis about the mid-fourteenth century monas-

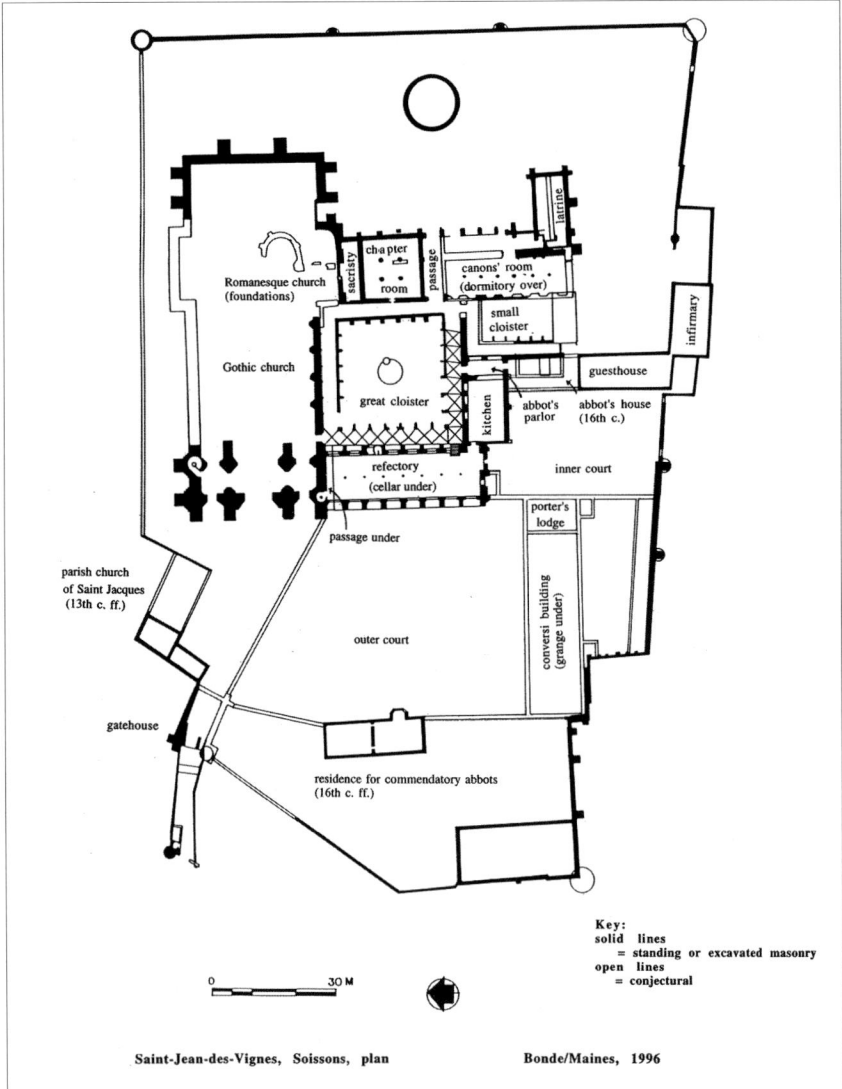

Figure 3.1a Site plan of Saint-Jean-des-Vignes showing all structures.

tery, with evidence elicited from excavated foundations, associated ceramic material and textual descriptions of the monastery. Other researchers may disagree, or may point to other forms of evidence to argue for a different dating or combination of buildings. Plans like this one are, thus, contested re-presentations of selected aspects of monastic existence, while necessarily omitting others.

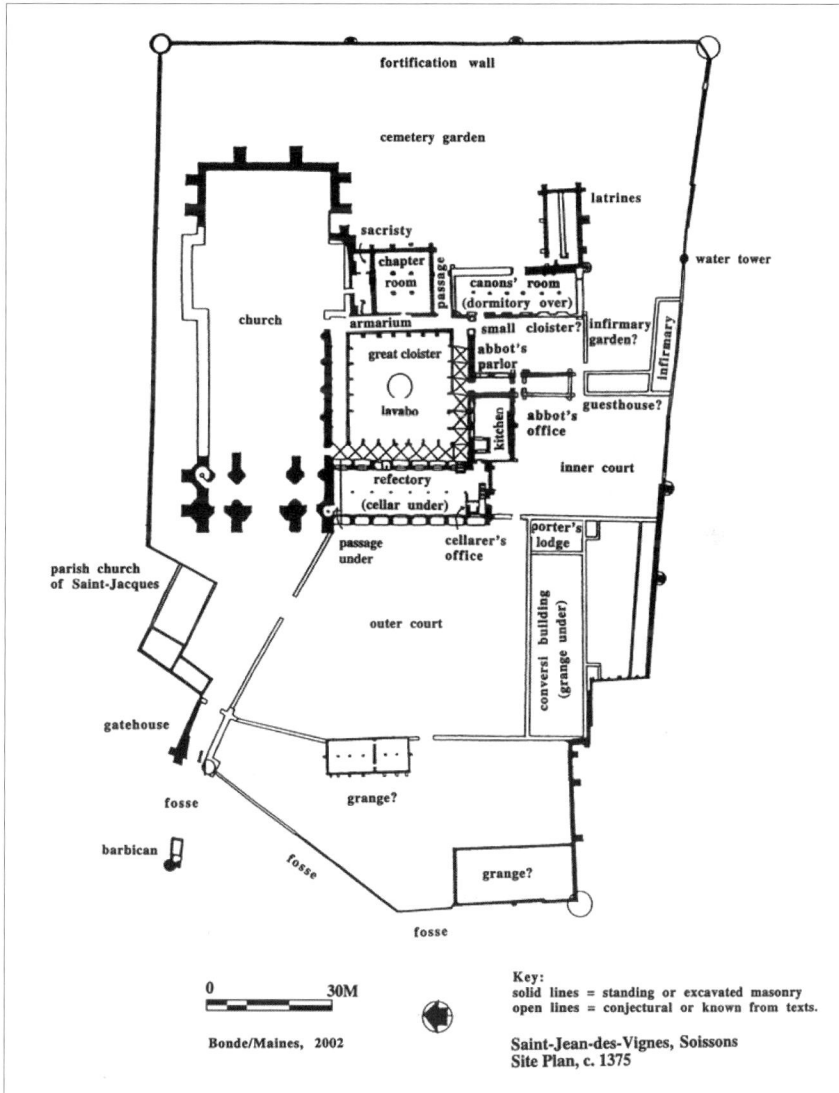

Figure 3.1b Site plan of Saint-Jean-des-Vignes showing only structures present in 1375.

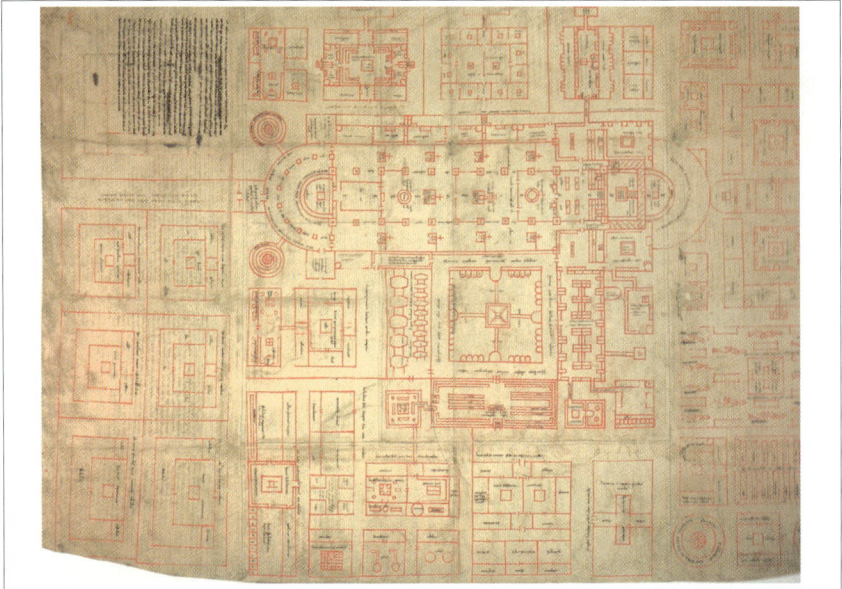

Figure 3.2   Saint Gall plan Sankt Gallen, Stiftsbibliothek, Cod. Sangallensis 1092, with
permission.

   The abundance of contemporary archaeological site plans stands in stark
contrast to the very limited number of plans produced in the medieval
period. Like modern site plans, however, medieval ones also tend to be panoptic. Best known among these are the famous ninth-century plan of Saint-Gall
(Figure 3.2) and the equally well-known plan of Christ Church, Canterbury,
of the mid-twelfth century (Figure 3.3) (Horn and Born 1979; Willis 1868;
Woodman 1992). The motivations for the production and function of these
two plans are disputed (see Barber and Thomas 2002; Hope 1902, on other
waterworks plans; consult Harley and Woodward 1987 and Harvey 1991, on
medieval maps). Scholars have noted the schematic nature of the Saint-Gall
plan (with its single lines for walls and the abundance of explanatory text
inscribed on the plan) and have argued that it was intended as an ideal image
developed in the context of the church reforms of 817 (Braunfels 1972:46).
Other scholars have suggested that it was paradigmatic, meant to be adapted
and executed by monasteries participating in the ninth-century reform (Horn
and Born 1979). The plan of Christ Church, Canterbury (Figure 3.3), presents
the buildings of the monastery from a variety of perspectives that defy a simple, naturalistic reading of the image. The monastic architecture functions as
a kind of background screen for the colorful water conduits running through
the site, which seem to be the principal interest of the image. This plan, in
fact, has been traditionally interpreted as a kind of plumbing manual for

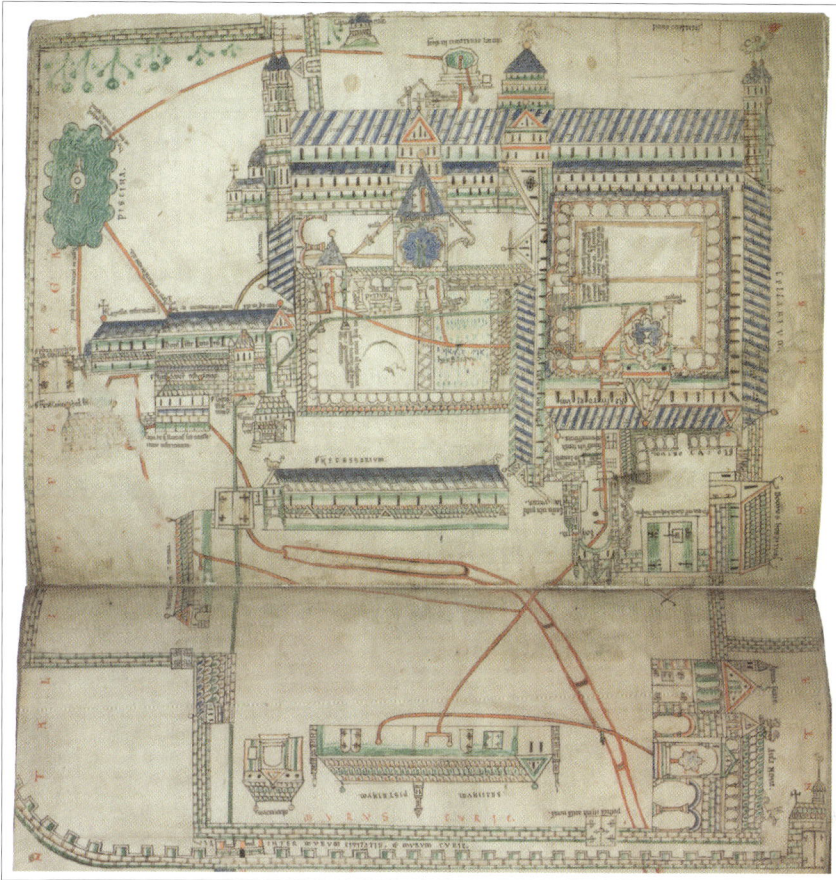

Figure 3.3 Eadwine Psalter (Ms. R 17. 1, fols. 284v and 285r (Drawing 1). Reproduced with permission of the President and Fellows of Trinity College, Oxford

repairmen (Willis 1869; Grewe 1991, 1996). In contrast, Peter Fergusson has recently proposed an alternative reading for the plan, suggesting that it may have been a commemorative image for the prior who was responsible for the construction of the hydraulic system (Fergusson 2008). Whichever reading is correct, the plan represented a panoptic view of all of the existing buildings of this particular site, including the (normally invisible) underground pipes that served its hydraulic system.

Closely related to site plans are early modern bird's-eye view engravings and paintings. In fact, many are identified as "plans" on their accompanying inscriptions and cartouches. Bird's-eye views constitute another form of panoptic representation. It is tempting to regard such views as "transparent" presentations of the monasteries at a single moment. To do so, however, is to overlook the function of these images in their own time. They often advanced a visual argument within a larger monastic reform movement. For example, dom Michel Germain's *Monasticon Gallicanum* was a collection of engravings of Benedictine monasteries appropriated as part of the Maurist reform (Courajod 1869; Germain 1967 [1871]). The *Monasticon* was not unique. Another set of bird's-eye views, plans and drawings exists but has not been systematically published or studied (Bibliothèque nationale de France (BnF), Paris, Est., Ve 20; Bibliothèque Sainte-Geneviève (BSG), Paris, Est., Cartons 74, 75, 147 and 148). These were produced for houses of regular canons affiliated with the Genovesan reform centered at the abbey of Sainte-Geneviève in Paris during the seventeenth century (Bolly et al. 1990; Petit 1991). Part of the purpose of the collection was to act as a pictorial record to guide the reformers in the physical renewal of their sites. In this sense, both the *Monasticon* and the compilation of views of Genovesan sites were panoptic *as sets*; that is, the compilations sought to represent both to their respective congregations, as well as ultimately to outsiders, the monasteries that formed the Congregation of Saint-Maur and the Congregation of Sainte-Geneviève.

Bird's-eye views, by their nature, lay claim to a visual omniscience. They provide a view from above that represents the totality of a monastic site, all of its buildings, gardens and waterworks, sometimes in a state of ruin, like the view of La Trinité de Tiron in the *Monasticon* (Germain 1967 [1871], Plate 58), sometimes, on stylistic grounds, evidently partially rebuilt, as is reflected in the two views of Notre-Dame de Bernay in the *Monasticon* (Germain 1967 [1871], Plates 108–109). This visual omniscience is typically enhanced by a cartouche containing a keyed list that identifies the function, and sometimes the "ownership" of particular buildings or areas of the monastic enclosure. These panoptic views also flatten and simplify the monastic site in the interests of clarity and communication.

Typical of the views is one that shows the Benedictine abbey of Saint-Crépin-le-Grand, located in the outskirts of Soissons (Figure 3.4). The view shows the abbey from the southeast in a way that emphasizes early modern buildings and gardens as much as it does the truncated Gothic church, which was clearly re-roofed after the thirteenth century and either never finished or partly dismantled at the west. The cartouche identifies the location of the dormitory, chapter room, and granaries as well as the abbot's house, among other buildings. The view also shows the "whole" site, including its fortified enclosure and some of the surrounding landscape. As such, it provides a comprehensive view of this venerable foundation, but one that shows nothing of the site's appearance from the north or west, and nothing of the differences in circulation levels that are known to us from contemporary studies (Ancien 1983). Bird's-eye views of monasteries, like Saint-Crépin and dozens of

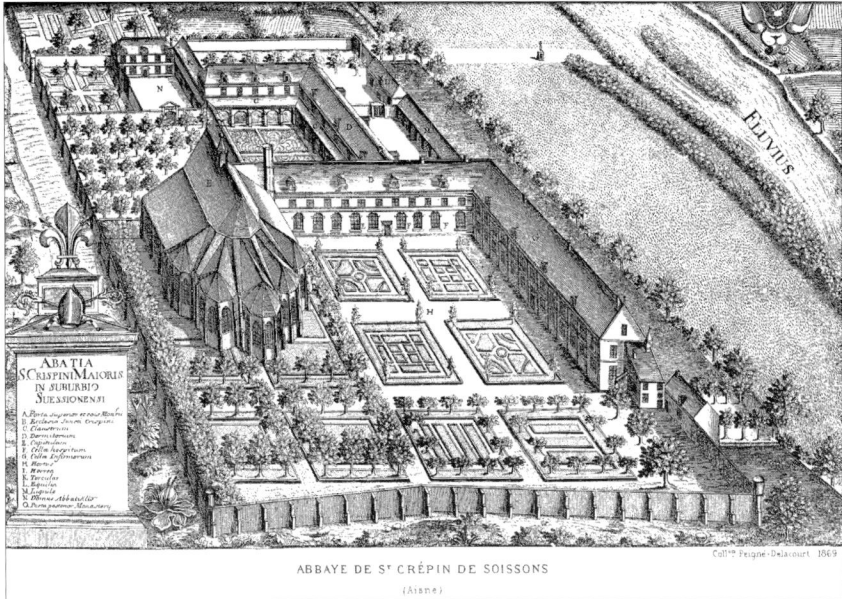

Figure 3.4 *Monasticon Gallicanum*, bird's-eye view of Saint-Crépin-le-Grand, Soissons.

others, were information-carriers, providing data about the state of repair of buildings, and the nature of new construction, as well as making visual statements of the congregation's identity as it attempted to redefine itself in terms of renewed religious precepts.

Modern aerial photographs, CAD reconstruction drawings, fly-through animations and Google Earth views may seem radically new, but they are in many ways the contemporary heirs to a representational tradition that is more than three hundred years old. The origins of aerial recording in World War II reconnaissance may reinforce the panoptic power we attribute to this omniscient viewpoint. Knowles and Saint Joseph commented on aerial photographs that

> Air photographs...lay bare the ground plan of a great monastery almost as
> completely as the most elaborate measured drawing; at the same time, by
> showing such of the elevation of the fabric as remains, together with the
> natural surroundings of the site, they give a more vivid visual impression,
> and a richer material for interpretation, than either a plan or a photograph
> from the ground can hope to do. (Knowles and Saint Joseph 1952, ix)

Even more authoritative in perspective is Google Earth where the viewer can zoom in seemingly from outer space to an archaeological site. Aerial views are necessary abstractions of a site and are, of course, totally a-historical in any experiential sense, since no monastic could ever have experienced the monastery from the air, at least not before the nineteenth century.

Although the study of representations is normally restricted to visual imagery, it is important to note that, particularly for the medieval period, texts also served as important re-presentations. In fact, texts were the predominant form of representation in the medieval period. Most monastic histories, whether in the form of chronicles or annals, were written by monks. These texts presented monastic communities and their ideas to the world at large. Other texts were directed inward, toward the community within the monastic enclosure. Such texts include monastic rules or the *ordo*, customaries and spiritual treatises. Monastic rules typically laid out precepts for monastic behavior, while customaries described the daily monastic routine, as well as job descriptions for the monastic officers. These *ordines* were all-encompassing and thus aimed to be panoptic in their scope.

Many other representations created by monastic communities about themselves belonged to our second genre, the *synecdochal*. Monastic seals are one such representation in which a part stood for the whole. Seals normally contain symbolically charged images pressed into wax and affixed by a linen ribbon to a legal document. Seals were an attestation of a person's or a community's participation in the legal agreement, echoing the recording of names of those same people in the document (Bedos-Rezak 2000, 2005; Pastoureau 1996). While the names (but not signatures) of persons participating in the legal agreement typically appeared on the document, sometimes accompanied by a mark (typically a cross), name alone seems not to have been sufficient to establish the accord of the individual or group. Instead, the seals served that authenticating purpose. Typical seals for a religious house might represent an image of the abbey gate or its church, or it might represent the patron saint of the house. As the use of seals increased in the second half of the twelfth century and into the thirteenth, both the abbot and the monastic community might have their own, different seals (Chassel 2003:63–99). This shift may be said to represent a fragmentation of monastic identity, or the legal recognition that groups within the monastic community might have competing areas of control, and might thus represent the monastery differently. Seals of the abbot might bear a symbol, or a building, or a person such as a saint or an abbot (Chassel 2003:82–83, Figures 79 and 80). For example, the mid-twelfth century seal of Saint Bernard of Clairvaux shows a forearm and hand grasping an abbatial crozier set within an inscribed frame (Chassel 2003: 85, Figure 83). As such, it is a relatively straightforward representation of Bernard's authority and power.

Monastic communities might elect to change the seals that represented their communities, as is revealed by the first and second seals of Christ Church priory, Canterbury (Figures 3.5, a and b). The architecture represented on each seal, presumably representing the church at Canterbury, probably

Figure 3.5   A. First seal, obv., seal impression, 1152, reproduced with permission of the Trustees of the British Museum B. Second seal, obv., 1155-58, Attached to British Library, Add charter 67123, reproduced with permission of the British Library

reflects changes made to the building between 1104 and 1161 (Heslop 1982: 94–100). As such, the later seal may be said to represent the priory's enhanced prestige resulting from new construction.

The monastic costume, or habit, constitutes another synecdochal representation of the monastery. Monks and nuns were immediately recognizable by the very clothing they wore. Cistercians, for example, were known as the white monks after their white habits, while the Augustinian friars were identified as Greyfriars for the same reason. The *Libellus de diversis ordinibus* observes that, "...what is seen in the monks of various orders, many of whom can be recognized by sight purely from the design of their clothing without being asked where they are from or of what order or monastery" (*Libellus* 2003:45).

But while each monastic *order* was distinguishable by its distinctive costume, the identities of individual *monks* were deliberately suppressed by the wearing of identical habits. The habit of an individual monk or nun thus represented both the corporate identity of a particular monastic community, as well as the negation of individuality. The habit signalled a specific monastic order and the form of monastic life that it practiced. The aspect of personal negation and the concomitant insistence on the value of community over individual is one that is highlighted by many monastic rules and customaries, and is essential to the synecdochal function of the habit. The Barnwell customary instructs the Augustinians of that house: "Without their habit, that is when they have taken off their outdoor cloaks, they ought not to be seen by seculars either standing, sitting or walking" (Clark 1897:105). The same customary records how a master is to teach a novice to "conceal his head within the depths of his hood" in order to be an anonymous monk, and not an individual (Clark 1897:127). In this case, clothing did make the man, but it made him part of a community and a religious order, separate from the secular world.

The property owned by a monastery also functioned as a synecdochal referent to the monastery itself. Every monastery sat within a bounded precinct that constituted a monastic site. Considered economically, however, a monastic site should be construed as a kind of corporate headquarters for the community's landed domain that might consist of dependent parishes, farms, mills, and ovens, as well as other possessions and privileges (Bond 2004). This monastic landscape also participated in a "negative" representational strategy as did the monastic habit. In his discussion of the negation of self in monastic life, C.H. Lawrence writes, "Property is an extension of personality. Its renunciation was a radical act of self-negation..." (Lawrence 2001:26). Lawrence was writing, of course, about personal property. Monasteries did, however, hold property—and lots of it—but they held it corporately. For a lord or peasant to come upon a farm, or a mill belonging to a monastery, was to encounter an economic part of a much larger monastic whole. Without recourse to iconography or inscription, awareness of ownership would have formed part of a common knowledge provided by oral tradition, and would have reminded the viewer of the monastic site and its corporate nature.

Like their clothing, the kinds of properties acquired and exploited by monastic houses varied deliberately. Monks used their properties to present their ideals to the world. Cistercians embraced rural life, and they presented themselves through their rural lands as a community of hermits consciously withdrawn into the "desert" and disengaged from intercourse with the world. Augustinians, by contrast, embraced urban life and parochial service. Through *their* properties, Augustinians represented themselves as apostles, involved in apostolic activities like preaching and care for the urban and suburban poor (Bonde and Maines 2003:49–53; Bynum 1982:22–58). Local knowledge of monastic ownership, often taking the form of obligations of payments in cash or in kind, contributed importantly to making the monastic domain an effective way of representing the monastery.

Contemporary popular representations of monasteries can be synecdochal or panoptic. The synecdochal "quotation" of monastic sites often appears in advertising or publicity documents. In the city of Soissons, for example, it is the ruined facade of the abbey church of Saint-Jean-des-Vignes that has come to signify the town on official letterhead, tourist brochures, flags, and other items (Figure 3.6), rather than the fully intact twelfth- and thirteenth-century Gothic cathedral that stands in the center of the town. The antiquity of the town is established by the presence of venerable ruins. "This is our past" is a claim made by local tourist boards—even though few of us can be direct descendents of medieval monks or nuns, for obvious reasons.

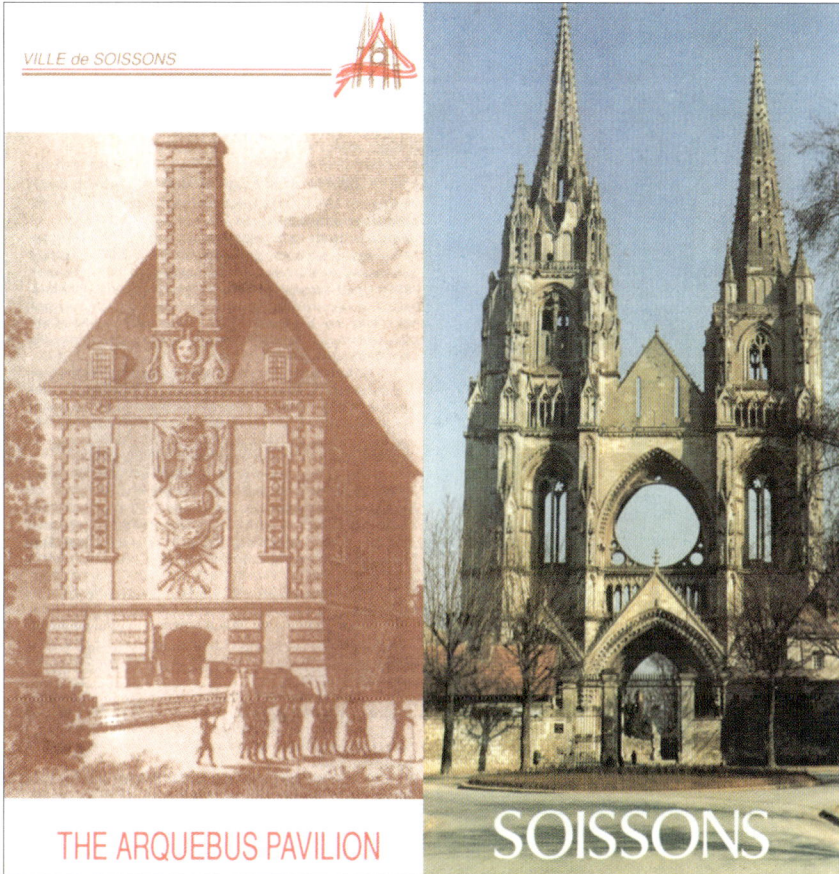

Figure 3.6 Two Soissons tourist brochures.

The creation of a monastic canon—a canon of orders, as well as a canon of monuments—has established a limited number of monasteries which are taken as representative. Canons have been constructed in a number of ways. Very influential are the textbooks that present the history of monasticism. The two most widely used historical surveys today are those by C.H. Lawrence (2001) and Wolfgang Braunfels (1972). Both aim at a comprehensive view: Lawrence of the religious and social history of monasteries, relying on archival material; and Braunfels of the architectural history, presenting the physical evidence. Studies such as these and other publications participate in the creation of a scholarly canon that is, in turn, part of the process of representation. It is notable that most monastic sites become canonical by virtue of the survival of their archives or their buildings, and their inclusion in influential publications like those of Lawrence or Braunfels.

In important ways, the monastic canon has been, and continues to be, a creation of monks and nuns. More than thirty years ago, Giles Constable discussed critically the role that monks have played in writing their own history, stressing that secular historians tended to be concerned with "external history"—the contributions of monastics to social, economic, intellectual, and artistic life in the middle ages—while monastic scholars were more concerned with "internal history"—the organization of monastic life with monastic spirituality (Constable 1974). While much has changed since Constable wrote, the essential point, that monastic self-representation is not restricted to the medieval period, remains as true today as it was in 1974.

A surprising amount of modern scholarly research repeats a very restricted canon. This limited canon has permitted Benedictine, Cistercian, and Cluniac houses to dominate our understanding of the monastic experience. In a survey we did for a conference in 2000—a kind of millennial stock-taking—we reviewed 2500 articles published over the 10-year period 1988–1998 (Bonde and Maines 2004). We found that published articles on male, rural Cistercian houses massively overshadowed attention paid to female convents or urban houses of orders other than those following the Benedictine rule. In fact, almost three-quarters (73%) of the surveyed articles were devoted to houses of the Benedictine tradition. It is worth remembering that there were over 500 monastic orders in the Middle Ages, so this proportion is strikingly overbalanced. The canon still over-represents orders with substantial written records or famous authors: in other words, the canon privileges the Benedictine orders whose self-representations remain persuasive to present-day readers.

Scholarship has also produced a canonical set of *images*. A comparison of the often-published plan of a "typical" Cistercian monastery and the plan of the abbey of Fontenay make it clear that the latter has become the canonical Cistercian site at the expense of more historically important houses of the order like Cîteaux (the mother house of the order from which it takes its name) or Clairvaux (where the first saint of the order, Saint Bernard, was abbot). This happened for several reasons. Fontenay is intact, and survives as a largely twelfth-century, Cistercian Romanesque site. By contrast, Cîteaux and Clairvaux are essentially destroyed, and were rebuilt or altered after their original phases. Fontenay was smaller and less successful than Cîteaux or Clairvaux, but its fossilized state has made it the perfect canonical referent for a Cistercian monastery.

Another canonical site is the famous abbey of Cluny, mother house and corporate center of the vast Cluniac order. Cluny was excavated and reconstructed by Kenneth Conant in the 1920s and 1930s (Conant 1954, 1968, and 1970). But his re-presentations of the abbey have been repeated with very little change by a host of recent CAD representations, where images of the church rather than the entire site predominate (see Koob 2006; Neiske 1997; Richner et al. 1993). Only in the last few years have excavations been renewed at Cluny, aimed at validating (or rejecting) some of Conant's more interpretive claims, and extending his work of seventy-five years ago to other parts of the site (Baud 2003; Vingtain 1998). While clearly important, this new work will do little to dislodge Cluny—or Conant's drawings—from the canon.

The Carthusian order gives us an interesting example of canon formation. Established at the end of the eleventh century, the mother house of the order, La Grande Chartreuse, remains a continuously active monastery with substantial portions of its surviving fabric dating to the seventeenth century. The site is, however, set high in the French Alps and is difficult of access. A few photographs of the site exist and are regularly republished, but no compelling reconstruction drawing or analytic surveys of the complex have ever been undertaken. Only one aerial photograph is known to us, and a site plan seems to have been produced only in 2002 (see Pacaut 1993, for the aerial photograph and Gröning 2007, for the plan). The editors of *Analecta Cartusiana* have taken steps to redress this problem by publishing a *Monasticon Cartusiense* as volumes in their series. Volume I, which will treat French sites, has not yet appeared but will treat the iconography of La Grande Chartreuse (see Schlegel and Hogg 2004).

Carthusian houses were never numerous, but in the fourteenth century, noble patronage produced more and impressive foundations. Few have been studied archaeologically, historically or art historically. This set of circumstances makes archaeological work at the Carthusian priory at Mount Grace (Yorkshire) all the more important. It has also meant that reconstruction watercolors of that site by Alan Sorrel and Judith Dobey have in turn become the canonical images of Carthusian monasticism (Sorrel's in Platt 1984:183, Figure 130, and Dobey's in Coppack 1991:36–37).

A recently released film by Philip Gröning, *Die Grosse Stille* (*Into Great Silence*) now brings the re-presentation of Carthusian life at La Grande Chartreuse to the big screen (Gröning 2007). Gröning's documentary strategies introduce movement to the representative palette, but strikingly, he does not include dialogue. The monastic idea of removing oneself from the world and taking a vow of silence is a radical one, and Gröning respects—and echoes—that choice in his filmed representation. In the silent world of Carthusian life, as represented by Gröning, only the sounds of footsteps on stone surfaces, the chime of bells, the music of moving water and voices raised in chant and prayer occasionally punctuate the quiet. There is no historical background, no voice-over, nor any explicit plot in this remarkable documentary. Gröning's style and editing reinforce the cyclical passage of the seasons, in which work, prayer and contemplation unfold in a timeless continuum. His is a

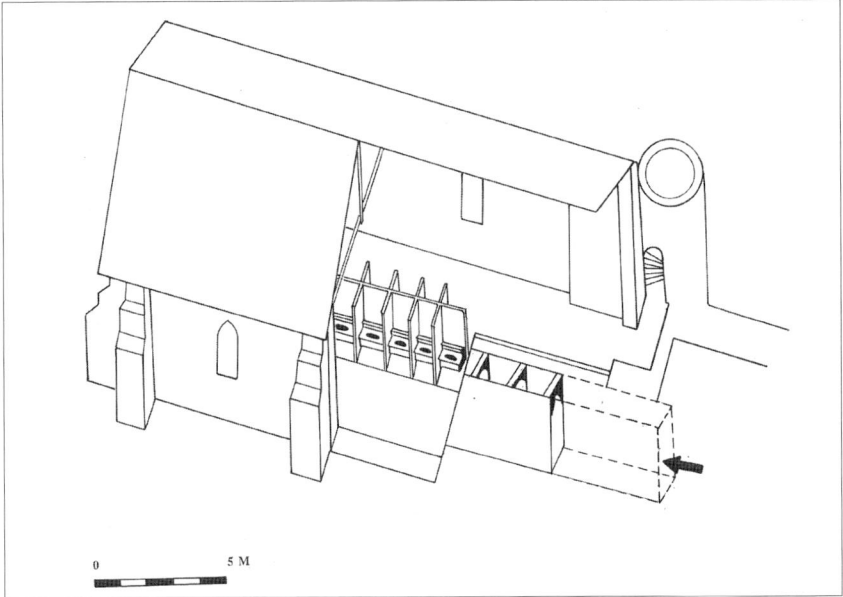

Figure 3.7   Saint-Jean-des-Vignes, reconstruction drawing, latrine building.

panoptic re-presentation—not just of La Grande Chartreuse, or even of the
Carthusian order—but even more comprehensively, of monasticism itself.
Gröning's image of monasticism is based upon the negation of the individual
(through silence and isolation) in favor of communal identity.

   Other referents besides sound are edited out in Gröning's version of monasticism. The film deliberately omits aspects of daily life from its representation
of monastic existence. Spirituality and prayer, rhythm and silence prevail. In
the film—as in most representations of the medieval monastery—monks do
not long to speak; they do not disagree with authority or deviate from communal ideals, and they certainly do not watch TV or go to the bathroom.
Our close association with living monastic communities, and our 25 years of
excavation and historical research at abandoned sites, demonstrate to us that
tensions over private space, individuality and methods of disagreement were,
and continue to be, important aspects of monastic life. The idealizing self-
representations promoted by dominant male monastic writers in the twelfth
century are still largely accepted and repeated in modern representations.
Future re-presentations of the important medieval phenomenon of the monastery and monasticism, we would argue, need to ask more critical questions
about monastic daily life, privacy, and dissent—and we end with one such
reconstruction (Figure 3.7) that not only puts the monk back in the monastery but in the spaces that are normally edited out.

— 4 —

Ping-Pong, Polygons, Virgins:
Graphic Representations of the Ancient Maya

Stephen Houston

> When there is a final truth of the matter, then what we say is brief, and it is
> either true or false. It is not a matter of representation. When…we provide
> representations of the world, there is no final truth of the matter
>   (Danilo Domodosala, in Hacking [1983:145])

The act of recording and reporting in archaeology is a complex business. Any
number of decisions informs the tasks of selecting, highlighting or dismissing
features that need to be described or reproduced. Most archaeologists accept
that this is a vexed process. They also understand that, to some unreflecting
readers, representations of the past extend beyond mere historical or hermeneutic interest—they *are* the past. This is because a photograph, drawing,
computer visualization, even an historical theme park, achieves a solidity and
"truth" that is not, in fact, warranted by the actual vagaries of preservation,
quality of evidence or evolving nature and substance of interpretation (Handler and Gable 1997). Images pass through the process of vision, held by
some scholars to be a dominant, Western means of verifying what is present
or absent, true or false (Gillings 2005:229). They gull the mind, often a com-
plicit one, into thinking that representations show the past as it really was.
For more thoughtful viewers, a representation is simply a claim. It is always
incomplete, indeterminate, and imprecise. We cannot know the past fully; a
near-infinity of detail needs to be winnowed to create a representation; and
mental processing of an idiosyncratic sort lies behind every image, either in
its making or reception (Ankersmit 2001:16; Favro 2006:321).

  Without a doubt, provisos about the power of images apply to the ancient

Maya, among the most graphically inclined of peoples in their fondness for image-making and, as stressed here, among the most imagined and imaged in popular and scholarly media. This chapter explores the Maya and their remains as representational targets, along with the precise ways in which they have been "re-presented" visually. Throughout runs a tension, never resolved, never fully resolvable, between an impulse to embrace mimesis and another to prefer clarity of presentation through the necessary reduction of detail.

The Maya as Representational Target

The Maya are a set of related peoples in and around the Yucatan peninsula, all speaking related languages. As the pottery evidence suggests, they first appeared in prehistory, perhaps in the second millennium B.C., but with only a clear linguistic presence, as registered in writing, by the final years B.C. (Saturno et al. 2006). They endure, by the millions, in present-day Belize, Guatemala, and Mexico. Nonetheless, "Maya" is an anachronism, for it is doubtful whether past speakers ever identified themselves collectively by such a description. During the "Classic period" (c. A.D. 250–850)—in itself a loaded term that implies singular achievement—the Maya consisted of a group of courtly societies, linked by trade, dynastic concerns, diglossia ("high" and "low-languages") that cleaved elites from non-elites, and theological precepts pulsing to different rhythms, with episodic convulsions that reorganized society and reordered populations (Inomata and Houston 2001; Houston et al. 2000). Continuities, often of stunning tenacity, appear alongside novelty and innovation that changed according to local conditions.

At present, the ancient Maya are also, as experienced in movies, magazines, tourist centers, and academic renderings, an interstitial creation shaped by many images. Clearly, no single scholar or member of the public will share the same set of notions with others, although there will be what might be described as "nodal" ideas around which many will cluster. The Maya of antiquity will always be a plural phenomenon. An essay on graphic claims of, and visual encounters with, the Maya could take many tacks: as a review of historical parks that exhume and present stone buildings and sculptures in photogenic and increasingly cautious manner (such structures are their own simulacra; Castañeda 1996); as a discussion of ethics regarding what is permissibly shown and responsibly displayed (Horsfield 2003:6, 10); as a study of the Maya in fictionalized media, from *Kings of the Sun* and *Apocalypto* to *Indiana Jones and the Kingdom of the Crystal Skull* along with various novels of lesser impact (see Hruby 2006); as an account of Maya self-representation, whether of pyramids depicted in graffiti or the ontology of depiction in the Classic period (Houston 1998); or as a report on the appeal of the Maya past in constituting new, often distorted fabulations that aim to preserve or evoke Maya tradition, whether in advertising or twentieth-century architecture (Ardren 2006; Gebhard 1993; Ingle 1989; with influence from Totten 1926). Instead, as one path of many, it charts general themes in graphic representation, both as to how they are made and how they condition perceptions of the ancient Maya.

Prestige and Credit in Mayanist Representation

The first observation touches on Mayanist practice, the ways and means by which scholars research and present results. A separate but linked matter is how Maya specialists learn attitudes and methods and pass them on to others. In such practice there tends to be a marked sociological devaluation of renderings over prose. Representations are held to high standard, and yet are often performed by lower-ranking staff, often female or foreign, as in the case of Antonio Tejeda in Guatemala (see below). In part, this practice acknowledges different levels of skill and efficient apportionment of labor, as not all professionals can draw to an acceptable standard. A comparison between a photograph and a rendering of a painted glyph in Tomb 7 at Río Azul, Guatemala, makes that point crystal clear (Figure 4.1; Adams 1999:Figure 3–14). But it goes beyond this, too. Several examples illustrate the marginalized role of drawing, ranging from the drawings of Annie Hunter for Alfred Maudslay (Graham 2002:221–222, although also with one "Edwin Lambert") to the water-colors of Adela Breton (McVicker 2005) and the reliance of the Carnegie Institution of Washington on Antonio Tejeda of Guatemala, (e.g., Kidder 1946:7), none of especially high status in the gringo-centric and *machista* world of early Maya archaeology. (Until the 1960s, for example, many North American Mayanists did not master Spanish [e.g., Kidder 1950:102].) For his opus on Maya glyphs, Sir Eric Thompson depended on otherwise unknown women ("Mrs. Huberta Robison...Mrs. Eugene C. Worman, Jr., Miss Kisa Noguchi...Mrs. Katherine B. Lang...[and] Miss Avis Tullock," [Thompson 1971:x; see also Thompson 1962:ix]). The Harvard work at Altar de Sacrificios and Ceibal, Guatemala, and Copan, Honduras, largely rested on renderings by non-archaeologists (e.g., Adams 1971:v–vi; Sabloff 1975:iii). The most important folio of Maya pottery stresses the names of the editors, not the artists who did the renderings (Gordon and Mason 1925–1943). The overriding impression is that prose-making was valued more highly than image-making. It was the effort most likely to receive credit on the cover page or bold lettering on the book jacket. Moreover, the author selecting images for reproduction played the role of impresario, coordinator, and paymaster, with claims to greater recognition than his or her assistants.

Figure 4.1   Comparison of drawing and photograph of painted glyphs, Tomb 7 at Río Azul,
Guatemala (Adams 1999:Figure 3–14 and George Stuart).

There are exceptions, however. A few archaeologists, aware of their debt, accord strong praise to graphic collaborators (e.g., M. Coe 1973:5). The celebrated career of Frederick Catherwood (1844; von Hagen 1950), the nineteenth-century topographic artist who accompanied John Lloyd Stephens, or the architectural renderings of Tatiana Proskouriakoff (1946) show that, for certain kinds of work, the representational eye attracts far greater recognition. This may have been because such renderings were regarded as labor intensive, the product of multiple measurements in the field. The same holds true for the rubbings of Merle Greene (Greene et al. 1972) or drawings of Ian Graham and his associates (e.g., Graham 1979), in which text is lightly accented and the representations assigned higher weight. In these publications, the artist is also the impresario, the guiding force behind the books.

The other exception is map-making, which, in Mayanist practice, receives cover-page recognition (Carr and Hazard 1961; W. Fash and Long 1983; Folan et al. 1983). Some such crediting comes from precedents of a highly specific sort. The publication of the map of Tikal by Carr and Hazard (1961) expressed the importance and scale of that city. It also reflected the accent on settlement research in the Maya region after Gordon Willey's appointment in 1950 to the Bowditch professorship at Harvard. Under strong institutional pressure, particularly from Alfred Tozzer, doyen of archaeology at Harvard, Willey had shifted to Mayanist work from his earlier emphasis on settlement studies in Peru and his growing, but subsequently thwarted, interest in Central America (Willey 1988:271, 288–289). After his appointment, there was a certain incongruity to Willey's later monographs, as he began to concentrate, not on settlement, which he increasingly apportioned to students, but to descriptive reports on artifacts (cf. Tourtellot 1988 and Willey 1972). This may have occurred because he tended to spend less time in the field, a necessity for his many writing projects, but, as a matter of scheduling, unsuited to any extensive mapping. Nonetheless, under glow of heightened prestige and excitement over its novelty and promise, mapping was seen to deserve monographic presentation, usually as folia of loose sheets. The bulk and expense of these folia were further warranted by the enlarged coverage of archaeological sites, from maps of central locations with sculptures and monumental architecture out to the faint edges of detectable settlement. The cost of production has since led to digital dissemination, in which representations of settlement become accessible in more supple and economical form (e.g., Barnhart 2001a, 2001b). The non-material nature of digital media—and, it must be admitted, comparative lack of peer review and editing—challenge Mayanist, and indeed all archaeological, practice, which traditionally esteems a tangible object, a book, as the chief measure of scholarly productivity.

Mimesis and the Clarity of Convention

In the act of rendering comes unavoidable input from personality and skill. The topography of Heywood Sumner, a member of the arts and crafts movement and devotee of a romanticized rural England, set a tradition of survey that was emulated in part—British archaeologists continue to show topography by means of stylized triangular wedges of varying length (e.g., Adkins and Adkins 1989:Figure 4.5)—but not in its incorporation of witty vignettes beyond the ability of most draftsman (e.g., Sumner 1988:21, 88, 97, 148, Plate 1). Sheila Gibson's (1991) renderings of Classical buildings reflect a lifetime of labor as an architectural draftsman, and the atmospheric, almost chiaroscuro renderings of Alan Sorrel (1981) come closer to John Constable and other lyricists of the landscape than do the flat tones of Google's Sketch-Up software. At core, these works are affective in that they convey stories and mood. Yet their level of skill is approximated in the Maya area by figures trained in the arts (B. Fash 1992; Heather Hurst, in Miller 2002) and in archaeology, especially at the University of Pennsylvania (W. Coe 1959, 1990). To a surprising extent, much-maligned figures like Jean-Frédérick Waldeck, guilty of inserting elephants into his images of Maya art, reveal themselves to be far more careful draftsman in their penciled originals (Baudez 1993:Figures 8, 9, 12, Plate 23).

The key figure here is William Coe, who taught at the University of Penn-sylvania. Unusual for archaeologists, he devoted large amounts of time to rendering of all sorts, from buildings to maps, artifacts to burials at the major city of Tikal, Guatemala (Figure 4.2). This was made possible by his appoint-ment to a position that required relatively light teaching. But the impulse behind it arose from Coe's evident understanding that to draw was to see. Drafting drew attention to detail and thus furthered interpretation of com-plex sequences of deposits—a laser cut through the axis of a building encap-sulated most of the information he wished to retrieve (Fowler and Houston 1991). As part of a chain of practice, this example was followed with minor adjustment by his students or by those influenced by him (e.g., Chase and Chase 1994) and differed from the less mimetic practices employed by Brit-ish archaeologists and their students and colleagues in Belize (e.g., Ham-mond 1991). It continues to be the standard in much Guatemalan archaeol-ogy (e.g., Fitzsimmons et al. 2003:Figures 5 and 6).

Coe was not the first to practice mimesis in section lines. This goes back to early explorations at Chichen Itza, Yucatan, by Augustus Le Plongeon, who excavated the Platform of Venus in 1883 (Desmond and Messenger 1988:95). Through a detailed profile that showed fill of varying sizes of stone, LePlongeon demonstrated sensitivity to stratigraphy that was not mirrored in his somewhat hallucinatory explanations of the site. Thereafter Mayanist stratigraphy took two directions until Coe arrived on the scene. One was a kind of simulated stratigraphy that showed "typical" features through a laser cut of a building, all done in mimetic style. This was as the archaeologist

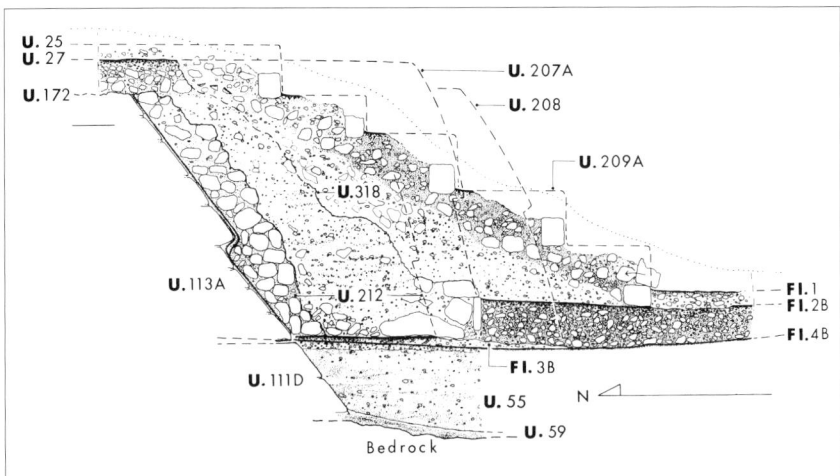

Figure 4.2   Profile by William Coe, North Acropolis, Tikal, Guatemala (W. Coe 1990:Figure 222a).

imagined a building should be, and could be highly instructive, if misleading in nature (Figure 4.3; e.g., Holmes 1895:Figure 5). "Typical" structures remain a feature of some archaeological publications (Martos López
2002:Figure 5). The other direction was perfected by the Carnegie Institution
of Washington, particularly at the site of Uaxactun, in excavations reported
most fully by Ledyard Smith (1950:Figures 73, 79). Stones were shown in all
their irregular detail, in immense profiles made possible by trenching (Smith
1950:Figure 9; see also Black 1990).

It is puzzling that later work by Smith, especially at Altar de Sacrificios and
Seibal, Guatemala, now as the field director of Harvard projects, regressed
from these standards. Strata were either shown in hesitant lines or appeared
in too strongly or conventionally asserted a manner (Figure 4.4; e.g., Smith
1972:Figures 6–15, 1982:Figure 18). This seems to have come from the final
years of Carnegie excavations, in this case at Mayapan, Yucatan, where profiles were shown as hybrid sections with three-dimensional properties, stones
shaded to enhance their mass; most profiles were idealized, rectified, even
collated from diverse examples (Proskouriakoff 1962:Figures 3 and 4; Smith
1962:Figure 4). For his part, Coe was clearly influenced by the Uaxactun
conventions yet seems to have introduced them at a relatively late date, after
the inception of fieldwork at Tikal. This may have occurred because the first
director of the Tikal Project, Edwin Shook, left his position and Coe took
over as principal archaeologist (W. Coe and Haviland 1982:10, 45). The first
published sections from the Shook period combined vertical profiles with
three-dimensional features, a feature difficult to reconcile with any "laser-
cut" notion of an archaeological profile (Adams and Trik 1961:Figure 38), or
they consisted of over-schematic and stylized drawings (W. Coe and Broman
1958:Figures 3, 8).

As anecdote has it, Coe enjoined students to draw stones as they were, in all
their jagged outlines. There should be "no ping-pong balls," no over-regular
representations of stones in structural fill. Casual and quick drawing was dis-
favored; mimesis, deposits as the eye saw them, took pride of place (W. Coe
and Haviland 1982:45). What resulted from this were highly variegated and
minutely textured profiles, relative darkness of soil indicated by density of
stipple, and eschewal of vegetation as distracting detail. Excavations could
be so driven by the need for clarity that, according to one critic of the Tikal
Project, they destroyed or dismantled buildings so as to enhance opportunities
for well-lit photographs and interpretable, tidy sections (Berlin 1967). The
focus on standardization was strong in the Tikal research, partly in response
to the participation of people with diverse ability on large projects. For Coe,
conventions had to be mimetic enough to achieve a high standard of representation, but not so difficult as to excuse most archaeologists from the process of

drawing. By any standard, Coe's was a large achievement in Maya archaeology. Few sites have such well-published or interpretable stratigraphy.

Yet ultimately the mimesis was illusory or partial. Each drawing was satu-

FIG. 5. TRANSVERSE SECTION OF AN ORDINARY YUCATEC BUILDING.

The upper part of the pyramid is shown with the stairway at the left.
a.   Lower wall-zone pierced by a plain doorway.
b.   Doorway showing squared and dressed stones of jamb.
c.   Wooden lintels cut midway in length.
d.   Doorway connecting front with back chamber and showing position of cord holders.
e.   Inner face of arch dressed with the slope.
f.   Ceiling, or cap-stones of arch.
g.   Lower line of mouldings, a survival of the archaic cornice.
h.   Decorated entablature zone.
i.   Upper mouldings and coping.
j.k. False front with decorations, (occasionally added).
l.   Roof-crest with decorations, (occasionally added).

Figure 4.3   Section through an "Ordinary Yucatec Building" (Holmes 1895:Figure 5).

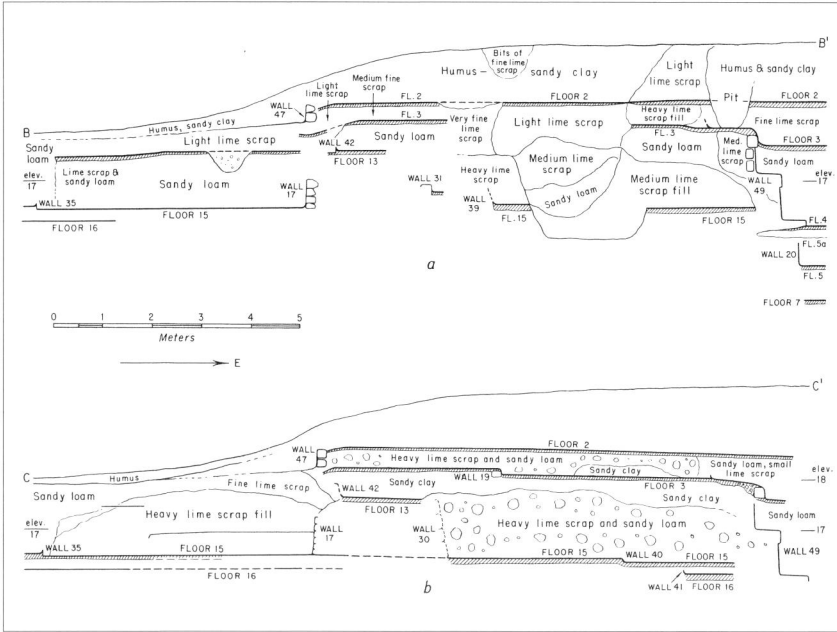

Figure 4.4   Later profiles by A. Ledyard Smith, at Altar de Sacrificios, Guatemala (Smith 1972:Figure 6).

rated with prior decision-making about what to include and what to ignore. They contained no color, an obvious component of visual experience, and lines were sometimes hardened so as to enhance clarity. Light came from a predetermined angle, with effects on stipple, heedless of actual viewing conditions at the time of drawing. The outlines themselves carried information about whether they represent faced-stones or not. Few scientific renderings can escape what has been called the need for "working objects" or "exemplary things," as in the ideal bile duct of a human being or bird of this or that genus, or a stone of consistent outline and plaster floor of uniform thickness (Daston and Galison 1992:85–86). These "working objects" impose, through rendering, a certain uniformity or standardization so as to facilitate comparison between images. Mimetic drawing has the aim of narrowing the distance between the observer and the actual deposit. Through mimesis, the rendering purports to show things as they "really are." But what is shown is always an interpretation—note, for example, the difference between standard epigraphic drafting, which focuses on line, and the stippled drawings in some works, which subsume line within the often irrelevant irregularities of a continuous carved surface (e.g., Hammond et al. 1999). The disciplined regulation of convention makes drawings resemble each other, but it is likely that archaeologists would see the same feature differently. Alternatively, a few renderings seem to improve on reality by offering whole bones and sharp, consistent lighting, as in certain burials at Altun Ha, Belize: the verisimilitude is both useful, showing details unavailable to the naked eye, and deceptive, by adding details not visible in situ—it is not so much a record as a reconstitution (e.g., David Findlay, in Pendergast 1979:3, Figure 67).

For that reason, epigraphic drafting at Copan, Honduras, has begun, under Barbara Fash's guidance, to insist on three different checks of a pencil drawing, itself, necessarily, a reduction of complex, three-dimensional surfaces. A long-term goal is to apply scanning technologies in the field so as to achieve minute topographies of carved surface (Powell 2007; also Doering and Collins 2005). As a complete record of a sculpture, these defer interpretation to some future time, when selected elements can be highlighted to respond to certain questions. A clever and effective ricochet between reconstructed shapes and actual heaps of masonry appears in Proskouriakoff's (1946) volume on Maya architecture, which presents the first as wash or watercolors, the second as line drawings. The dissonance between the two is deliberate and meant to induce caution in viewers who might place too much weight on the reconstruction drawing of a ruined building (e.g., Proskouriakoff 1946:Plate 2).

Mimetic Predicaments in Mapping

The tensions of mimesis come to the fore in the representation of large surfaces through maps. For Mayanists, maps typically represent a scorched surface, devoid of vegetation that abounds at most Maya sites (e.g. Carr and Hazard 1960; Weeks et al. 2005:401–409). From an early date, archaeologists have felt torn between a mimetic need to show the surface with minute detail, usually as hints of slopes or as more accurate contour lines, or as stylized shapes that display monumental architecture in the form of faceted or beveled polygons. The former defers interpretation by suggesting the varied elevations of Maya sites, likely to be structures but not always clearly designated as such. For some archaeologists, this remains the standard mode of representing a Maya site (e.g., López Camacho 2006:Figura 3). It also belies Nelson's (2000:9) claim that the eye of modernity claims the ability to craft omniscient panoramas, hardly the case here. The latter commits to an interpretation of massed forms as Maya buildings, stylizing to an extent that allows large structures to be shown by a few angled forms. Both approaches have implications for fieldwork, in that contours or elevations can involve large amounts of survey, obstructed by dense vegetation, while faceted shapes can be quickly delimited by compass mapping, if at the expense of structural detail and nuances of surface. One of the largest Preclassic Maya cities, El

Mirador, was first presented in this way (Graham 1967:Figure 29), mapped almost single-handedly by Ian Graham. A seldom-used alternative involves the creation of vertical profiles of sites, an archaeological profile that focuses on varying surfaces across large areas (e.g., Tozzer 1913:Plate 34; clearly of influence to Satterthwaite 1943:Figure 2).

The delineation of elevation appears in some early works, including an early view of Uxmal by Brasseur de Bourbourg (1865:255). But, with a few exceptions, little attempt has been made to distinguish between natural and artificial surfaces, other than to trace the buildings themselves. A marked advance comes with the publication by Charnay and Viollet-le-Duc (1863:Figure 8), the over-enthusiastic restorer of Carcassonne in France. Here, in clear view, are the geometrical forms that become the dominant convention in Maya mapping, along with shading to impart mass and three-dimensionality to pyramid shapes. Thereafter, maps in the region become hybrid productions: slopes in the Charnay style when details are unclear; lines to demarcate certain terraces, walls, and standing buildings, and contour lines to convey topography. Examples include Merwin's map of Tikal, done in 1910, and Tozzer and Merwin's plan of Nakum, not far away (Figure 4.5 [top], Tozzer 1911:Plate 29). This was the template for most later maps of Maya sites, although there are a few exceptions, including an effort that stylizes mounds to the point of illegibility, perhaps because that scholar did not seem to learn her craft through apprenticeship on Maya projects focusing on architecture (Ford 1987:131–144).

Equally aberrant and deficient are the maps of Maler, who imposed an excessive regularity on plans and, paradoxically, showed the precise lay of terraces yet dashed them to indicate uncertainty about such features (Figure 4.5 [bottom]; e.g., Maler 1908:Figure 14). In a separate tradition, Maudslay (1889–1902:Plates 1 to 3) had made stucco models of sites like Copan, photographed them with raking light, and then commissioned artists to touch up the image with text and selective accents. Photographed from different angles, these models presaged far later computer graphics yet served as an example to few other scholars other than model-makers of individual buildings (e.g., Fane 1993; Graham 1967:Figure 28). Another neglected if admired example were the topographic vistas of Holmes, an early employee of geological surveys in the American west, where he created majestic views of natural formations. A distinguished artist in his own right, he served as member of the Bureau of American Ethnology, and, for a few years, as curator at the Field Museum before leaving for the Smithsonian (Holmes 1895:Foldout). The viewer floats about 100 m above ground, looking towards the ruined, vegetation-covered city of Uxmal. The skill of the rendering, from the hand of a topographic artist who knew just how much ink to use, and no more, is

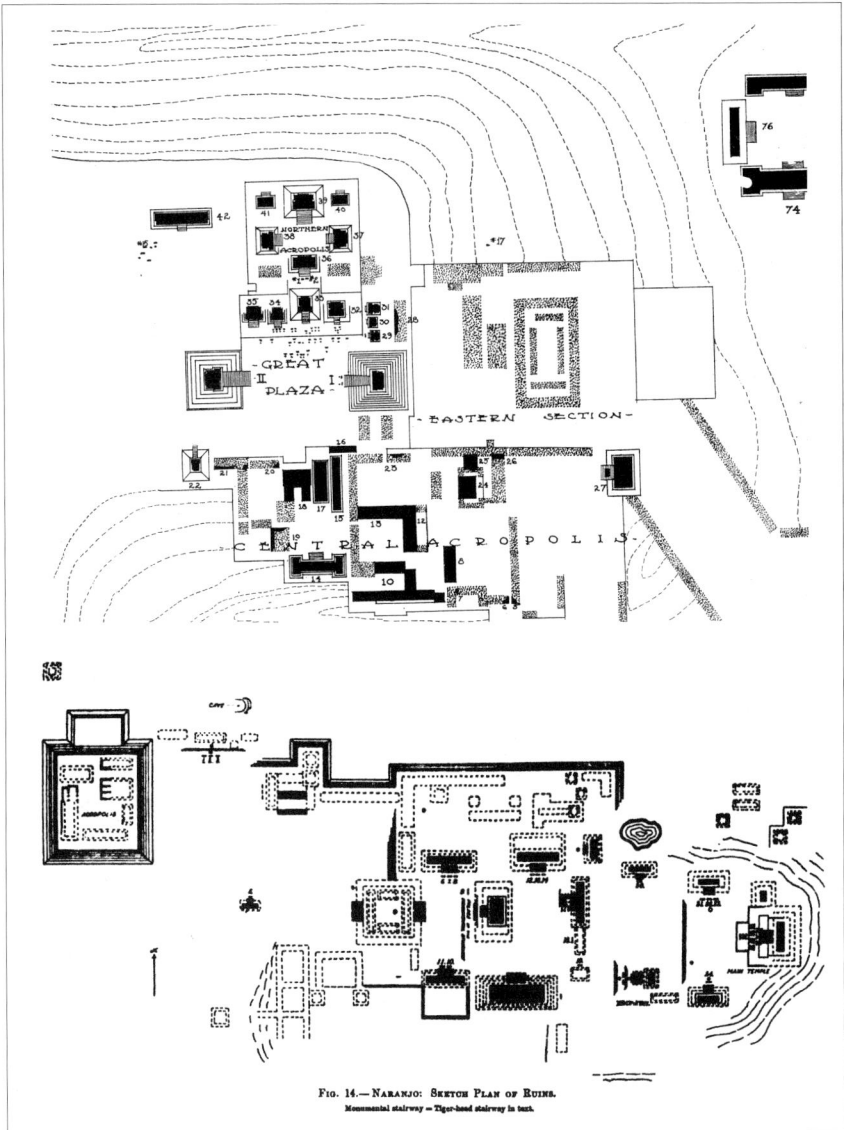

FIG. 14.— NARANJO: SKETCH PLAN OF RUINS.
Monumental stairway = Tiger-head stairway in text.

Figure 4.5   Maps of Maya sites, by varying methods: (top) Tozzer and Merwin, of Tikal (Tozzer 1911:Plate 29) and (bottom) Maler, at Yaxha, Guatemala (Maler 1908:Figure 14).

of such quality that few other archaeologists could achieve the same effect. It surpassed common skill and had few successors for that reason. One of the few is a group of Catalan architects, creators of "San Rafael," an impossible site merging, in chronological sequence, elements of El Mirador, Tikal, Antigua Guatemala, and Guatemala City (Hernández et al. 1992).

There is a strong suggestion that maps are done in the way they are less because of influence from published examples than from practices inculcated at particular excavations or academic programs—the "guild" structure of archaeology, in which "apprentices" learn certain practices and "masters" exist to enforce them. Thus, in a stream of Mayanists: Tozzer and Merwin to students at Harvard, including those who worked for the Carnegie (Smith and the influential Alfred V. Kidder [Willey 1988:309–313]), then by diffused practice to the University of Pennsylvania and its archaeological progeny. Whatever the tradition of apprenticeship, however, map-makers seldom acknowledge that the surfaces they represent are but one of many such possible renderings. By the very nature of their craft, archaeologists will continue to toil at the border between mimesis and interpretive conventionalization, the former literally unachievable, the latter disinclined to transcending or trumping the external thing it wishes to show.

To Make "Just-Like-Us" and "Not-Quite-Like-Us"

A final aspect of Mayanist representation concerns the animation of scenes, the injection of affect and of people to make those scenes come alive. Renderings can no longer be done by archaeological draftsman of modest ability, but must rather come from trained artists. Here, too, the presence of conjecture increases rapidly, as does the problem of balancing images of people who are both "just-like-us"—recognizably human, empathetically so—and "not-quite-us," engaging precisely because they are not like the viewer (Berman 1999:288). In such projections of the past the claims become particularly grand. The images purport to offer reliable snapshots of former times, a difficulty compounded when the artist was of exceptional ability, as in the case of Zdeněk Burian, consummate illustrator of early humans (Wolf and Burian 1978). In fact, Burian's paintings accentuate debatable hypotheses about ancient behavior or appearance. For the Maya the main purveyor of such images is *National Geographic* magazine, held by some critics to be problematic at best, culturally offensive at worst (Lutz and Collins 1993). Typically, the artists chosen for Maya assignments have prior interests in "Western" art, the depiction of past lifeways in the American West: Roy Andersen [b. 1930] is one such figure, but also Herbert Herget [1885–1950], who depicted a terrified virgin hurtling into the Well of Sacrifice at Chichen Itza (Morley 1955:197). An exception is Peter Spier (1975), children's book illustrator and, in one issue of the magazine, revivifier of Tikal at its height in the Classic period (P. Spier and Hall 1975). For all the delightful whimsy of Spier's publications, including *People* and *Christmas* (P. Spier 1980, 1983), Spier spent several horrific years in Nazi concentration camps, together with his father, the Dutch cartoonist, Jo Spier (1978). His humanity, unaffected or perhaps accentuated by appalling personal experience, flows through scenes of pets, conversation, and loving family life. Veering from people "just-like-us" to the fundamentally weird, the magazine has since returned to portrayals of deeply exotic Maya (Gugliotta 2007). Most such depictions, excepting a few by Terry Rutledge, whose work is filed under "surrealistic art" on one server (Chaplin n.d.), treat architecture as rigidly polygonal, with hard lines, consistent colors, in peak condition of conservation, not a slump or irregular surface in sight. The plans mirror Maya buildings as modern architects might design them, a fact expressed clearly by certain renderings of structures at Copan, as done by the pen of a professional architect (Hohmann 1995: Abbildungen 4, 446–449).

Conclusion

It has become commonplace in studies of past image-making to speak of "visuality," modes of seeing and, by extension, depiction that dominate in certain societies, and in varied ways as "pattern[s] of cultural constructs and social discourses" (e.g., Elsner 2007:xvii, 289; inspired by Bryson 1988:106–108). This concept has some broad utility in addressing shared traditions of image-making and image-viewing, but skirts the historical challenge of looking at chains of image-makers, working in tight communities that preserve attributes of apprenticeship. Unavoidably, these chains of image-makers confront problems of how to deal with complex things in the world, from strata to ruined buildings, and, more ambitiously, reanimated vignettes of Maya life and historical events. Mimesis, an impulse to show things as they are thought plainly to be, bumps against a need for uniformity in large projects and wider intelligibility to technical audiences. On further consideration, mimesis founders on the impossibility or inadvisability of comprehensive representation. In this area of collision and tension, archaeologists find themselves beset by a need for closer attention to why they represent things and people from the past as they do, and a requirement for supple, multiple presentations that supplant and enrich the Mayanist trove of ping-pong balls, polygons, and virgins.

— 5 —

Visual Time Machines:
Nineteenth-Century Photographs and Museum
Re-Presentations in Maya Archaeology

Barbara W. Fash

For decades archaeologists have relied on earlier explorers' snapshots of their archaeological fieldwork to illuminate now-altered landscapes and the exact conditions and context of discoveries, rather than resorting to the embellishments often found in nineteenth century lithographs or paintings. This has required peering and squinting with magnifying lenses in order to make out details of the photographed scene. Digitization of early photographic collections has changed all that. Now, with new techniques, it is possible to zoom in and out of a scene in a blink—allowing our brains and visual faculties to activate an image that was once static and remote. This permits the sensation of entering into the image, especially if the places depicted are very familiar. So sharp are the details in these digitized versions that they are in the best cases transformed into visual time machines, allowing the viewer to closely inspect people, their clothing, the textures of objects and the surrounding landscapes, while inviting the imagination to conjure the temperature, the smell of the air, or hear the wind. Whether they record artifacts, tombs, a wall, fallen sculpture or inscriptions, old photographs enable us to revive a moment of discovery or illuminate details that may have been overlooked at first glance, once the material has been removed from its context (Shanks 1997).

Large-scale models and recreations in museums also provide opportunities to visualize and re-present the past. Photography and reconstructions together play dominant and overlapping roles in recent archaeological projects at the Classic Maya kingdom of Copan, in southwestern Honduras. These two approaches have been utilized extensively to both advance the archaeological work there and make it accessible to a larger public. Ongoing projects there continue to utilize the unique photographic archives from the early expeditions to the site to study the ruins, the results of which in turn are re-presented for visitors and students through museum exhibitions and diverse media. The process serves as an example of how combining the rich body of photographic information with modern investigations can offer creative and significant new insights into the past (Shanks 1997). It also prompts us to reconsider how today's cultures will be viewed and portrayed in the future, and the importance of leaving behind a clear and accessible record.

In my documentation and reconstruction work with the carved stone sculpture at Copan particularly, rarely does a field or lab day go by without reference to a photograph as an aid to understanding the ancient past. Untouched photographs can be trusted more than many other documentary tools, as the most accurate method and honest tools to re-present and revive the past. Both approaches, photographic documentation and physical reconstructions, will be treated here with a preliminary analysis of their impact on our understanding and visualization of the past.

Glass Plate Negatives

The high resolution of large-format, glass-plate negatives from the nineteenth century was remarkable for its ability to capture extraordinary details in rugged field conditions. Their transport and preservation from archaeological site to museum archives along mule trails and shipping lines alone are wondrous considering the plates' extreme fragility. With the advent of digitization we can now appreciate their superior qualities in comparison to later photographic formats. And as such they open new avenues of investigation to information that might otherwise have remained locked in minute form.

The glass plate technology used in the early Copan expeditions was a "dry plate" process introduced in the 1870s that coated the plate with a light-sensitive gelatin. Different expedition photographers approached their work with varying degrees of scientific accuracy and social interest. Images range from strict excavation photos to social images of an expedition, often with the "excavation space treated almost as a backdrop of a stage, before which stand members of the excavation party in various groupings" (Bohrer 2005:189), a widespread nineteenth century preference (Figure 5.1). The digitized images coupled with journal writings, photo captions, and excavation reports bring forth the voices of early explorers via a visually enhanced format. Although much of the insider's knowledge about the subject or events may be lost, the potent combination of these exceptionally sharp images and surviving texts produces an indelible memory that neither could accomplish alone.

Figure 5.1   The Peabody Museum of Archaeology and Ethnology at Harvard became the first U.S. institution to conduct archaeological research at a Maya ruin in Central America and Mexico. Their work at Copan ran from 1891 to 1900. Shown here are Ismael Vallecido, George Byron Gordon, George Shorkley and photographer Edmund Lincoln on Shorkley and Lincoln's last day in Copan, April 1893. Photo courtesy of the Peabody Museum, © President and Fellows of Harvard College, no. 2004.24.520.

Ancient stone monuments were perhaps constructed and carved to preserve a moment in time much like photographs. But because these "images" are interpretations laden with symbolism and biases, just as the texts and embellishments of the first explorers who recorded them, as opposed to unaltered activities captured on film, we can rely on the monuments and early archaeologists' notes with much less certainty as to their veracity. Hence, initial photographic scenes captured prior to an investigation can help verify accuracy in the condition of the archaeological record, in some cases betraying contextual evidence for ancient propaganda or intervention of carved stone remains.

The Copan Hieroglyphic Stairway Project

Copan boasts a very visual archaeological record, well known for its abundant high relief sculpture and—until recently—elaborate and enigmatic hieroglyphic writing (Baudez 1994; W. Fash 1991, 2001; Maudslay 1889–1902; Morley 1920). The famed Hieroglyphic Stairway at Copan, the longest ancient inscription in the New World, collapsed in the centuries after the aban-

donment of the city (see Figure 5.2). Its early nineteenth- and twentieth-
century investigations resulted in over half of the text and sculptural remains
being restored out of order from 1936–1945, and it was an intractable puzzle until recent epigraphic decipherments and archaeological detective work
have succeeded at re-ordering over seventy percent of the blocks (B. Fash
2006; W. Fash 2006; Stuart 2006).

In attempts to sort out the original order of the inscription and understand
its historical context, archaeological projects have been probing the structure
it adorns (numbered 10L-26 in the Copan mapping system) since the time
of its ill-fated reconstruction in the 1930s and 1940s. In the past two decades
especially, tunnel excavations and numerous previous photographic records
have been put to use to document and analyze the inscriptions and structure. With each new effort we have inched closer to an understanding of the
monument and what the eighth-century dynastic rulers intended when they
constructed and reconstructed this pyramid and text in a huge effort to honor

Figure 5.2 The 1891–1900 Peabody Expeditions uncovered the incredible Hieroglyphic
           Stairway, shown here in the background with a local family group, possibly a
           wedding party posing by removed stair blocks, 1893. Photo by Edmund Lincoln,
           courtesy of the Peabody Museum, © President and Fellows of Harvard College,
           no. 2004.24.452.

Figure 5.3a The earliest image of the Copan Hieroglyphic Stairway. Photo by Marshall Saville, courtesy of the Peabody Museum, © President and Fellows of Harvard College, no. 2004.24.144.

their ancestors and patron gods with the hope of ensuring their own legacies for the future (W. Fash 2002).

The glass-plate negatives of the Stairway taken in the 1890s during the Harvard Peabody Museum's expedition to the site contain a vast treasure-trove of information no longer available to us on the original monument today, in large measure due to the carving's subsequent erosion. With support from a grant from the National Endowment for the Humanities, the Peabody Museum completed Phase I, in 2007, of a two-year project to scan its entire collection of glass plate negatives (approximately 10,000 in number), and 19,500 nitrate and acetate film images (Peabody Museum 2007a). This technological advance came at a welcome moment in the archaeological research at Copan and during a renewed attempt to reconstruct the inscription's original order.[1]

---

1. The author organized several conference workshops and field research trips to Copan in 2006–2008 with epigrapher colleagues David Stuart, Stephen Houston, and Simon Martin, and archaeologist William Fash, to renew attempts, initially conducted from 1985–1996, to reconstruct and document the inscription and archaeological record. The results of the workshops were presented by all five participants at three conferences: 2006 *Stairways to Immortality: Ancestors, Heroes, and Warriors.* The Peabody Museum Weekend of the Americas; 2007 *Investigaciones de la Escalinata Jeroglífica, la historia y el arte de los antiguos Mayas.* Public symposio, Municipalidad de Copan Ruinas, Honduras; and

Figure 5.3b Zoomed-in detail of the Copan Hieroglyphic Stairway. Photo by Marshall Saville, courtesy of the Peabody Museum, © President and Fellows of Harvard College, no. 2004.24.144.

The digitized glass plates allow us to zoom in and see details that before were too small to see in photo enlargements or contact prints. Quantities of valuable information come to light in each image, especially considering so much of the inscription is eroded today, and their close inspection effectively allows us to virtually step back in time (Peabody Museum 2007b; Figure 5.3a–b).

The Stairway was not found as visitors see it reconstructed at the site today. The upper three-fourths of the 64 stairs became dislodged by earthquakes, with fifteen steps from the upper part sliding down over the lower part at the base. Many blocks splayed out or were broken in this process of deterioration and collapse. In one of the earliest images of the Stairway taken in 1891 the excavators lifted these massive blocks from the ground, trying their best to lay them out in order on the adjacent plaza. Later on, in the 1930s, the Carnegie Institution of Washington (CIW) project repositioned the blocks on the building to the best of their ability at the time, but since only the calendric portions could be deciphered their reconstruction left the stairway text 70% out of order. In 1946, CIW architect and epigrapher Tatiana Proskouriakoff painted the twentieth-century vision of how the monument once looked, constituting the first re-presentation of the Hieroglyphic Stairway (Figure 5.4). It is from this jumbled state and the fixed reconstructed image embed-

2008 *Copan Archaeology and History: New Finds and New Research,* 32nd Maya Meeting, University of Texas at Austin.

ded in many minds that scholars continue to wrestle the blocks back into their original order and into a new representation.

Close attention to details of the glass plate photographs revealed a time lapse in two images that appeared to be contemporaneous, but in fact were

Figure 5.4   Reconstruction watercolor of the Hieroglyphic Stairway, Copan, by Tatiana Proskouriakoff 1946. Photo courtesy of the Peabody Museum, © President and Fellows of Harvard College.

taken two years apart. The scenes captured in each image showed that the blocks forming nearly six full steps of the overlying slumped segment that was found in its original order, were later dislodged by the rains. This event therefore, caused them to be removed out of order two years after the first image was taken (Gordon 1902). The displacement meant that they were not set back in their proper sequence decades later by the unwitting Carnegie team. Although seemingly insignificant in comparison to the Stairway's entire corpus of 64 steps, the six "rediscovered" steps identified during the 2006 research of the 1892 and 1895 photographs proved to be an instrumental piece in jump-starting the epigraphic reconstruction process. The resolution of the glass plates and the keen eyes of the epigraphers David Stuart, Stephen Houston, and Simon Martin enabled identifications of the mis-restored blocks from their improper positions, and the reordering and resetting of them in their original positions, at least on paper (Peabody Museum 2007b). This giant step forward led to a series of linkages with previously "floating" text segments that David Stuart and Linda Schele had reconstructed years before. Stuart and his colleagues proceeded to build on the phases, now achieving approximately 71% reconstruction of the original order (B. Fash 2006; W. Fash 2006; Stuart 2006).

It is possible the misplaced blocks might have been recognized earlier had the most complete frontal images of the Stairway at this stage not been relegated to the background of several shots. Instead, the still in situ stairs only appear in the distance behind scenes of local people posing around removed stair blocks in the adjacent plaza. Frustrating as it might be, the record underscores how a crucial piece of the puzzle today was a mere backdrop to personal narratives a century earlier.

Despite the progress in decipherments, the environmental degradation of the stone is so advanced that large amounts of the text and iconography have already been lost forever. With the physical condition of the Stairway blocks so dire, if the blocks are removed and reset they will be even further damaged. Here is where line drawings, another representational tool employed in the recording and decipherment process, come into play. When followed closely, established standards in drawing conventions leave little question in researchers' minds about glyphic details, so a drawing need not be deciphered to retrieve crucial information. These coded re-presentations of archaeological illustration appear side by side with photographs—one to enhance and corroborate the other.

In keeping with many earlier well-intentioned attempts to halt the Stairway's deterioration, new efforts were begun to this end in 1997. The Honduran Institute of Anthropology and History (IHAH) asked the author to investigate how to make a completely faithful copy of the inscription without touching the fragile and friable stones. About the same time the Getty Conservation Institute was engaged to make a detailed condition study of the cause of the deterioration and provide the IHAH with recommendations for how to preserve this monument into the future (Getty Conservation Institute 2006). In 1998 3-D laser scanning tests were conducted at the Harvard's Peabody Museum, to establish if the technology could be applied to the Stairway (McCluskey 1998). At that point in time the technology was still very cumbersome and expensive, yet it resulted in a 3-D model of one block and a virtual model of the entire composite group of sculptures brought to the Peabody in the 1890s. Naturally the 3-D technology has advanced considerably since our initial attempt. In 2007, the author and a research team

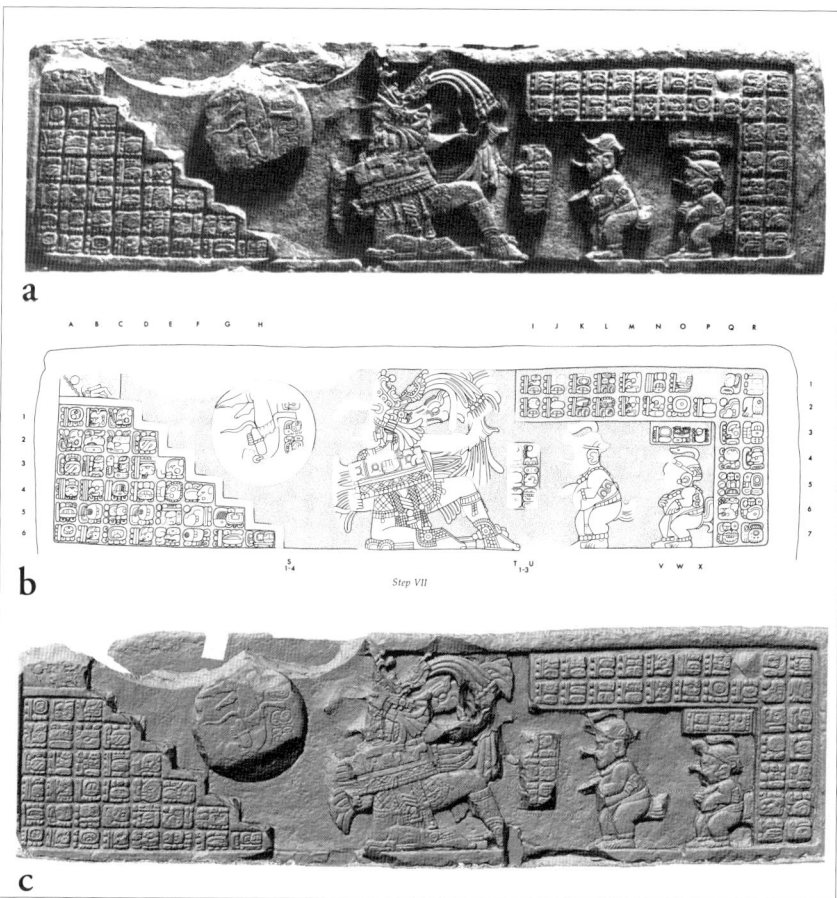

Figure 5.5 Three ways of representing an inscribed block from the Hieroglyphic Stairway at Yaxchilan, Chiapas, Mexico, a) traditional 2-D photograph, b) a line drawing, and c) a 3-D digital image. After Tokovinine and Fash, 2008, 20.

tested a now available 3-D optical system in the remote tropical setting at the site of Yaxchilan, Chiapas, Mexico (Figure 5.5; Powell 2007a, 2007b, 2007c). The system complements and enhances the existing representational tools of photography and line drawings, with the added benefits of manipulating light direction, object rotation, and the ability to generate replications from the data at varied scales. As of this writing, the system is being deployed to scan the entire Copan Hieroglyphic Stairway, which will enable the new reconstruction of the inscription to be produced in a virtual model. The virtual model can be converted to a solid model, at any scale, through a variety

Escalinata Jeroglifica, Bloque 4 (detalle), 11/11/08 ©President and Fellows of Harvard College

Figure 5.6 Three different angles of lighting on a 3-D model of a Hieroglyphic Stairway block (2008). Corpus of Maya Hieroglyphic Inscriptions Program, Peabody Museum, Harvard University.

of production techniques now commercially available (Figure 5.6).

Following the 3-D data capture and post-processing, the next step will be to unite to the nineteenth century images and the 3-D data. Although not intentionally captured as such, stereoscopic images that occur in the 1890s photos can be texture-mapped over the new 3-D scans and effectively reverse time, by restoring eroded details. If successful, it is hoped a solid model of the stairway with this additional lost information added can be reproduced for Honduras, preserving the inscription and its history into the future.

The 1890s Peabody expeditions also made casts of the blocks, functionally the equivalent in the nineteenth century of our 3-D digital scans today. Vast cast collections enabled many museums of the nineteenth century to have a varied and useful sample of art for artists and students to draw inspiration from, and for connoisseurs to appreciate. Motivated by convenience, economy, iconographic meaning, as well as aesthetic appeal, ancient reproductions—whether cast or copied—transmitted visual representations to a larger audience in a way photographs and now electronic images do today. Eventually the tides changed, and many casts were removed from exhibition halls to make way for original works (B. Fash 2004; Whitehall 1970).

With a new appreciation of the value of the plaster casts today, it is imaginable that the digital scans will have an equally important role in the future. Universities and museums seem to be the best place to preserve such records, which will require data migration to new formats as software becomes obsolete in the future. Unlike object collections, storage and periodic cleaning of digital data will not be the issue, but data migration will continue indefinitely and demand a renewed focus on the material with each permutation. Collection mangers will not only be custodians of physical objects, but virtual ones as well. Access to and reproduction of digital images and 3-D data require thoughtful standards, so that careless use or loss of originality are not issues.

Even as scholars struggle to recreate stories and information from past images, teasing out feelings and unwritten events, it is important to make every attempt not to decouple today's histories from modern visual records. Local people in Copan are just becoming acquainted with these century-old images of their community. Most people have no mental picture of what the town or ruins looked like before it was built up or the ruins were reconstructed. Looking upon the old images stirs new feelings of community and a desire to become more familiar with their history and cultural patrimony.

Reconstructions in the Copan Sculpture Museum

Inaugurated in 1996, the on-site Copan Sculpture Museum was conceived of as a means of conserving many of the monumental stone stelae and altars and

Figure 5.7   Interior of the Copan Sculpture Museum with the Rosalila replica at center and façade reconstructions on the edges. Photo by the author, 1996.

an opportunity to display the numerous new reconstructions of stone mosaic sculptures accomplished by the work of the Copan Mosaics Project and the Proyecto Arqueológico Acrópolis Copán (PAAC) to the world at large (B. Fash 2011). The exhibitions represent the best-known examples of building façades and singular sculptural achievements from the ancient Copan kingdom (Figure 5.7). Over 150,000 national and international tourists visit the ruins of Copan every year, a UNESCO World Heritage site.[2] Development and completion of the sculpture museum not only serves to preserve the Classic Maya sculpture from the archaeological site, but also re-presents the ancient achievements in a manner that both fosters cultural understanding of the past, and enhances a local and national sense of identity (B. Fash 2011).

As a case study, the Copan Sculpture Museum demonstrates that on-site archaeological museums may provide multiple benefits to a community and its cultural heritage by advancing the shared goals of cultural heritage preservation, education, and tourism. It accomplishes this by providing a place for interpreting and re-presenting ancient cultures, art, and world-view, while simultaneously helping to protect the archaeological site. Enhanced local

2. Data provided from records kept by Professor Oscar Cruz Melgar, Regional Director for the Instituto Hondureño de Antropología e Historia.

identity and a strong appreciation of the past are generated by community involvement with the museum at all levels. The process of constructing an on-site museum sets in motion a change of attitudes locally towards cultural property ownership and its curation by creating a dynamic new museological approach to heritage preservation and interpretation with a potential for promoting social change (B. Fash 2007).

The museum allows ample space for reconstructing many varied and lively sculptural façades to the public for the first time in over 1,000 years. By assimilating the ancient architectural sculpture, visitors come to appreciate the artistic achievements of the past and can marvel at what was accomplished using only stone tools. Making a heap of confused jumbled sculptures once again into objects of visual interest creates a sense of wonder in the viewer, stirring emotion just as the building may have in the past. Once the viewer's attention is attracted in such a manner, the exhibitions take on a resonance beyond the museum (Greenblatt 1991). The convenience of keeping the sculpture physically near to the ruins in an on-site museum maintains it as close as possible to its original context. Visitors to the site can retain the original context as a fresh experience from which to contemplate these sculptures and buildings in the museum setting. Complicated on-site logistics and risks that would have arisen from moving the immense sculptures greater distances are reduced by the museum's proximity to the ruins.

The centerpiece of this museum is a full-scale recreation of a masterpiece of Copan architecture and artistry, a magnificent Early Classic Maya structure dubbed "Rosalila" by archaeologist Ricardo Agurcia, who discovered it buried beneath the final version of Structure 16 in the Acropolis (Agurcia and B. Fash 2006). Local artisans reproduced the modeled stucco sculptures faithfully in a carefully controlled way, using photographs and drawings of the original under the author's supervision, while scholars worked together to determine the original colors of the constituent parts.

With this conservation and museum mission, in collaboration with Hondurans of various ages, backgrounds, and regions, a new level of cultural hybridization in progress was experienced (B. Fash 2007), one "where culture is generative and innovative, offering possibilities for change and continuity, not merely the replication of either old or new cultural forms" (Kreps 2003:15). The creation of new hybrid cultural forms demonstrates local communities' capacities for reshaping and redefining the past to meet their own interests and purposes. Cristina Kreps feels that "there needs to be further movement away from static notions of conservation that have been embedded in salvaging and rescuing paradigms" (2003:14). But rather than abandon these practices, which I see as still necessary, I have attempted to implement an *integrated system* that allows for both past and present to share resources and energies, so rescue operations of the past may give purpose and meaning to the "living knowledge, customs, and traditions associated with material culture" of the present (Kreps 2003:14). In the Copan Sculpture Museum this integration is most evident by the years of rescue operations, analysis, and training that preceded the museum's construction. Now, where fallen façade blocks were once left in jumbled heaps and ignored by most visitors, the reconstructed sculptural façades are again available to visitors, bringing history back to life for the many schoolchildren that visit yearly. Conservator Charles Rhyne (2006:168) notes that the Copan Sculpture Museum's re-presentation of Rosalila is a highly successful example of how replicas can be immensely informative when the originals are properly studied and preserved (Figure 5.7). With these reconstructions it is hoped that visitors will come to realize that the ancient Copan sculptors produced some of the finest and most animated buildings and temples in the Maya area, in addition to the stunning freestanding monolithic monuments people have admired for many years.

Although computer graphic reconstructions can be useful tools, the sculpture museum provides us with an alternative format to present our findings utilizing the actual sculptures and building façade stones. At the archaeological site, strict reconstruction codes laid down by the Venice Charter of 1961 prohibit any restoration on the original building at an archaeological site, other than what was specifically found intact or can be proven by clear, well-documented physical evidence and the anastylosis process. In the end, these are all a work in progress, using all the structural and iconographic clues available to us to carry out the reconstructions to the very best of our ability. By using the original excavated sculptures and faced stones in the museum we hope to bring to light a sample of the numerous lively buildings that once graced this ancient city rich in the sculptural arts, and leave them in a semi-permanent setting for protection and study.

In the near future it is possible to imagine a reconstruction of Copan's Hieroglyphic Stairway in the Sculpture Museum once the 3-D model is complete. If so, it will open a new chapter on the convergence of nineteenth century photographic methods with today's latest imaging technology. Preservation of the information in the original monument would be achieved without moving the original indoors.

Concluding Remarks

This essay examined how the computer technologies of digitization and 3-D scanning are reutilizing photographic records and replications from a century ago and advancing the way we understand and re-present the past, specifically for reconstructing some of the New World's greatest jigsaw puzzles and unlocking the history they contain. It demonstrates the way efforts to recreate and represent the past in a museum setting have an impact on larger social issues today. If we reflect on where a century of development of representational tools has brought us today we can only imagine the uses that lie ahead for our students, and theirs in turn. Will future generations find our virtual realities quaint precursors to their methods? Will people one day have the ability to metaphysically project into reconstructions through their imaginations? Will this be the way we learn about history, and if so how much more profound will our experiences be as a result? I agree with Mark Gillings (2005: 223) that VR has fallen into a specific niche in archaeology, "a form of flexible reconstruction drawing...that is both lacking in imagination and limiting in scope." One wonders if virtual realities will stop at architectural models and monuments—or will people, activities and senses, pleasant or not, be standard projections as well? Reflecting on other studies of re-presenting the past in this volume, the question remains for how the twenty-first century will deliver its sights, smells, and sounds for future researchers so these intangible qualities are not left to the imagination in their reconstructions of us.

— 6 —

Of Imaging and Imagining:
Landscape Reconstruction at Piedras Negras

Cassandra L. Mesick

For the past two decades or so, the development of digital technologies has significantly impacted the field of archaeology. Methodologically, many archaeologists have begun to rely, for instance, on digital photography, video recording, and three-dimensional computer modeling to document fieldwork activities (Pollefeys et al. 2003). Several of these tools are similarly employed in the subsequent laboratory analysis of artifacts and other archaeological features. Archaeological survey has been similarly affected by increased reliance on Global Positioning Systems (GPS) (Barratt et al. 2000; Leech 2008; White and King 2007:61–66), while the mapping of sites and terrain is often aided by (if not wholly undertaken through) the use of Total Stations and Geographic Information Systems (GIS) software (e.g., Allen et al. 1990; Forte and Kay 2003; Wheatley and Gillings 2002). The archaeological application of these technologies is not limited to field methodologies, but rather extends to the presentation of data. In fact, the advent of computer programs such as AutoCAD and other modeling software have influenced how archaeologists are able to reconstruct and re-present ancient sites, artifacts, and peoples to academic and public audiences alike (e.g., Barceló et al. 2000; Forte 1997, 2005; Frischer et al. 2000; Higgins et al. 1994; Moscati 2007; Niccolucci 2002). The shift towards digital technologies therefore carries with it both methodological and representational consequences.

As archaeologists have begun to explore these new modes of imaging the past, they have simultaneously examined the broader representational practices adhered to within the discipline, often from a critical perspective. In general, these discussions tend to upset the notion that images convey information and meanings that are universally "self-evident" to viewers (Gillings 2005:224). Instead, these debates demonstrate how the cultural knowledge and multiple messages encapsulated in images may disrupt presumed assumptions about their accuracy, realism, and objectivity (Molyneaux 1997:1). Although historians and archaeologists have developed this argument in reference to archaeological representations varying from photographs to illustrations to written site reports (e.g., Bradley 1997; Hodder 1989; Shanks 1997), it has been rather forcefully articulated with respect to the growing number of Virtual Reality (VR) and interactive computer reconstructions archaeologists have created to re-present ancient structures and sites.

In this particular context, discussions often focus on defining the aims and purposes of VR applications (e.g., Gillings 2005:228; Kantner 2000; Reilly 1991), delineating specific methodologies and techniques employed in the production of digital models (e.g., Barceló 2000; Gillings 2000), and questioning the relevance of concepts such as objectivity, authority, and verisimilitude in the production and reception of these models (Delingette 2002:90; Favro 2006; Gillings 2005:229–231). Despite a burgeoning literature about the archaeological adoption of these technologies, archaeologists appear to hold varying opinions about the current state of affairs. For instance, Mark Gillings cautiously maintains that, at present, VR has been primarily exploited as a "sophisticated means of creating ingenious pictures" (Gillings 2005:223). In contrast, Maurizio Forte boldly asserts that his edited volume containing VR reconstructions of archaeological sites offers "the most faithful re-presentation of the ancient world possible: highly realistic in information and with a high scientific content" (Forte 1997:10).

This chapter addresses many of these concerns about the roles and limitations of digital technologies in archaeology by presenting a synopsis of work undertaken to image the Classic Maya kingdom of Piedras Negras, Guatemala and its hinterlands through the use of ArcGIS and computer animation software. After providing a brief history of past research at the site to contextualize this more recent work, it describes the process of (re)mapping Piedras Negras and subsequent efforts to use these spatial data to create a digital three-dimensional reconstruction of its elite and non-elite architectural remains and their relationships with the natural landscape. The explanatory emphasis emerges, first, from a perceived need to promote transparency concerning the ways in which new imaging technologies are being used in archaeological research and data (re)presentation, as well as the problems they engender.

History of Research and Background

The Classic Period Maya site of Piedras Negras, Guatemala has enjoyed a long history of exploration and excavation. Although first documented and named by Ludovic Chambon in the 1890s (Golden 2002:4), Teobert Maler produced the first photographs and maps of the site, published in 1901 (Maler 1901; Satterthwaite 2005[1943]:170). Somewhat later, between 1910 and 1920, Sylvanus Morley visited Piedras Negras, recording its monuments and drawing a sketch map of the ruins (Morley 1920, 1937–1938). The publication of Morley's materials increased archaeological interest about the site, eventually resulting in its systematic excavation by a team of University of Pennsylvania archaeologists between 1931 and 1939. During this time, members of the Penn project focused primarily on excavating public architecture, documenting monuments, and mapping the site core; the significance of their work should not be underestimated. Despite the lack of attention to small, non-monumental architecture (Z. Nelson 2005:16), the project did produce what has until recently been the most authoritative map of the site, created by architect Fred P. Parris from 1931 to 1933, with later amendments by Tatiana Proskouriakoff in 1939 (Figure 6.1; Satterthwaite 2005 [1943]:170–171).

Approximately half a century later, excavations at Piedras Negras began anew with the Proyecto Arqueológico Piedras Negras, an archaeological project jointly led by Stephen Houston and Héctor Escobedo. The project undertook four consecutive seasons from 1997 through 2000, completing fieldwork with a final season in 2004. Throughout the duration of this project, a small team of archaeologists conducted local survey in an attempt to (1) expand the limits of the 1939 map and (2) create a digital version of the revised map (Escobedo and Houston 1997a:iii; see also Escobedo and Houston 1997b, 1998, 1999, 2000). The following section details how these goals were achieved.

Imaging the Maya Landscape at Piedras Negras

When Fred Parris created the original map of Piedras Negras, he employed a theodolite, paper, and pencil, triangulating the position and orientation of each building and the surrounding topography (Satterthwaite 2005 [1943]:170–171). It took nearly three years to complete this project, and it required still more effort by Proskouriakoff to correct and expand Parris' work. With a densely settled site core that encompasses about two square kilometers, Piedras Negras covers an area large enough to daunt even an experienced surveyor, challenging any attempt to complete this task expediently and accurately. Owing in part to the expansive and complex nature of the site, the most recent efforts to record natural and built features of the site made use of newer equipment and methods.

On-site Survey and Mapping

Between 1997 and 2000, Nathan Curritt, Timothy Murtha, and Zachary Nelson collaborated to expand and digitize the map of Piedras Negras created

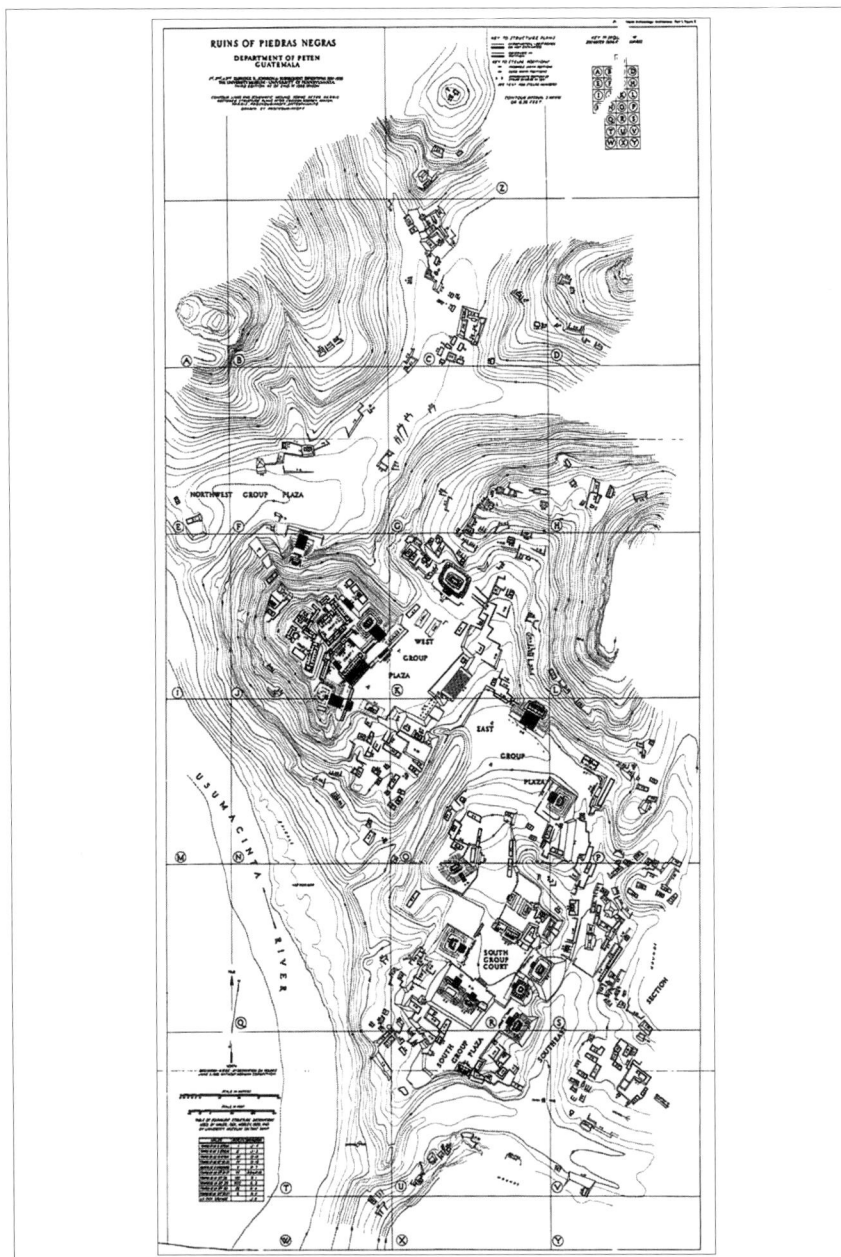

Figure 6.1   Map of Piedras Negras, created by Fred P. Parris between 1931 and 1933 and
Tatiana Proskouriakoff in 1939. Digitized by the Brigham Young University
Geography Department.

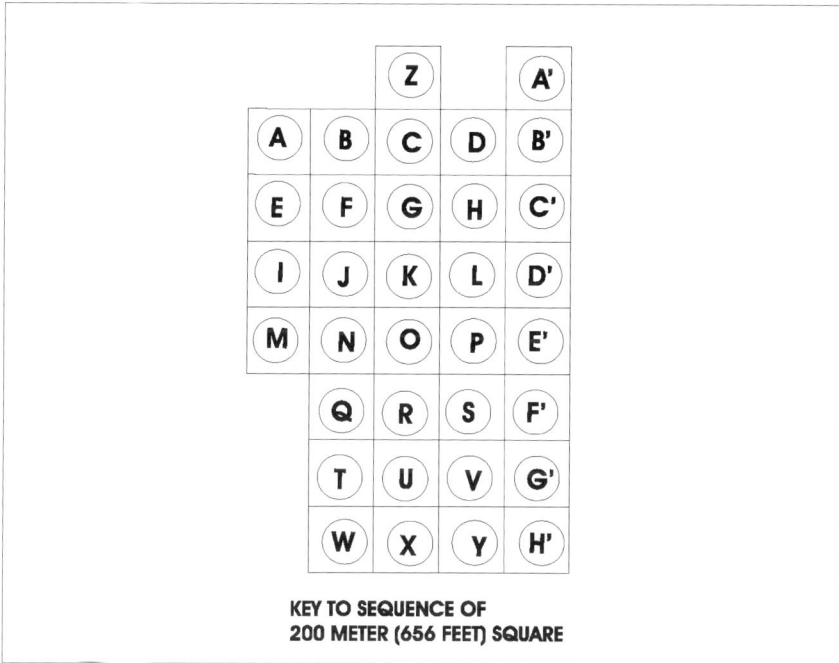

Figure 6.2   Revised grid system employed by the Proyecto Arqueológico Piedras Negras (Z. Nelson 2005:42, Figure 4.1).

by Parris and Proskouriakoff in the 1930s. This original version employed a grid system consisting of twenty-six 200 meter squares, each of which was superimposed onto areas of the site then known by Penn excavators. Each square of the grid was assigned a unique alphabetic designation. This labeling system presented Curritt, Murtha, and Nelson their first logistical challenge, because its nomenclature did not readily allow for expansion of the map. Consequently, Curritt concentrated his efforts in the areas of excavation undertaken in 1998, most of which were in the site epicenter, and focused on establishing a new grid for the revised map. This grid is oriented towards magnetic north, with its origin located 5km south and 5km west of an existing surveyor point (5TT121982) positioned at the base of Structure K-5, a monumental building located in the northeastern corner of the West Group Plaza. Elevation, arbitrarily placed at 100 meters above sea level, was determined from this same point. The revised grid retained the same basic structure as the original, with the addition of a single row of primed letters on its eastern edge to account for features discovered outside the boundaries of the 1930s map (Figure 6.2). Murtha was responsible for surveying beyond the southern and northeastern limits of the Penn map, thereby connecting excavations in the "rural" hinterlands to the site core (Z. Nelson 2005:41). Nelson worked at the south edge of the site and created the new digital map of Piedras Negras (see Z. Nelson 1999, 2005).

The mapping team used the same equipment during all field seasons, which included a Topcon Total Station with laser sights, a Mark VI data collector, and a laptop computer with all necessary software applications (in this case, Notepad, WordPerfect, QuattroPro, Minicad, CorelDraw, AutoCAD, and ArcGIS). First, the Total Station was set up at a series of stations, or points with known geographic coordinates; these were marked with wooden stakes, each of which was tied with blue flagging tape for visibility and affixed with a metal identification tag. The ID tag recorded (1) the X, Y, and Z coordinates of the stake, (2) the name of the station, (3) the date it was placed there, and (4) the initials of the individual responsible for taking the points. Using the Total Station, its sight laser, and a pole-mounted prism that reflects the laser back to its point of origin (in this case, the Total Station itself), a series of points—designated by N, E, and Z coordinates—was taken.[1] After recording hundreds of NEZ points from dozens of stations, the entire area of Piedras Negras was mapped. Data pertaining to architectural features was first hand-drawn using a tape and compass, and the sketches were then used to facilitate the coordination of architectural data with Total Station points.

The NEZ coordinates generated by the Total Station were subsequently loaded through a serial cable into the Mark VI data collector, which stored them until ready for download onto the laptop. This data transfer, from Total Station to data collector to laptop, occurred daily on-site, allowing any possible problems to be addressed and corrected in the field. For instance, Total Station mapping with the particular model used during the 1996–2000 field seasons requires the surveyor to manually input the NEZ coordinates for each station; if entered incorrectly, all points taken from that station will be inaccurate and can distort the entire map. Each point collected during mapping had to be moved from the data collector onto the computer individually. After formatting the NEZ data into a comma delimited file (ASCII), the resulting document was saved first as an Excel (.xls), then as a DBASE file, the latter of which is compatible with ArcGIS. The data were then opened in ArcGIS,[2] allowing the creation of digital maps directly from the Total Station coordinates using the suite of ArcGIS programs.

Few serious impediments arose during this stage of research. Limited visibility, particularly in peripheral areas of Piedras Negras where vegetation was

1. In the Total Station coordinate system, N designates the Northing (or North/South coordinate), E records the Easting (or East/West coordinate), and Z provides the elevation.

2. ArcGIS employs an x, y, z coordinate system. Translating from the NEZ system of the Total Station is simple: x=E, y=N, and z=Z.

dense and uncut, made it difficult to obtain the necessary sight lines for the Total Station laser to reach the pole-mounted prism. In addition, the necessary reformatting of data was tedious and at first time-consuming, although with practice and training it was completed expediently.

Post-Fieldwork Imaging: Creating the Maps

Before three-dimensional recreations of Piedras Negras were created by Zachary Nelson using ArcGIS, Penn's original map was digitized by the Brigham Young University Geography Department—no small feat given that the physical document is over 5 feet in length. This digitization allowed for comparison between the new points gathered by the Proyecto Arqueológico Piedras Negras and those obtained by Parris and Proskouriakoff in the 1930s. The immediate result of this comparison was the "discovery of distance errors in the original Piedras Negras map," in some places as discrepant as 20m (Z. Nelson 2005:44). The distortion resulted in shortened distances between buildings,[3] which, in turn, presented difficulties for incorporating newly documented structures into the map, since there was inadequate space in which to do so.

To compensate for this problem, Nelson correlated the digitized Penn map with the coordinates taken by the Proyecto Arqueológico Piedras Negras team along a north-south axis (originating at Curritt's Str. K-5 survey point [see above] and running to a large ceiba tree located at the southern periphery of the site, southeast of the South Group Plaza). New data from the 1997–2000 and 2004 field seasons were then added (Figure 6.3). The result was a digital image of Piedras Negras that incorporated many of the errors that plagued the Penn map. Nonetheless, the compromised version sufficed, at the time, for two reasons. First, architectural survey points were too scarce to position buildings recorded in the 1930s onto the corrected map. Second, contour information was sufficiently lacking to ensure a reliable topographic context. Thus, when Nelson undertook this project in 2004, it seemed as though any further correction of the map would compel the time-consuming task of remapping the entire site. Despite the ultimate shortcomings of the mapping project, it was not without obvious merits, since more than 90 mounds were added to the Penn map—primarily in the southeast quadrant—increasing the number of known structures by 25%.

Nelson created additional maps using a combination of CorelDraw and ArcGIS. The former rendering program allows the user to create multiple layers, which can be hidden and made invisible or activated and made visible.

---

3. Despite the errors in Penn's map, it is still largely accurate, especially given the equipment and conditions at their disposal in the early 1930's. Nonetheless, it should not be consulted for authoritative data concerning the distance between structures even if their relative placements are accurate.

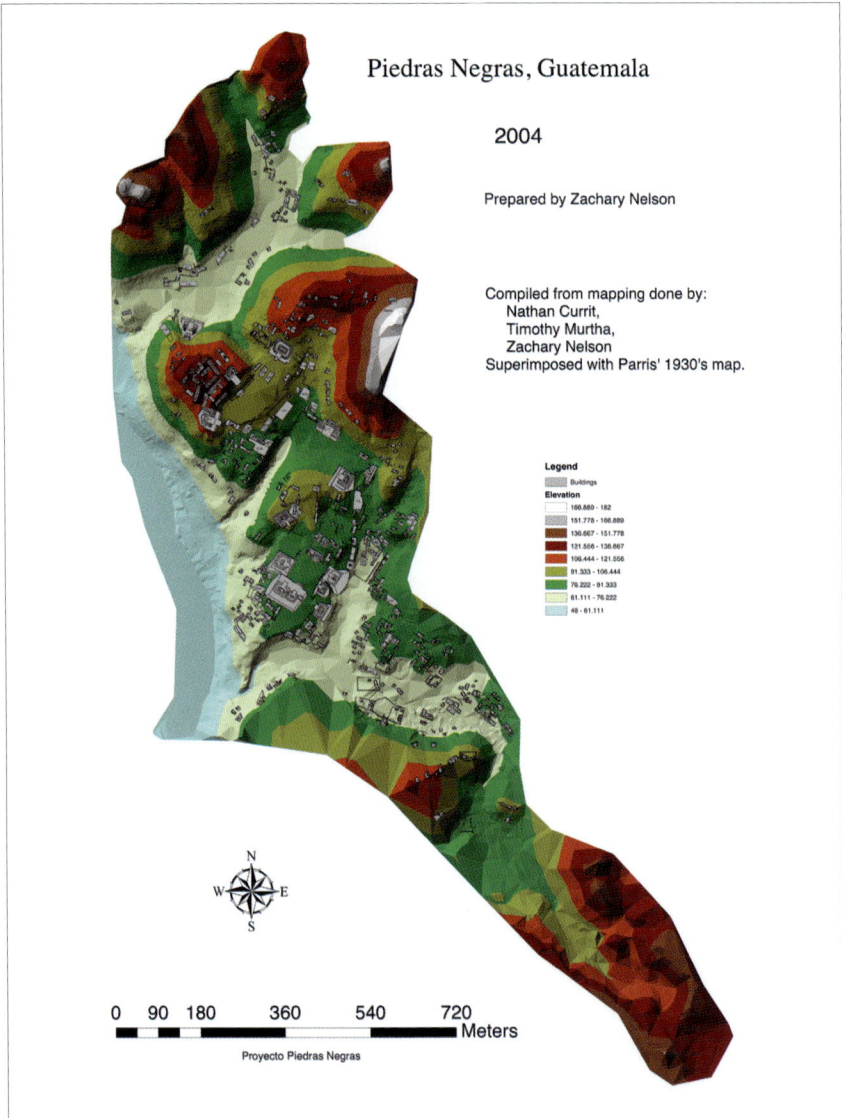

Figure 6.3   Digitized map of Piedras Negras showing contoured topography and site structures superimposed on the 1930's map (Z. Nelson 2005:41, Figure 4.0).

This allows incremental complexity and flexibility in a single image. Thus,
rather than creating several different maps to illustrate desired features (e.g.,
contour lines, structures, water sources, etc.), it is only necessary to create
different layers, which can then be viewed in any combination.

The types of computer-generated maps discussed above highlight some of the most salient paradoxes of employing sophisticated new technologies to re-present the past with greater accuracy. First, despite the fact many archaeologists and professional surveyors consider the coordinates from Total Stations to be precise measures of a given landscape, the maps produced using these data were still considered "compromises" by those who created them. The maps are not wholly accurate, which stems in this case from the fact that—however immersed in new technologies contemporary archaeological practices may seem—practitioners of these new methods and media still engage with and rely on older, more established traditions. Members of the Proyecto Arqueológico Piedras Negras referred back to the Penn map, created with a theodolite, pen, and paper, with near constant frequency. In this way, the methodological and representational shortcomings of this earlier project were never fully divorced from the more recent attempts.

Second, one of the great promises of ArcGIS (arguably one of the most familiar and least "new" of the technologies available to archaeologists) is its ability to represent the three-dimensionality of a landscape without the highly conventionalized contour lines typically employed to indicate elevation. The 3-D landscape is meant to look and be experienced as more "real" through the application of this program. Yet the images it produces are still static, and they can only be experienced via a two-dimensional medium (e.g., the computer screen or paper). The Proyecto Arqueológico Piedras Negras attempted to mitigate the fixity of these representations by using ArcScene, one of the applications comprising the ArcGIS suite, which allows the viewer to manipulate the map by dollying, tumbling, and panning it. Of course, to reproduce the supposedly more interactive, dynamic maps in traditional media such as books, articles, or reports, "stills" must be created, effectively relinquishing any sense of interactivity or dynamism. As of yet, the problem of two-dimensional mediation of supposedly three-dimensional images has only been resolved through immersive virtual reality simulations, which have not been employed with the Piedras Negras data (for other case study examples, see papers collected in Barceló et al. 2000; Frischer et al. 2000; Kenderdine 2004).

Imagining the Maya Landscape at Piedras Negras

In late 2005, Zachary Nelson began exploring possible ways to correct the unresolved problems of the digital map of Piedras Negras without returning to the site to survey and remap it. In consultation with project director Stephen Houston, Nelson determined that he would be able to identify and adjust the spatial distortions between structures by creating a virtual reconstruction of site architecture and topographic landscape (e.g., Forte 2003).

The virtual model of the site's buildings would be based on coordinates taken with the Total Station and measurements recorded during the most recent excavations, for which adequate photographs and fieldnotes were available for consultation. The expectation was that this model could then be compared, on a computer, to the digitized map created from Penn excavation data. This process thus required rendering software compatible with ArcGIS data. After researching various options, Houston and Nelson purchased Alias Maya 7.0, computer animation software that met all necessary requirements, with the joint purpose of (1) allowing for corrections to the digitized maps of Piedras Negras created by Nelson and (2) facilitating three-dimensional reconstruction drawings of the site's architecture.

Interventions and Corrections

Primarily employed by animators and filmmakers, Maya 7.0 has not yet received much attention by archaeologists. In some respects, it differs significantly from more familiar computer rendering software such as AutoCAD, CorelDraw, or Google SketchUp. For instance, while such programs allow the artist to create drawings or wire frame images in two-dimensions with the possibility to view them in three-dimensional, isometric perspectives, Maya 7.0 forces the artist to create "scenes" using solid, three-dimensional shapes. All reconstructions must therefore always be conceptualized and created through the use of simple and complex polygons defined by x, y, and z coordinates.

Yet many of the program's core features share similarities with aspects of the more popular programs. Most importantly in this context, Maya 7.0 permits its users to create and hide rendered elements in a variety of combinations, similar to the use of layers in CorelDraw. Consequently, in attempting to correct the errors in the newer Piedras Negras maps, two of its digital versions were imported into Maya 7.0 as discrete layers: (1) a relatively simple plan of the site containing only its architectural features; and (2) a three-dimensional view of the natural topography created in ArcGIS. When the second layer is activated, the site plan is invisible; the topographic overlay obscures it entirely (Figure 6.4). For much of the corrective work, both layers were hidden, allowing computer reconstruction of architecture to occur without visual confusion from the other data.

Using this software program in conjunction with architectural measurements extracted from excavation data, Nelson created three-dimensional reconstructions of monumental architecture, focusing on large structures in the acropolis area. The choice of structures first targeted for reconstruction derives from the fact that (1) they were excavated by the Proyecto Arqueológico Piedras Negras and were consequently associated with more data; and (2) the area surrounding the acropolis suffered from the greatest distortion in

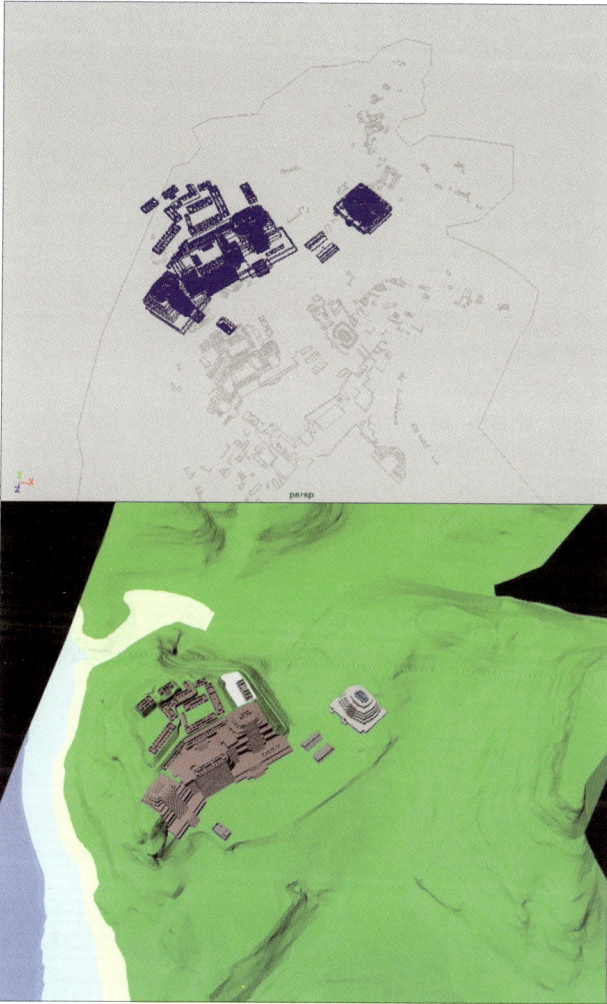

Figure 6.4   Views of the two layers in Maya 7.0: (upper) Bird's-eye view of the acropolis and surrounding topography (in blue wireframe) above the digitized 1930s map (in gray); (lower) same view with topographic layer activated in solid surface. Prepared by Zachary Nelson.

Penn's map.[4] Imaging efforts began with the reconstruction of K-5, located to the east of the acropolis complex. To render its terraced platforms, a series

---

4.   This probably stems from two factors. First, the monumental architecture around the acropolis is the most complex and dense at the site, making accurate mapping difficult. Second, the acropolis was one of the locations where the original leafs of the Penn map were stitched together (Zachary Nelson 2007, personal communication).

of cubic polygons were placed atop one another, with height, length, and width adjusted according to measurements taken in the field. The scalloped contours of the terraces, common in the architecture at Piedras Negras, was achieved by overlapping three-dimensional cylinders (proportioned so as to match the degree of curvature witnessed at the site) in the squared corners of the cubes. The three-door structure atop K-5 was similarly rendered through the combination of polygonal cubes, joined together to create interior spaces of the same dimensions as those measured on-site. The width and height of the cubes creating the walls were also based on in-the-field measurement.

Since Str. K-5 was re-created based on field data from the Proyecto Arqueológico Piedras Negras, its size, orientation, and dimensions were considered accurate. The same process was repeated for other structures in the acropolis complex. Once this expanse of the site had been recreated, the first imported layer—the architectural plan of the site based on the Penn map—was activated, and the newly reconstructed three-dimensional architectural map of the site was overlaid and compared to the site plan. Errors, consistent with those observed during the remapping process with ArcGIS, were encountered. Several months were spent determining where, exactly, the errors in the Penn map occurred, as well as their magnitude. In other words, the three-dimensional reconstructions were being used as accurate points from which to correct the distortions of the original map. Ultimately, we hope that this will result in a more accurate resource for use in determining distance between structures—which, as noted above, had not existed prior to Nelson's efforts.[5]

The next stage in this imaging project sought to integrate Nelson's corrected and three-dimensional architectural configurations of Piedras Negras with the natural landscape. Thus, the second imported layer—the GIS-based topographic map—was activated. The reconstructed architecture had previously been anchored in their x and z coordinates based on the GIS data, but were arbitrarily placed on the y (vertical) axis within the Maya 7.0 template. In other words, their N and E locations, as mapped using the Total Station, were correct, but the Z (elevation) was unaccounted for. The buildings were, in effect, floating somewhere above an artificial plane. The topographic layer was consequently positioned so that its lowest elevation point would correlate with z = 0 in the Maya scene. With the "bottom" of the 3-D landscape aligned with the artificial plane created by Maya, the reconstructions were simply moved along their z-axis until they appeared at the surface of the

5. In an interesting note, Nelson also scanned in Tatiana Proskouriakoff's reconstruction drawings of Piedras Negras architecture (several of which appear in her volume, *An Album of Maya Architecture* [1963]) and was able to compare her hand-drawn reconstructions of isolated structures with his own computer-generated ones. Although incorrect in some places, her drawings were impressively accurate.

landscape. The resultant elevations accorded with those taken on-site with the Total Station.

The result of these efforts was a three-dimensional, corrected map of Piedras Negras complete with areas of reconstructed architecture (Figure 6.5). Little guesswork was inherent in this stage of imaging, since all buildings contained extant walls and measurable dimensions. However, the majority of the Maya 7.0 map remained a blank canvas of hills and valleys. The final stage of imaging sought to address this by filling in the architectural landscape via the same software and methods used in the acropolis area.

Filling in the Gaps

In January 2007, I was trained to use Maya software in order to replicate efforts undertaken in the acropolis area of Piedras Negras in both public, civic areas as well as non-elite, domestic sectors of the site. Although the monumental architecture of the site core is more complex and time-consuming to render, reconstruction of house-mounds and *plazuelas* is not without attendant difficulties: with little standing masonry and few archaeological data upon which to base reconstructions, this endeavor was fraught with educated guesswork and speculation. As a consequence, the level of authority and confidence with which these architectural groups were created remains low. However, accuracy was not the ultimate aim in this portion of the project.[6] Rather, the goal was to experiment with this new technology as a means of visualizing, even imagining, what a fully, architecturally populated landscape might have looked like to the ancient population at Piedras Negras. Because Maya 7.0 allows for interactivity through dollying, panning, and tumbling, sight lines can be accessed from any given vantage—from atop the acropolis looking across the landscape to the interior of a domestic structure gazing out its entryway. To date, little such effort has yet been undertaken using these specific methods and technologies in the Maya region.

The process began by creating three archetypal models of a Maya house, each of which differed from the other with respect to their dimensions and the number of rooms they incorporated. This resulted in single-room, double-room, and triple-room structures, each saved as their own scene. Following a pattern observed at Piedras Negras, a bench was added to the center of the rear wall in triple room buildings. The highly linear nature of residential platforms and architectural furniture at the site facilitated attempts to recreate these structures: cubic polygons were created and joined to form the outer walls, while thinner cubes were connected to the outer walls to make interior divisions.

6. This is not to imply that undue liberties were deliberately taken: in my opinion, the reconstructions may be hypothetical, but they are also conservative.

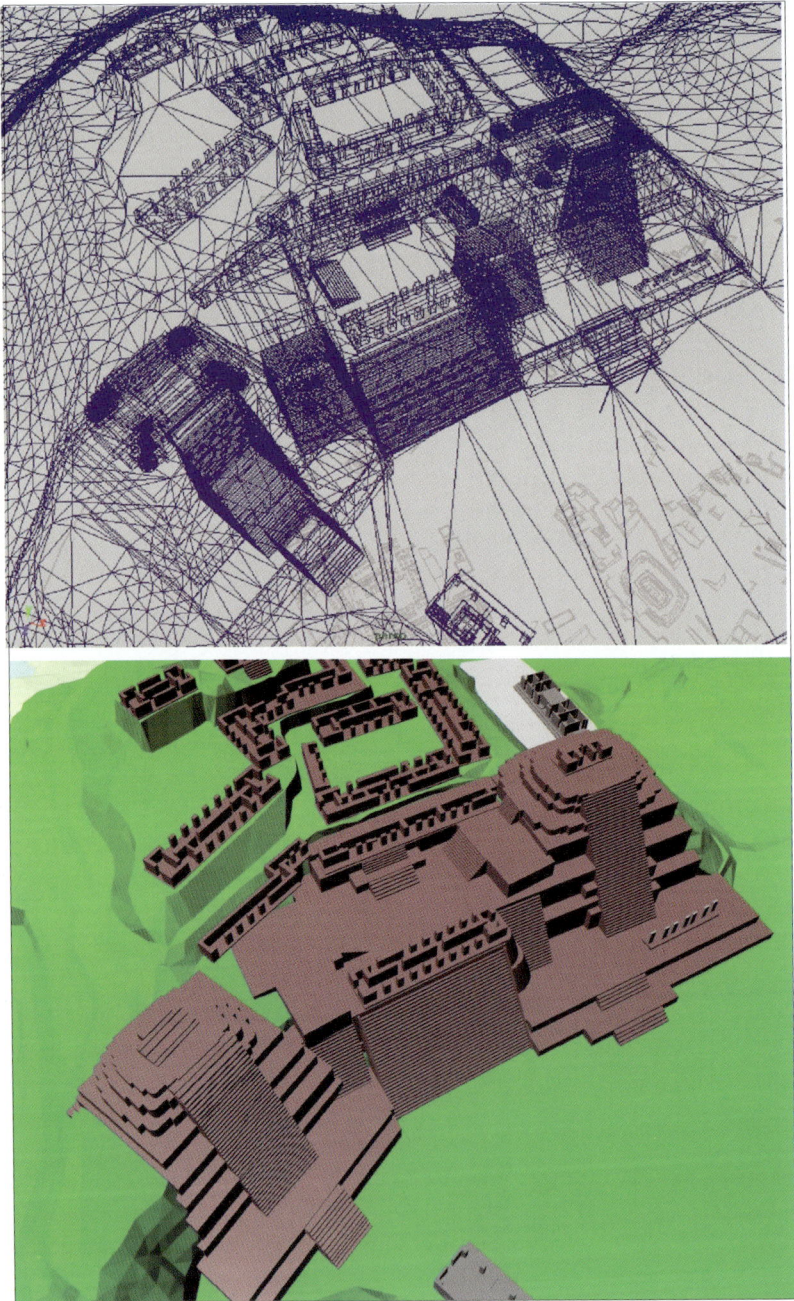

Figure 6.5   Reconstruction drawing of the acropolis in: (upper) wireframe and (lower) solid
            surface.

A steep, sloping roof with rounded edges on the short side of the structure, measuring approximately 1.5 times the height of the house, was added to each. The eaves protruded approximately 1 meter from the exterior walls. Although these roof configurations are estimates and disallow heterogeneity of form, they were based on historical and ethnographic analogy by necessity: made of thatch, these architectural components do not survive in the moist, tropical environment of the northwestern Peten.[7] From a technical standpoint, the roofs were created through the conjoining of a prism and two half-cones. The lower and interior faces of these shapes were removed to create an undivided, hollowed interior rather than the solid shapes Maya software offers as defaults (Figure 6.6). To experiment further with this visualization, a photograph of thatch was imported into Maya as a Texture File, which was then superimposed onto the entire roof surface in (an admittedly artificial) mimesis of thatch.[8]

Once the prototypes were complete, the Maya 7.0 map was opened, and all layers except the site plan were hidden. One by one, residential and non-monumental architectural remains were targeted. Based on relative size and, in some cases, the indication of room divisions, one of the three house models was copied onto the correct x and y coordinates to overlay, roughly, the desired structure on the plan. The dimensions were then adjusted for a correct "fit." Some prototypes were expanded in length and decreased in width while others were made squarer to account for the formal variety witnessed at the site. Additionally, some structures were selected at random for the application of minute modifications, e.g., a different placement of the entrance or positioning and size of an interior bench. While not necessarily based on archaeological data (since little exists for the smaller patio groups and residential buildings), this attempted to account for variegation and diversity doubtlessly present in the layout of houses at Piedras Negras.

Once the prototypes had been overlaid and modified to fit with the site plan template, the second layer was then activated. As with the acropolis architecture, the houses were moved along their z-axis until they reached the

---

7. See Kantner 2000:47–48 for a critical discussion of how the inclusion or omission of perishable architectural features such as roofs may affect the reception and interpretation of virtual reconstructions.

8. The ability to import photographs into Maya means that it would be possible to reconstruct a building stone-by-stone if each masonry block were photographed or scanned on-site, individually imported as a Texture File into Maya, and correlated with the individual cubes standing in for masonry blocks. Although the utility of stone-by-stone reconstructions, or even the overlaying of 'realistic' textures in VR imagery, is not necessarily clear (Gillings 2005:226), this is a largely unexplored use of technology in Mesoamerican archaeology.

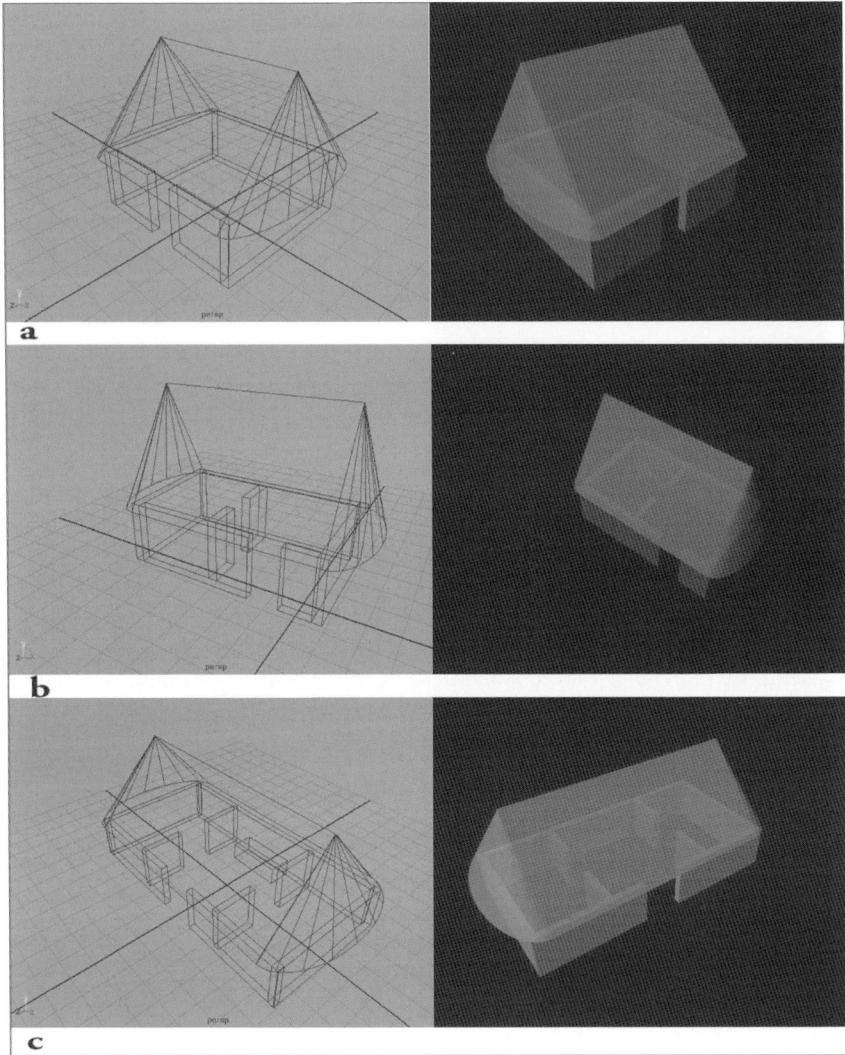

Figure 6.6   Reconstructions of domestic prototypes in wireframe and solid surface views: (a) one room; (b) two room; (c) triple room. Prepared by Cassandra Mesick.

surface of the reconstructed topography. The result is a small segment of a landscape populated with domestic structures (Figure 6.7).

Many potential problems with this undertaking should be apparent. First, this project took well over a year to complete, and efforts remain ongoing still. This significant investment of time owes to the intricacy of architecture at the site, the complexity of the software, and the relative inexperience of both myself and Nelson: though proficient with other computer rendering programs, we were at the time novices with Maya 7.0. Since the training required to master Maya is considerable and far more intensive than what is typically needed to learn other rendering programs, its applicability in mainstream archaeological projects may be limited or relegated to specialists.

Second, imaginative license was taken in some of these reconstructions, particularly with respect to non-monumental architecture. Although imagination and a sense of aesthetics are not "necessarily a sin" (Favro 2006:332), they are devalued and treated with skepticism by most archaeologists (Favro 2006:328–332). Indeed, my own personal ethics of representation were called into question, and at times I believed knowledge of and authority over the ancient Maya landscape inadequate. Although this aspect of imaging Piedras Negras may be interpreted negatively, it can also be construed as a strength for a reflective archaeologist. As John Kantner notes, it "is much more difficult to gloss over missing information when one is creating a 3D model of a prehistoric structure…With 3D models, unknown aspects of the prehistoric architecture cannot be easily avoided" (2000:47). This direct confrontation of gaps in our collective archaeological knowledge may compel innovative research into questions that are difficult to answer but irresponsible to ignore, such as the perishable or ephemeral aspects of ancient life.

Nevertheless, the virtual reconstructions of Piedras Negras make no claims to authenticity. The deliberately bright and garish colors of buildings, the angled contours of a landscape that appears smooth in reality, the superimposition of obviously "fake" textures onto roofs ultimately serve not to make these reconstructions more realistic, but rather to remind us that they are not real at all (e.g., Favro 2006). The improved, the corrected, the architecturally populated maps may perhaps bring archaeologists one step closer to *imaging* what the ancient landscape at Piedras Negras might have "really" looked like—yet this image of the ancient site still remains firmly tethered to that act of *imagining* the past, not necessarily to the act of experiencing or knowing it.

Evaluations and Conclusions

This paper aimed to provide an explanatory description of how the site of Piedras Negras has been imaged and the role that new representational capacities have played in creating these types of archaeological maps. From the beginning of such processes in the field, access to Total Stations and computers have revolutionized the ways in which maps are created: they can be completed more quickly, with corrections made in the field, and can be presented with flashy graphics through programs such as ArcGIS. Furthermore, they are (putatively) more accurate, based on mechanized lasers and compu-

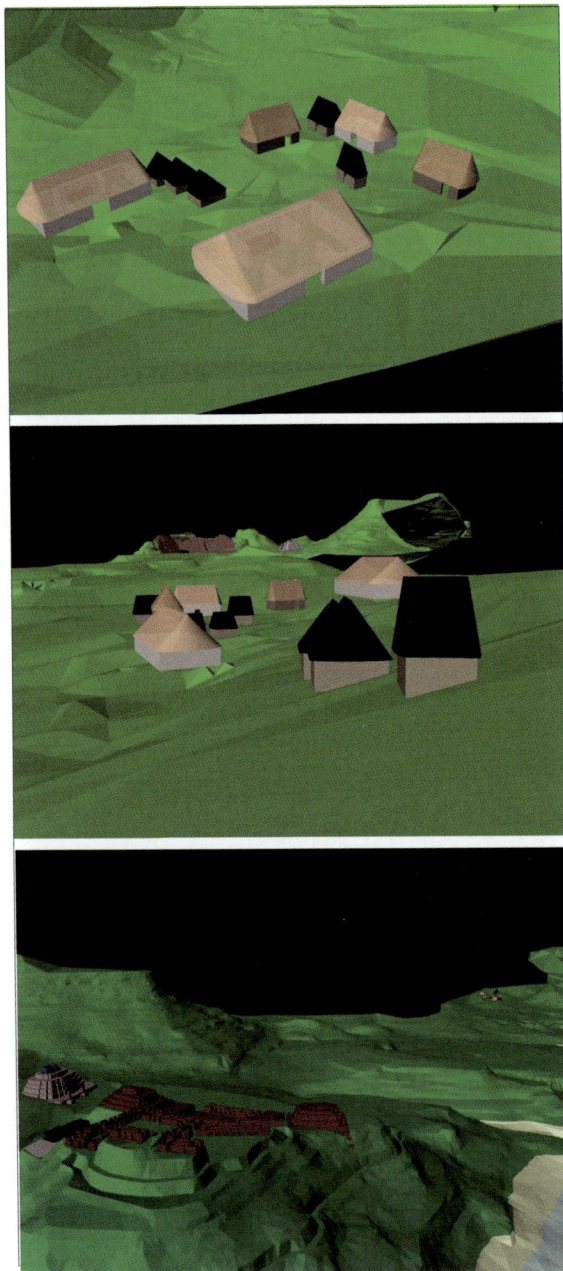

Figure 6.7   Area of reconstructed domestic houses: (upper) View from the southeast; (middle) Vista from the houses towards the acropolis; (lower) Vista from the acropolis towards the houses. Prepared by Cassandra Mesick.

ter data rather than the potential and perpetual fallibility of the human eyes and hand (Daston and Galison 1992; Wise 1995). Subsequent manipulation of such data with new and complex computer programs permits nearly infinite possibilities for visually appealing re-presentations and re-constructions of the past.

Yet, by touching on some of the pitfalls encountered in recent efforts (to achieve greater accuracy, to offer enticing images), it should be remembered that although new technologies affect archaeological practice in seemingly positive ways, they also raise just as many new issues to be tackled. Problems of time, labor, and financial investment, acquisition of training and specialization, notions of authority and "reality"—all emerge from this single case study. Much of the growing literature dedicated to archaeological representation and new representational media seems polarized between enthusiastic advocates of these new imaging technologies who champion their potentials without critically examining their shortcomings, and the skeptics who deride their current uses, sometimes without realizing that representations of the past have always been mediated, that at one point in time any given technology was new (Smiles, this volume).

Nevertheless, it seems that archaeologists have recently come to occupy a middle position on this spectrum, recognizing that while many of these new applications are not without associated problems—whether practical, financial, or intellectual—they may also provide fodder for future research questions. It seems as if creative combinations of different technologies may offer innovative ways to approach the past, and equally innovative means of re(-)presenting it.

Acknowledgments

I would like to express my gratitude to Stephen Houston and Sheila Bonde for allowing me to participate in this discussion, as well as for their helpful, encouraging feedback and support. Zachary Nelson also deserves special credit for his patience while teaching me to use Maya 7.0 and for collaborating with me on the Piedras Negras architectural and landscape reconstructions. Without his generosity and willingness to share his knowledge, experience, and resources I would not have been able to complete this project. Any mistakes or omissions remain my own.

7

A Political Economy of Visual Media in Archaeology

Michael Shanks and Timothy Webmoor

Archaeology abounds in visual media, both media artifacts from the past, as well as means of documenting and studying those artifacts. Classic and long-established approaches to visual media include iconography and iconology (semantics and the identification of visual content), semiotics (the systems and structures of communication, signification and meaning), as well as graphics, cartography, planning and charting (communicative efficacy, the geometry of 2-D to 3-D translation, and information compression).

We shift emphasis in this paper away from communication, iconology, and visuality per se, the content and structure of imagery, toward the way visuality works in archaeology, from visual media as material forms (graphics, maps, photographs) to the work that visual media perform in archaeology. Along the way we present a criticism of the stress placed in much discussion of visual media on their representational qualities, that is, their fidelity to what they are taken to represent, to their mimetic qualities and their degree of correspondence to what is represented.

It is not that we consider such inquiry to be wrong, but rather that communication and meaning are often secondary functions of media. Ironically, what often matters most about visual media, we would claim, is not what they represent, but the way they fit into archaeological work on the remains of the past. In this development of McLuhan's old adage that it is the medium that matters, we focus attention on practice and discourse, drawing particularly on the field of science and technology studies (STS).

This emphasis upon the way images work is why we term our interest one in the political economy of visual media—recovering the work done by visual media in archaeology through networks of production, distribution and consumption. This leads us to identify some of the implications of new digital media, not for more spectacular summations of data about the past or photorealistic simulations, but as open fora for the co-production of pasts that matter now and for visions of future community.

The Importance of Media in Archaeology

We should start with the basic premise of all archaeology: that archaeologists need to record and publish what they find, otherwise the past is lost. Archaeology is based upon the unrepeatable (and "quantum") experiment where intervention in the present, through collecting, excavating, conserving, or even just visiting, fundamentally affects and changes what archaeologists are interested in—the remains of the past.

In the archaeological relationship between past and present that lies behind this idea of the unrepeatable experiment is a distinctive experience of immediacy—a notion of *discovering* the past in its material remains. This is the time of connection or engagement, the *relationship* between past and present. Two terms which describe this temporality are "actuality," the juxtaposition of two presents, that of the past "as it was" back then, and that of the present, as we turn with interest to the past, and "kairos," the time of connection, between past and present (and that key opportune moment when the past appears to us).

The "kairotic" time of the unrepeatable experiment drives an archaeological ethic. The notion of the loss of the past, whether through natural processes of decay or through human intervention, is a component of a broader anxiety that compels preservation, conservation and documentation or publication. A conservation ethic drives the global heritage industry—that the past should be looked after as a legacy of cultural property, with such a past often even considered a human right, according to which people deserve a genuine past of their own, not one made up for them, but properly documented and fairly represented to them or by them. A democratic heritage for all.

The archaeological nature of the relationship between past and present is not often explicitly recognized: we are referring to the material relationship of decay/loss and rescue/restitution at the core of this contemporary historicity and the anxiety just outlined. Such an archaeological sensibility refers to matters of presence and absence, of genuine representation and fake replication, of trust and authenticity in documentation. It reaches far beyond the discipline (Shanks 2009).

So while archaeology may rest upon sites and artifacts, visual media are indispensable in this process of documentation, of turning the past into manageable and manipulable forms. From reconnaissance survey, to excavation of features, to laboratory analyses and interpretation of glyphs, the work archaeologists perform could not be accomplished without proxies of our vision of the past. This holds from research methodology and project planning all the way to information design and presentation of results. Understanding the past, making knowledge, is primarily about the process of making and using media.

Archaeology is about working on what's left of the past; archaeologists do not simply discover the past. Taking it up, sorting, classifying, counting, drawing and measuring so that we might distill relationships, patterns, quantities and changes are what archaeologists spend much of their time doing. This is an especially important part of designing quantitative information (Tufte 1997, 2001). But it is no less an integral part of engaging with the past through more affective means; the theme of the ruined past in the present, for example, has been a consistently prominent component of landscape imagery in the west since the seventeenth century (Andrews 1999; Makarius 2004).

The archaeological process can be described as moving through a continuity of material worlds that run from ruins and remains to the materiality of media "proxies," the world of our media. It is less about "discovering" the past and more about crafting what remains of the past into "deliverables" (Shanks and McGuire 1996). Into text, graph, map, drawing and photograph: this is the work of visual media in archaeology. We all too often sell ourselves short. Much effort is required to produce these deliverables. It ought to be recognized as a highly skilled process akin to (reverse) engineering. Yet archaeologists tend to truncate this long sequence of working on the past, these "serial orders of representations" that get us from the archaeological ruin, feature and artifact to the monograph, article, report and website (Lynch and Woolgar 1990:5). Archaeologists focus on the final products, particularly those that summarize and argue for a particular point of view or interpretation. We elide the process of transformative steps linking different media. We "black box" the archaeological process as if there were only "inputs" and "outputs" with little inspection of the messy middle (Latour 1999:304). For example, we now acknowledge the skilled and unskilled laborers who rarely appear in authoritative archaeological publications that instead highlight the unified voice of the project director or principal investigator (Berggren and Hodder 2003). Archaeologists, skilled and unskilled laborers, technicians, consultants, curators and the many other specialists involved in archaeological engineering never act alone, however. Archaeology's productive forces involve the actions of a complex host of characters. A political economy of media would recover the work done by our mundane media.

This elision is, of course, most often a practical necessity. Research cannot return every time to raw data sets, to first principles, to the minutiae of every project archive. We do have to rely on media architectures that gather and articulate dispersed sites, collections and archives. Our point is that unpacking the work done in these architectures has profound implications for our archaeological research.

Archaeology's Commitment to Mimetic Media

The actuality of archaeological work, its "kairos" is, we maintain, connected to an ethical imperative to record authentically, with fidelity. Because archaeologists change the past in their work, even discard and destroy the contexts, they most often give epistemological primacy to the material remains: a drawing or photograph is considered secondary or supplemental to the actual materiality of the past, even though we could not construct knowledge of the past without such media. This makes visual media supplemental in a Derridean sense (Derrida 1976). The archaeological image is like a prosthesis—an artificial substitution to replace a loss or absence. But it has a double significance: the image supplements a deficiency, the loss of context, while signaling also a deficiency in the past itself. The past cannot be known without media. Archaeology works in this charged middle ground—a fundamental point that lies behind our elucidation of the political economy of archaeological media.

The epistemological deferment to the "original" past accompanies a strong commitment in archaeology to a particular kind of representational accuracy, one that is technologically enabled and based upon a correspondence theory of fidelity. The translation of experience of archaeological remains, with all their complex qualities, into media proxies frequently relies upon certain technologies (such as remote sensing and photography), instruments, and upon reproducible procedures and standards (such as cartography and architectural survey, or even finds drawing) that are taken to guarantee fidelity. There is thus a distinctive technophilia in archaeology, exemplified in early adoption of media technologies, whether it was the printed illustrated book, or systematic cartography, aerial photography, remote sensing, and, more recently, architectural and virtual reality (VR) software. An example was the hope placed upon the "pattern recognition work" of technology to remove, bearing the caveat of "junk in, junk out" in mind, the subjective archaeological observer ("first order observation") (e.g. Binford 1989:35; see Galison 1997 on "noninterventionist objectivity"). Media artifacts produced with the aid of technology are most often evaluated in archaeology according to their degree of correspondence with what they represent, their mimetic qualities.

Critiques of Mimetic Media

We will take a contemporary theme in archaeological visualization in order to examine the features of this commitment to mimetic fidelity. Since the 1980s archaeologists have taken up with enthusiasm software that allows 3-D modeling and rendering. Coming out of professional architectural and engineering practice (computer-aided design) and the media industry (computer-generated imagery), increasingly affordable systems allow the creation of photo-realistic simulations of ancient buildings and landscapes on the basis of archaeologically generated data. And not just on a computer screen; wearable media devices offer the possibility of more immersive simulations: Pompeii regenerated on a visor display, in the ruins themselves (Raskin 2002; Siewiorek, Smailagic and Starner 2008; and see Witmore 2004). Fidelity can certainly and appropriately be correlated with photorealistic accuracy, because photography effectively mimics the external appearance of things. If the past is decaying and being lost, the attraction of a photorealistic record is evident.

But this fidelity is precisely superficial. David Lowenthal (1996) has criticized the contemporary heritage industry for its reliance upon voyeuristic recreations that offer eye candy rather than insight. Nevertheless, the desire for sophisticated visualizations is increasing. Is this visual fetishism? We will investigate this point.

VR experiences, typical of gaming and entertainment software, are making their way rapidly into archaeology and cognate fields (Forte and Silotti 1997; Frischer and Dakouri-Hild 2008). In the last quarter of 2008, for example, Google offered 3-D modeling of Ancient Rome, superimposed upon their topographic and satellite imagery in Google Earth and based upon archaeological research and data processed at the University of Virginia. Visit Rome on your computer and you can fly through the ancient city of 320 AD. The visuality of such projects is highly complementary to CAD simulations. Second Life, an online world, has grown rapidly since its launch in 2003 to become one of the Internet's most discussed manifestations of VR. It has several archaeological and "recreational" sites of antiquity. To explore the issues of VR in archaeology, in 2006 the Metamedia Lab in the Stanford Archaeology Center, in affiliation with Stanford Humanities Lab, undertook an experiment in constructing an archival facility in Second Life (Figure 7.1).

Life Squared, built on an island in the online world Second Life, is an archaeology of an artwork made by Lynn Hershman Leeson and Eleanor Coppola in 1972. In the Dante Hotel in San Francisco Lynn created an installation of artifacts, traces and remnants, posing questions of who had been there and what had happened. In 2005 Stanford University Special Collections acquired the artist's archive which included what was left of the installation—texts, photos, artifacts. As part of the Presence Project (Gianacchi et al. 2010), an international interdisciplinary collaboration researching the archaeology of presence, the Daniel Langlois Foundation funded the reconstruction of the 1972 art installation at the Dante Hotel in 2006 in Second Life. This "animated archive" has since appeared at the Museum of Fine Art Montreal and San Francisco Museum of Modern Art (Frieling 2008).

Life Squared thus addressed questions of how to treat archaeological or archival sources as the basis for the reconstruction, replication, or simulation of an "original" experience and event: questions of how we might revisit the "presence" of an experience or event, in a "kairotic" connection, as defined above. A context is the future of the art museum in the absence of a self-contained artwork (how to curate "an experience"). Conspicuously, Life Squared is an experiment about modeling and simulation—those core epistemological practices in archaeology.

An obvious option was to photorealistically simulate the hotel of 1972 so that avatars might re-walk the corridors as if they were there back then. Most of the VR experiences in Second Life aspire to photorealism. But we chose another option. In order to remain faithful to the fragmented remains, and in order to open up the 2006 experience to new associations (the actuality of the past), we created an ichnography. We traced out the surviving floor plan of the building and located the archived images and documents of the 1972 installation in a skeletal wireframe that was reconstructed only to the extent attested by the sources. The fidelity to the original hotel of 1972 is highly selective; the hotel of 2006 in Second Life does not look anything like the original, yet it is empirically sound and contains nothing that cannot be verified. The result is something of a dissonance with the sunny photographs we have of the San Francisco street of 1972. Instead, it shares the ghostly light of Second Life of 2006 filtering through the digital ruins of a building hardly witnessed now in any record or archive.

With respect to visualization, rather than a stand-for, substitute or replica of the original, we chose to treat the "virtuality" of this online world as an opportunity for re-iterative engagement, for people to come to a fresh participatory experience (Frieling 2008), connecting then and now. The intention was to open up the past to new interests and involvement, with avatars in Second Life revisiting and reworking the past on the basis of the surviving traces. The implicit proposal is that photorealistic simulation is actually not particularly faithful to the past and closes off opportunities for such engagement, because such simulation appears to be finished, the past—if that is what it is—over and done with.

A broader argument concerns the transitive character of information. Life Squared is based upon the premise that the information rooted in archival sources needs to be worked upon if it is even simply to survive. Left in museum boxes, sources will molder and decay. Information requires circulation, engagement and articulation with the questions and interests of a researcher. Information, as active data, is a verb. Life Squared was explicitly treated as an experiment in "animating the archive."

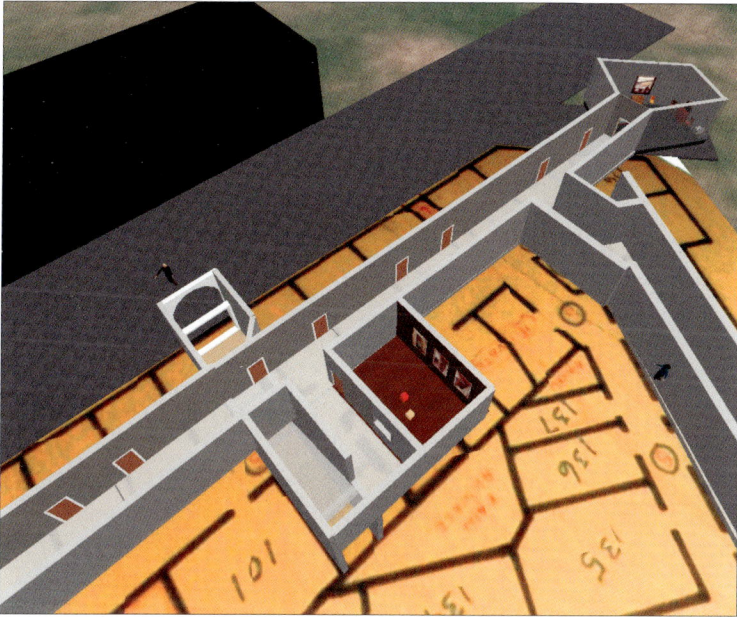

Figure 7.1   Building the Dante Hotel in Second Life as part of the Presence Project's Life Squared.

Second Life, like an archaeological excavation, is a space for performance, as well as being indebted to certain visual media. We treated the space not as a representational medium, an animated 3-D image, but as a prosthesis, as we defined above, a cognitive instrument for probing this particular connection with the past. This shifts attention from visuality per se, the experience of forms and textures and the quality of the photorealism (aspiring to the response that "it surely did look like that"), to the specifics of how the traces of the past connect with the present, the avatar visiting the "hotel" of 2006 in a particular encounter located in the expectations and experiences of that avatar and their owner. This is to treat such a 3-D world as a mediating space, and the construction of an archive as a co-productive project involving curator, the artifacts and the visitors or users.

Another context for this project is the genre of theatre/archaeology, defined by Pearson and Shanks (2001) as the re-articulation of fragments of the past as real time place/event, and sharing an interest in memory practices as part of a distinctive trend in contemporary fine and performing arts (Enwezor 2008; Gianacchi et al. 2010; Kaye 2000).

Tri Bywyd (*Three Lives,* Figures 7.2–3), for example, a work in 1995 by performance company Brith Gof, was an ambitious work of such a theatre/ archaeology (Kaye 2000:125–138). It was an assemblage of three portfolios of evidence relating to three deaths in west Wales—Sarah Jacob, the "Fasting Girl of Wales," Lynette White, murdered in Cardiff in 1988, and an anonymous farmer's suicide. These portfolios were mediated through five performers, three architectures, an amplified sound track, various props including flares, buckets of milk, a bible, a revolver, and a dead sheep. Tri Bywyd was set in the archaeological remains of a farmstead deep in a forest plantation.

The explicit purpose of the work was to visualize and make manifest the subtleties of these archaeological/forensic narratives, but not to simulate or represent, nor indeed to explain. The work's aesthetic, in common with much contemporary art, was not at all mimetic. "Three Rooms" (Shanks 2004) was another experiment in the documentary articulation of three forensic portfolios that eschewed any mimetic visuality, plot or character, but hinged on performance and the burden of work carried by memories and traces, albeit set in the long tension between urban and rural experience.

We needn't look only to the contemporary visual and performing arts for a critique of photorealistic mimesis. The impact of Foucauldian notions of discourse and the growth of the interdisciplinary field of media studies has resulted in a substantial body of critical reflection upon representations in archaeology (Clack and Brittain 2007; Joyce 2002; Molyneaux 1997; Smiles and Moser 2005). For instance, Moser (2001) has brought discourse analysis

Figure 7.2 *Tri Bywyd* (*Three Lives*)—site specific theatre/archaeology.

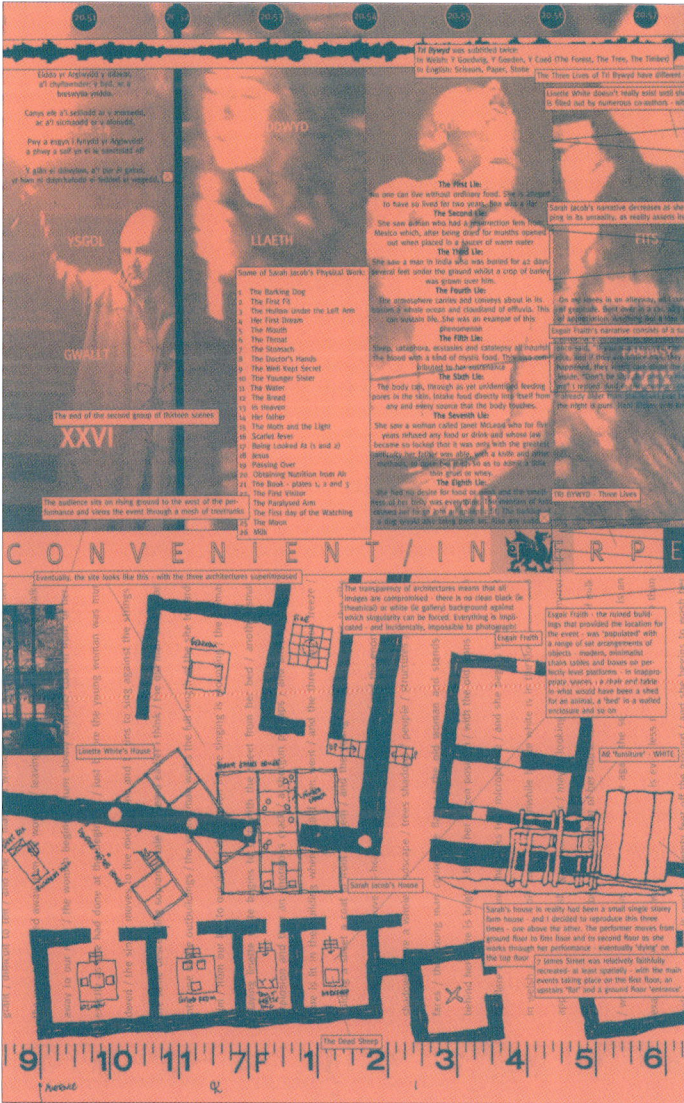

Figure 7.3. *Tri Bywyd*—image and document.

to the visual conventions or visual language of archaeology. Clack and Brittain (2007) have taken a cultural studies approach, highlighting the manner in which popular appropriations of archaeological information have a "dumbing down" effect on representations. (On the other hand, they equally emphasize that archaeological representations must be communicable to an increasingly interested public). This critical examination of archaeological representation is important. Indeed, a self-critical orientation steers us away from historical and cultural biases—such as the portrayal of Pleistocene "man the hunter" or other conceptions based upon patriarchal, sexist values (Gero and Root 1990).

Such appraisals generally end with separating off "popular" and "pedagogical" representations from "inter- and intra-specialist" representations (Clack and Brittain 2007:31). This seems to imply that certain representations remain closer to the data while others, geared toward popular communication, inevitably stray from certainty. But perhaps a broader question would simply ask: just what are we representing with our visual media in archaeology? Of course it will depend upon the image or graphic, but ultimately we can ask whether there is a datum that can be taken as the origin of a representation? We will come back to this question.

Correspondence and Evaluation

Certainty and assurance also motivate archaeology's desire for photorealism. The belief in representing the past with fidelity, as it was, is coupled with the need to discriminate between different renderings. Expressions of archaeological epistemology have variously revolved around the notion of epistemic fit to the material past (Wylie 2002). In a concern to achieve more accurate or nuanced representations of the past, archaeology has moved in a historical trajectory in the development of its theory and methodology along with other natural and social sciences. Driven by ocular analogies, the pursuit of the "mirror of nature" (Rorty 1979) has involved the sciences in perennial questions of "representation and reality" (Putnam 1988). Philosophers of science have characterized such inquiry as the *summum bonum* of modernist epistemology. The reasoning and motivation is not misplaced: such a principle of representation grants evaluative capacity to knowledge claims. Better representations are judged to match, hook onto or mirror, to correspond to, an external reality. Therefore, better representations may be evaluated by peers as superior according to how they fit with the past.

There have risen a complex host of problems associated with such a one-to-one notion of representation, as well with how to achieve consensus in the judgment of such representation—through predictive success, instrumental efficacy, coherence to other representations and so on (Hacking 1983). We mention here the interesting history of modernist notions of vision as representation (Berger 1984; Foucault 1990; Gombrich 1960). This notion is a legacy owing much to the scientific canonization of Galileo and his ocular amplification, and to Leon Battista Alberti and his rendering of the world in two-dimensional "windows" through single-point perspective. The critical issue in terms of epistemic solidarity, of building alliances around knowledge, has been the idea that settling disputes in knowledge claims hinges upon "seeing-it-as-it-really-is." Indeed, this was the beginning of Boyle's experimental method for science and the importance of demonstrations in early modern science (Shapin 1984). Unblemished and cleansed of distortions, either on the part of theoretical conception or methodological apparatus, Nagel's (1986:9) climb to an unpolluted "view from nowhere" might enable us to represent the world with fidelity.

Such a conception of knowledge is very difficult to get to work. Or, more specifically, knowledge claims do work; they just don't work by demonstrating any epistemologically privileged relationship with an external and removed reality. We would sidestep the problems by refusing the radical distinction between the past and our claims to know it. This is not to question the reality of the past by asserting that we construct it. It is simply to question a modernist epistemological tradition that presumes an ontological rift between people and things, between internal minds and external reality, between the past and the present, between what we do (as archaeologists) and how we represent this practice. And if we sidestep such a deeply rooted epistemology, we avoid a theory of correspondence that bolsters a faith in representational proxies. As Hilary Putnam puts it, "the idea that truth is a passive-copy of what is 'really' (mind-independently, discourse-independently) 'there' has collapsed under the critiques of Kant, Wittgenstein, and other philosophers, even if it continues to have a deep hold on our thinking" (1981:128).

In this shift away from questions of epistemology the answer to the question of whether there is a datum, an origin to archaeological "mediawork" and representation, is clear. The idea of a "record" waiting to be passively recovered and represented is too simple. It begs the "Pompeii Premise," an assumption that there is an inert "past" to be represented free from distortion (Binford 1981; Schiffer 1976). Thoughtful archaeologists have been long aware that the archaeological record is something created through the work of making media. Transforming the dynamic and materially complex ruins in the landscape into media artifacts releases them into mobility as "immutable mobiles" that may be taken back to our laboratories and archives (Latour 1990; see also Lucas 2001; Witmore 2006).

Several discussions are relevant here regarding the complexity of archaeological science: Shanks and Tilley (1987) introduced the notion of archaeology's "fourfold hermeneutic" to capture these transformations; Binford (1977, 1989) and Schiffer (1988) debated the character of the "middle-range theory" required to articulate remains that had been subject to processes of transformation of natural and social origin with past socio-cultural process; Patrik (1985) and Barrett (1988) contested even the reality of an "archaeological record." The ethics of heritage interests and their impact upon what is left of the past are in the forefront of concern in archaeology's professional sector today. Visual media and representations occur throughout this manifold of operations performed upon the past.

Asking whether there is something that ultimately we are representing in our archaeological work, questioning the nature and origin of the archaeological record and determining our epistemic relationship to it certainly provokes us. The particularity of archaeological work centers upon the "kairotic" temporality we have outlined above, upon the relationship of artifacts and sites to social, cultural and historical change, and upon the processes of decay and entropy that remains of the past undergo.

This transformative power of visual media is amplified through the algorithmic alchemy of digitization. And the extraordinary power of digital media is perhaps encapsulated in Geographical Information System (GIS) and VR software. Software which offer the potential of connecting data to spatial coordinates, fleshing out site and landscape, and rendering simulated pasts in photographic detail, all on the scale of world building—as complete a model of the past as can be possible; a "digital heritage" (Webmoor 2008). We might become enthralled with the "cool factor" and get caught up in a technological optimism that would aim at such simulation and accept mimetic correspondence as achievable, at least in some circumstances. But the epistemological conundrums remain, and we suggest it is better to think of archaeological work in a different way, not as mimesis, modeling, simulating, or representing, but as a fundamentally transforming mediation or translation, work done in the spaces between past and present.

Force for this view of representation in archaeology comes from a range of work in science studies and cognitive science. Early modern experimental science was wrapped up in "natural magic." Pre-scientific instruments were frequently popular parlor tricks. Magic lanterns, the camera obscura and Robert Boyle's vacuum pump were employed for entertainment and edification. Francis Bacon and John Locke were distrustful of these instruments and the visual rhetoric that they produced (Hankins and Silverman 1995). Nevertheless, such popular technologies came to be valued for their capacity to augment the human senses and inscribe what they registered at the boundaries of human perception. Early demonstrations to gatherings of peers were intended to show, through viewing and witnessing the instruments themselves, the matters of fact under consideration. These ocular demonstrations relied upon common and shared experience for the settling of disputes concerning hypothesized entities and natural philosophy.

As considerations of nature became more abstract, delving into matters of cause and effect, instruments had to increasingly produce visual outputs.

By the end of the eighteenth century, demonstrations gave way to recording instruments that mechanically translated relationships into visual media that were not modeled upon ocular perception. An example was James Watt's indicator diagram of 1796. A gauge attached to a locomotive engine physically translated the pressure in a cylinder into an inscriptional graph of volume versus pressure. These instruments translated a world not visible by the unaided senses into "self illustrating phenomena." They produced visual media that were abstractions of physical processes. And ever-increasing amounts of background knowledge and assumptions were required to "read off" the invisible processes. They "showed" results, but through non-mimetic transformation.

Developing from William Playfair and Johann Lambert's earliest diagrams, graphs, charts and other visualizations so common now to scientific endeavor retain little physiognomic or iconic relationship to their subject matter. Instead, these visual media enable cognitive work to be performed. They have become cognitive prostheses rather than visual analogs for the world around us (Hankins and Silverman 1995; Tversky 1999). Visual media help us think and work as tools. They only "represent" in a very loose and often highly abstract manner. In step with the increased sophistication of instrumentation, our capacity for "intervention" comes to be the epistemic guarantor of our results. Ian Hacking, a prominent advocate of scientific realism, states the matter this way: "experimental work provides the strongest evidence for scientific realism … because entities that in principle cannot be 'observed' are regularly manipulated to produce a new phenomenon and to investigate other aspects of nature." (1983:262). Fidelity may be futile, whereas pragmatic criteria, the ability to get work done and accomplish specific tasks in research, are what count.

Consequently, visual media are valued for their indispensable role in making modern science work (Latour 1999; Lynch and Woolgar 1990). Emphasis has shifted from debating whether information conveyed visually corresponds with the world, toward information design and effectively expressing research with specific modes of engaging that information in mind (Tufte 1997, 2001). We reiterate that correspondence is a difficult road to take with archaeology's visual media. It robs media of their active role, begs wearisome epistemological questions, and encourages a passive "past voyeurism" on the part of the public. Media are far from copies.

Walter Scott and the Anxiety of Mediation

We will continue with another more archaeological illustration of the active role of media. Let's indeed put to one side the epistemological conundrums and return to the early nineteenth century and the antiquarian tradition.

Walter Scott was a magistrate, antiquarian, musicologist, novelist, essayist, collector, landowner, poet, bestselling author in the book trade of the early nineteenth century, inventor of the historical novel. His focus was a border-land between Scotland and England, between past and present. In 1814 was published his *Border Antiquities of England and Scotland*. The two volumes, profusely and wonderfully illustrated with engravings in classic picturesque style, are subtitled *Border Antiquities—Comprising Specimens of Architecture and Sculpture, and other vestiges of former ages, accompanied by descriptions. Together with Illustrations of remarkable incidents in Border History and tradition, and Original Poetry*. It is a gazetteer of archaeological interests.

A long introduction takes the reader through an historical narrative of the borders. On pages xviii–xix Scott is dealing with the Roman border and Hadrian's Wall: "The most entire part of this celebrated monument, which is now, owing to the progress of improvement and enclosure, subjected to con-stant dilapidation, is to be found at a place called Glenwhelt, in the neigh-bourhood of Gilsland Spaw."

He adds a footnote:

> Its height may be guessed from the following characteristic anecdote of the late Mr. Joseph Ritson, whose zeal for accuracy was so marked a feature in his investigations. That eminent antiquary, upon an excursion to Scotland, favoured the author with a visit. The wall was mentioned; and Mr. Ritson, who had been misinformed by some ignorant person at Hexham, was disposed strongly to dispute that any reliques of it yet remained. The author mentioned the place in the text, and said that there was as much of it stand-ing as would break the neck of Mr. Ritson's informer were he to fall from it. Of this careless and metaphorical expression Mr. Ritson failed not to make a memorandum, and afterwards wrote to the author, that he had visited the place with the express purpose of jumping down from the wall in order to confute what he supposed a hyperbole. But he added, that, though not yet satisfied that it was quite high enough to break a man's neck, it was of eleva-tion sufficient to render the experiment very dangerous.
>
> (Scott 1814:xviii–xix).

Was it that Ritson, a noted literary antiquarian, hadn't read the many accounts of the Wall published since the sixteenth century in that fascinat-ing lost genre—chorography? Unlikely. Had he forgotten? Or was it rather, as Scott suggests, that his "zeal for accuracy" meant he had to visit and wit-ness the very structure in order to authenticate the written accounts of the remains? He clearly assumes that there was or had been a Wall: ancient authors and sources document it. What he disputes is that there was anything left. This tension between text and monument is very characteristic of anti-quarian debate, and Ritson was renowned for his skepticism regarding claims for the authenticity of ancient manuscripts and historical documents.

Alexander Gordon's *Itinerarium Septentrionale* was published through private subscription in 1726. It deals with Roman remains in the north and goes into great detailed description of the surviving remains of Hadrian's Wall. Ritson may not have read it. He may have known it, but still doubted the description of Hadrian's Wall. We may assume that Scott had read it: his copy is still in his library at Abbotsford. Figure 7.4 shows part of a page from this account of "A Journey thro' most of the Counties of Scotland and those in the North of England."

Gordon literally paces out and records every boot-marked trace of the Wall in his itinerary. He might not have jumped off the Wall, but you can almost hear every crunch of his boots through the pages of his expensive folio.

The book sets the "northern journey" in the context of accounts in ancient texts of the Romans in the north. Gordon knows his classical authors. The engravings are revealing. He illustrates many rectangular monuments in their various relationships with straight Roman roads. The monuments are all unexcavated and comprise simple earthen features—tumbled down overgrown ramparts. Gordon's illustrations mark out nothing except rectangles and lines; though they have, significantly, been paced-out. The engravings of sculpture show only sketched-in figures, focusing instead on the transcription of the inscribed text.

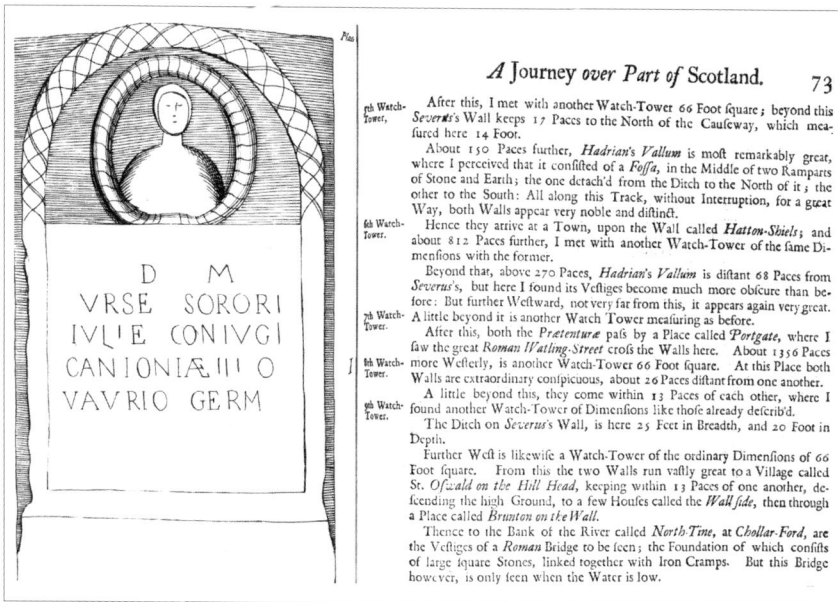

Figure 7.4   Alexander Gordon — *Itinerarium Septentrionale*.

Ancient authors, epigraphy and the antiquarian's boot—the topic here is the fidelity and authenticity of different kinds of witnessing of antiquity and its relics. This witnessing, representation if you like, is in an indeterminate and debatable relationship to voice, text, image and figure.

Scott's own writing represents a miscellany of voices articulating past and present. His bibliography includes: ethnomusicological collection of medieval bardic epic poetry; his own poetry; medieval historical novels (most notably *Ivanhoe* [1983]); the antiquarian gazetteer; historical novels dealing with Scottish themes in recent memory (such as *Waverley* [1892] and *Guy Mannering* [1892]); essays and non-fiction in various genres. Many of these were illustrated with the latest in steel engravings.

Scott consistently elides fact and fiction in his examination of traces in the present of the past (archaeological, memory, textual, placenames, landscapes). We should note here a recurrent theme in literary antiquarianism in the eighteenth century—establishing the authentic voice of the past—from Thomas Percy's *Reliques of Ancient English Poetry*, an edited edition of antiquarian manuscript sources, through to Macpherson's Ossian, the wholly fictitious creation of a medieval bard (see Stewart 1994 for a fascinating treatment of this issue). A related interest is the transition from voice (oral poetry, verbal account, memory) to text (a new version of the old song, the annotated transcription/edition, the historical novel, historical narrative). This is inseparable from address to the transition from the land to the illustrated book—how the witnessing pace of the antiquarian, how sites and their names, how place-events become itinerary, chorography, cartography, or travelogue.

Conventional notions of media (as material modes of communication—print, painting, engraving, or as organizational/institutional forms—the media industries) are of limited help in understanding what Scott and his contemporaries were up to in mediating authorial voice and authentic traces of the past. We can consider the rise of cheaper engraved illustration, the popularity of the historical novel in the growth of the publishing industry, developments in cartographic techniques and instruments. But in order to understand how all this and more came to be archaeology—the field, social and laboratory science—we need to rethink the concept of medium.

Scott, Ritson, Gordon and their like are making manifest the past (or, crucially, are aiming to allow the past to manifest itself), in its traces, through practices and performances (writing, corresponding, visiting, touring, mapping, pacing, debating), artifacts (letter, notebook, manuscript, printed book, pamphlet, map, plan, plaster cast, model), instruments (pen, paint brushes, rule, Claude Glass, camera lucida, surveying instruments, boots, wheeled transport, spades, shovels, buckets), systems and standards (taxonomy, itinerary, grid), authorized algorithms (the new philology, legal witnessing), dreams and design (of an old Scotland, of a nation's identity, of personal achievement). Making manifest came through manifold articulations. And "manifestation" was a complement to epistemological and ontological interest—getting to know the past "as it was, and is."

Visual media, in the conventional sense (print, engravings, maps), are involved, but also much more that challenges the premises of communication and representation underlying the concept of medium. What we are seeing, we suggest, is a reworking of ways of engaging with place, memory (forever lost, still in mind, to be recalled), history and time (historiography, decay, narrative), and artifacts (found and collected) when the author's voice was undergoing question and challenge (Who wrote the border ballads?—Is this our history?—Whom do you trust in their accounting for the past?), when ownership of land and property, and the traditional qualities of the land were being altered under rational agricultural improvement, when property was being reinvented as landscape, when the status of manufactured goods was changing rapidly in an industrialized northern Europe. That dinner with Ritson and the visit to Gilsland are establishing what constitutes an appropriate way of engaging with the past. It is only later on that Scott gets called a historical novelist, Ritson is marginalized as an irascible literary antiquarian, largely forgotten, and archaeology becomes the rationalized engagement with site and artifact through controlled observation, "fieldwork" and publication in standardized media and genres.

In this debate over appropriate ways of engaging with the past, medium is better thought of as mode of engagement—a way of articulating people and artifacts, senses and aspirations, and all the associative chains and genealogical tracks that mistakenly get treated as historical and sociopolitical context. Scott presents us with a fascinating laboratory of such modes of engagement, one that runs from field science to romantic fiction through to what was to be formalized as altertumswissenschaft by German classical philology.

By the mid nineteenth century the debate about mediating the past had quietened into an orthodoxy of modes of engagement that came with standardization of practice and publication—an orthodoxy of measurement, inscription and illustration with which we are now very familiar.

Maps as a Cognitive Tool

Spatial tracing and the notion of information as a verb bring up the map: a touchstone medium for archaeology. Indeed the map directs most other methodologies at archaeological sites. Maps have become an organizing informational framework—much like a Microsoft Windows Operating System—within which information must be rendered compatible. Considerable investment has been made in the digital evolution of the map into GIS, maps combined with databases.

The map is a very indirect compression of certain qualities of the material world. This "information" is selected from the total synaesthetic possibilities of experiencing place. So, far from simply a mimetic model or objective simulation of an archaeological location, a map augments certain visual relationships while minimizing or not registering others. It reduces out the noise of background phenomena. This is, of course, suited to many purposes. And maps work well in being purpose-driven.

Work by one of us at Teotihuacan, Mexico—an incredibly complex and monumental site—underscores why maps should be treated as cognitive and perceptual prostheses. Along the lines of visual information as a verb, they should not be regarded as stand-alone representations of archaeological features and landscapes. Let us illustrate again the contrast between visual representation and mediation.

The Teotihuacan Mapping Project (TMP) is an exemplary case of archaeological surface survey and mapping (Figure 7.5). It was begun in the early 1960s and completed in 1973 with the publication of a two-volume, four-part compendium, replete with pockets and a total of 147 pull-out maps at a scale of 1:2,000 covering an area of over 20 square km (Millon et al. 1973). The smaller scale, overview map ("Map 1") has become a rock star poster of mapping in archaeology more generally and working at Teotihuacan specifically. So let's ask: when does a map become a great map? And what makes the TMP map a great map?

We can compare the TMP with the unique history of mapping at Teotihuacan over the course of five centuries—a media cascade—and begin to identify important qualities. As early as 1560 we have the so-called "Mazapan Map," a copy from a lost original, which formed part of sixteenth-century Spanish records of farmlands and land ownership in New Spain (see Arreola 1922). A "map" complementary to the Mazapan was published two decades later in 1580 as part of the *Relación Geográfica de San Juan Teotihuacán*. This "map," rather than landholdings, emphasizes imperial infrastructure: that of the Spanish grafted upon that of the Aztec. By the time of Ramón Almaraz's 1865 work we can confidently remove the quotes from around map. There is a standardized, consistent quality that is facilitated by the "view from nowhere." There is also a selective fidelity going on: what to visualize and what to leave blank. Gone are the personages found on the Mazapan depiction, the stylized church façades of the relación geográfica and the individual maguey cactus and other rich particularities of nineteenth century "maps" (such as those of Brantz Mayer in 1844 and Désiré Charnay in 1887).

What has been gained and what has been sieved away through mediation?

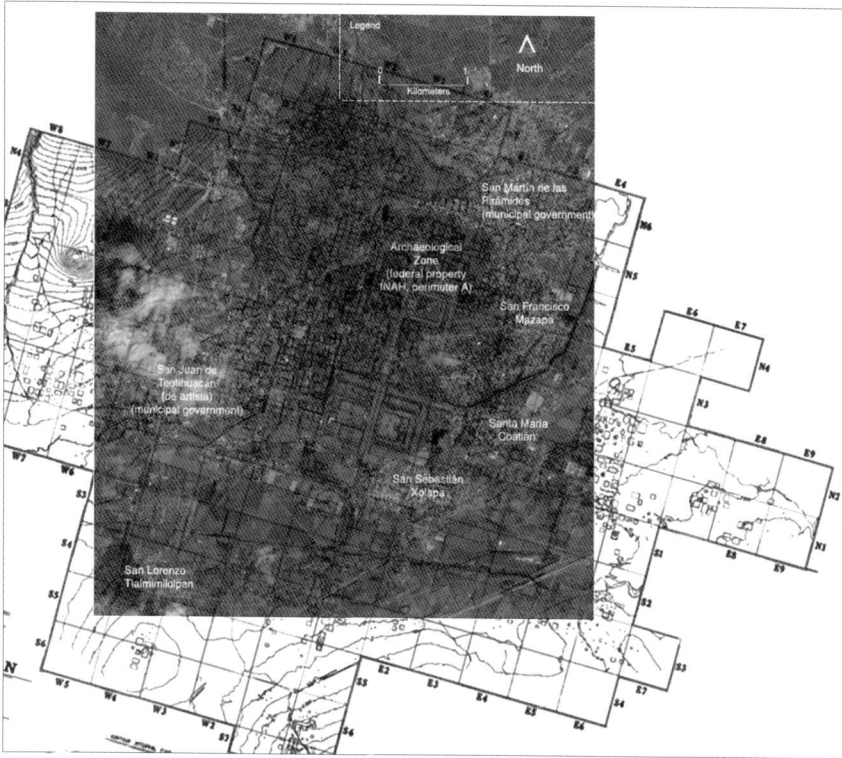

Figure 7.5   Teotihuacan Mapping Project's "Map 1" mixed with satellite imagery of Teotihuacan (adapted from Millon et al. 1973).

Over the course of five centuries of mapping the same ruins we arrive at some key goals or vectors in making maps: compression of data; micro-macro combination; optical consistency; fungibility/combinability; extensibility; light-dark contrast/presentation. Its superlative attention to these qualities make the TMP a paragon of archaeological mapping.

The precision and detail of putting on paper what was there in the 1960s at Teotihuacan is no doubt part of this. The team found and mapped the boundaries of the site—a monumental undertaking in surface survey. But it is how the map serves the goals of the future, how it creates affordances for future research projects, that makes it great. All subsequent depictions of the site, from 3-D "fly throughs" of a virtual La Ventilla apartment compound to stratigraphic profiles from a trench in the ciudadela, may be inserted to "hang" on the scaffolding of the TMP map. Like a house, it is a media architecture built for future generations. The map is also, contrary to the crisscrossed appearance of its analog and static lines, fluid. Extensible, it can infinitely expand its grid outward to cover macro features; conversely, it can fold the micro details of burial offerings deep within the pyramid of the moon into its sliding scale. It is mercurial media at its best.

The TMP map also works as a prosthetic device (Webmoor 2005). Maps work through the inextricable relation between perception and schematic visualization (Figure 7.6). Maps convey information as visual short-hands. But in practice maps only work, only allow navigation and way-finding, via linking this abstracted information beyond the immediate perceptual and cognitive capacity of a map-reader to what is available perceptually on-the-ground—an analog version of "wetware" (Gell 1985; Muehrcke and Muehrcke 1998). The perceiving map-reader becomes a conduit for coordinating information offered directly through perception—of features, plazas or pyramids—and indirectly through the schemata that are maps. One cannot operate effectively without the other. This is cyborg ontology—the articulation of "naturecultures" with device and human body engaging in purpose-driven practice (Haraway 2003; Manovich 2006). In this sense, maps are indeed better understood as prostheses. Restoring, supplementing and augmenting human perceptual and cognitive capabilities; engagements with media that far outstrip the overburdened notion of "representation." We reiterate that mediation is less what we do with information—to convey, condense or distribute—and more how we intimately function through visual media.

Certain visual qualities are, to be sure, carried from the material world and inscribed on maps. But thinking in terms of correspondence doesn't get at

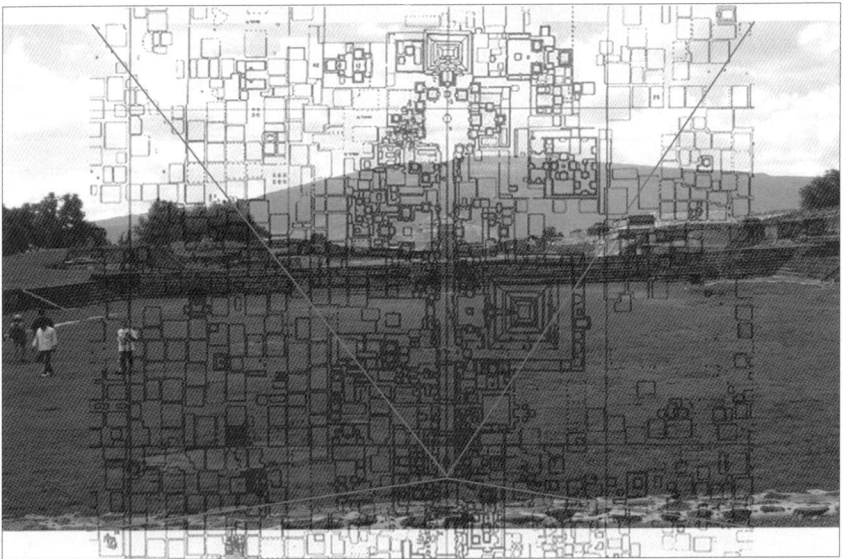

Figure 7.6 Mapwork at Teotihuacan, Mexico — photograph and map, rendering in analog how maps work in navigation by linking perception with schema.

why the TMP map is an excellent map. It may be accurate with respect to what it depicts. More importantly it is useful. Corresponding to the world may afford utility. But, as students and historians of science have learned and we have noted above, judging visual media by correspondence holds us spellbound by the modernist epistemological conundrum (Webmoor 2007). We must be more pragmatic with our media.

Mediation not Representation

In directing attention away from the communicative and representational function of media we are arguing for a more performative appreciation of archaeology as work done on the past, productive labor directed often toward building knowledge of the past, where such knowledge is an achievement, not a discovery.

That the "archaeological record" of sites and remains is an outcome of archaeological practice rather than a datum seems now well-established (Hodder 1999; Lucas 2001; Patrik 1985). The past, in its archaeological traces, is assembled through engagements with it, operations performed through instruments, archives, networks of institutions, and, of course, visual media. In this archaeological work, representation and "accuracy" come second to the critical need to move back and forth, to retrace the connections between the material remains, the evidence, and their stand-ins or proxies, the texts and visuals. The measure of media is their ability to afford such movement, such engagement, and to what extent they afford the possibility of future action upon and engagement with the past. One way that media may do this, somewhat ironically, is that representation can provide closure upon a piece of research. A convincing rhetoric (Gross 1990) of text and image, a marshalling of evidence and study can "blackbox" research such that it can be taken as given, work can move on, at least until the matter is reopened (Latour 1987). One aspect of such rhetoric involves visual media being treated as illustration, that is they may act primarily as visual support for statements made in a text (Webmoor 2005); photographs of an excavation, for example, may affirm the statements made about the structure of the site, rather than provide evidence for debate (Shanks 1997).

As corollary to this appreciation of active media(tion), the way media work with archaeologists, the paradigm of the archaeologist as custodian or steward of the past is under serious challenge. As in the eighteenth century, this challenge is to do with shifting definitions (legal included) of cultural property. Archaeologists are again having to address the political matter of re-presentation—that is, advocacy and witnessing, who is representing (in a constitutional as well as communicative sense) the past, for whom, and on what basis.

That the past is there as a datum to be represented is under question; though, of course, the traces remain, conspicuously prompting these questions. What one of us has elsewhere (Shanks 1999:9–36) called the "expressive fallacy" (that archaeological texts somehow "express" or represent the past) is being recognized and accepted, as archaeology moves towards a paradigm not of stewardship, but of co-production. We are all archaeologists, working, in different ways, on what is left of the past, sharing a modernist archaeological sensibility attuned to materialities and temporalities (Schnapp et al. 2004). The critical reflexivity so apparent even in that anecdote from Scott has been, of course, a feature of theoretically informed disciplines for several decades. The history of archaeology is becoming an extended disciplinary memory that recognizes negotiation and multivocality in situated knowledges. Archaeologists work with others in constructing pasts. We are indeed back with the eighteenth century in this awareness of the political economy of archaeological work on what remains of the past in the present.

The Potential of New Digital Media

This evolution of archaeology is connecting with deep changes associated with digital media, with the increasing ubiquity of media, their fungibility, and their own changing political economy (Webmoor 2008). Archaeology must find its value in a growing economy wherein the inherited roles of "producer" and "consumer" are beginning to merge with that of the participatory "user."

We can take a photo on our phones, send it as an email, post it on a blog, share it on a social web network, print it out, display it in a gallery in Second Life, add it to a lecture slideshow, add it to a home movie. This fungibility is part of an increasingly diverse political economy (you might call it a cultural ecology) of media. No longer is it quite such a regularized process of painting a landscape, publishing a site report, printing a museum catalog. The same "content" can lie behind very diverse media manifestations, different contexts of manipulation and consumption. We are very aware of contested property rights in relation to cultural creativity (Lessig 2008). There is considerable effort being made now to pin down cultural resources, imposing restrictions. Issues of access (who gets to produce and consume), however, now have less to do with ownership of the means of production (owning the printing press). In this new political economy, the notion of medium as mode of engagement prompts us to look beyond product (the image, the text), to the conditions of conception, manufacture, distribution, consumption and curation or discard. These are internal to the media object. A picture is such a distributed field, as well as a material artifact. Second Life is not a "virtual world," but a prosthesis, an extension of sociality into another synthetic and commoditized mode of engagement, usually alone in one's home, with screen, currency, server network, graphical objects, other residents, company managers.

Two key and contemporary concerns in this diversity of media and information are noise (spam) and trust (think of Wikipedia and Google searches). The issue of noise refers us to the sorting of value, to hearing the voice in the crowd, finding the archaeological artifact in the debris of history. The issue of trust is clear in the question of whether the voice or image we have found on the web is as authentic as we might wish it to be. These are constitutional issues of re-presentation, with constitution defined as the political settlement surrounding who can give voice, where and for whom, and who can listen and reply. These are also classic concerns of collegiality in the academy which has traditionally valued the open pursuit and sharing of knowledge.

This is the intimacy to us now of those eighteenth century concerns with the authenticity of ancient and modern texts, the voice of the author, concepts of community (region and nation), authentic pasts (whose pasts?), visiting remains, reanimating them in the present.

On the basis of these current changes, let us conclude by forecasting the future of visual media in archaeology.

There is a powerful trend towards high fidelity photorealistic simulation. This will continue in archaeology simply because of the spectacle it offers. But a counter to this celebration of surface texture is the realization that a user's commitment to a "virtual reality" may depend little upon such fidelity—the most advanced 3-D military simulations funded by the US Department of Defense's DARPA (Defense Advanced Research Projects Agency) identified a "threshold of commitment" to photorealism (see, for example, Lenoir and Lowood 2005; Lowood 2009 discussing military simulation). We have outlined some of the features of this non-mimetic mediawork. The importance of narrative is considerable, and different kinds of selective fidelity, imaginative dissonance and low resolution may be more important principles for visualization than would be expected, because they often engage the maker and viewer, listener or user more intensely and work effectively in community building and reinforcement.

This is particularly so given the trend towards sociality, narrative and networking, as much as technological wizardry, in new web-based media. We might contrast the remarkable achievements of the digital worlds in Hollywood movies and their offshoots in architectural graphics, such as the layer of ancient buildings on Google Earth's terrain map of Rome, with the island of Roma in the online world of Second Life. Roma, a kind of recreation of ancient Rome, exists through and for its community of enthusiasts; events and sociality are foremost in the life of this community.

The past is more than ever a collaborative project in social networking systems like Flickr and Facebook. Web 2.0 media satisfy a suite of functionalities quite different to mimetic fidelity, such as user-generated content, mixing and mashups, database proliferation, customization and collaborative architectures. We can expect these to fuel the rethinking of archaeology as the steward of the past, as the discipline moves further toward a mediating role in cocreative acts of heritage, just as memory practices are altering with the proliferation of web-based information. And this future of memory has a double sense: digital media can facilitate the collation of an enormous range of interests, including those living intimately with archaeological sites and finds, in addition to enabling a publishing platform for more orthodox professional and academic archaeological expertise. Museums are regularly seen now as in educational partnership with communities as well as repositories of rare goods and expertise. Trends toward the democratization of information (consider the debates around Google's scanning of academic libraries) promise to raise awkward issues concerning expertise and the ownership of intellectual property. So digital technology has certainly amplified capture (the amount of data now kept from an excavation, for example). But it seems that storage, retrieval, distribution, and, we should add, creative re-mixing or fungibility, are all magnified with new media.

The politics of this participatory heritage involve questions of access and control, of intellectual property and stakeholder interest, as well as questions of authenticity and expertise. We do not consider it an exaggeration to connect the profound changes associated with the emergence of the modern public sphere in the eighteenth century with these contemporary challenges to our archaeological desire to represent the past.

8

Representing the Medieval Festivals of Jaén Through Text, Enactment and Image

Thomas Devaney

As part of the festivities celebrating the Christmas season in Jaén in 1462, the Constable of Castile, Don Miguel Lucas de Iranzo, arranged a special visit. The king of Morocco, accompanied by the prophet Mohammed bearing the Qur'an and escorted by a strong contingent of knights (all characters were played by the Constable's knights with false beards and Muslim dress), entered the city and proceeded to the Constable's lodgings to deliver a *carta bermeja* (chancery letter). This letter praised the Constable for his martial success against the Muslims of Granada and, lamenting that these victories had driven Mohammed to despair, challenged the Christian knights of Jaén to a *juego de cañas* (a Muslim sport adopted by Spaniards in which teams of knights galloped at each other while flinging light spears). If defeated, the king of Morocco would convert to Christianity. The joust was held in the Plaza de Santa María and lasted more than three hours, until the horses could no longer move. It ended predictably, and the participants paraded across the city to the church of Santa María Magdalena. There, the King was ceremoniously baptized along with his knights while Mohammed was first thrown to the ground and then, with his Qur'an in hand, dunked into a fountain behind the church for a more theatrical baptism. The newly Christianized Muslims then made their obeisances to the Constable and joined their former foes for wine and fruit in his palace (Carriazo 1940:98–100).

Although the message of Don Miguel Lucas's none-too-subtle spectacle seems straightforward—that the Christian armies, led by their heroic Constable, would soon defeat the demoralized and infidel Muslims—the audience's reception of this message is less obvious. Teofilo Ruiz (1994:303), a modern scholar of the pageant, tells us that the "entire urban population" enjoyed the show, cheerfully absorbing not only the play-acting but also the political content of the show. But did all the people of Jaén really attend? Did they wait attentively for a glimpse of the Constable? Or did they talk amongst themselves and think of other things? Did they express approval or disapproval of the events in any way? Could they even see what was happening with nearly two hundred horses crammed into the confines of the plaza? Historians and anthropologists have carefully scrutinized the intended messages of urban rituals and festivals in medieval Iberia, but the reception of those messages remains comparatively unexamined. Especially for elaborate pageants, elites generally controlled the funding and therefore the content. However, popular expression of competing messages could be (and was) accomplished through heckling, lack of participation, and alternate spectacles. Scholarly representations of medieval festivals that neglect such aspects are not only incomplete; they present a version of the past that replicates the partisan views of the written sources on which they are based.

In this essay, I recount the ways in which both contemporary and modern authors have represented the Constable's spectacles of December 26, 1462. I begin with the perspective presented in the most detailed surviving eyewitness account of the festivities and move on to four quite different modern interpretations. I then consider the central problem raised by this analysis: how can historians represent enacted performances and oral popular culture known solely through textual means? The goal of analysis should be to move beyond the concerns of medieval chroniclers to approach, as far as possible, how participants and spectators experienced the event and understood that experience. The first step is to develop an understanding of who was there. Since our sources are silent on this issue, we must instead pose the question of who could have seen the pageant's processions and enactments. To that end, I present a limited analysis of the festival using Geographic Information Systems (GIS) mapping to trace the procession routes. Finally, I suggest that GIS, whose main application by medieval scholars has thus far been the study of land use and urban layout, can be a valuable tool for the cultural historian.

As most scholarly treatments of Don Miguel Lucas de Iranzo's pageants focus on their political significance, a brief summary of his career will provide context. Although the son of a minor noble, he rose quickly to assume a prominent role in the court of Enrique IV. In the course of this ascent, Iranzo made influential enemies and soon after receiving the prestigious post of Constable of Castile in 1458, found himself replaced as the king's favorite and imprisoned. Having escaped, however, he reached an accord with his rivals. In exchange for his title and the rule of any city in Castile, he would abandon court politics. He chose Jaén, a small city that abutted Nasrid Granada and marked Christianity's furthest outpost. When he arrived in Jaén in

1461, Iranzo faced dangers on all sides: powerful rivals in Castile who hoped to gain control of the war against Granada, social tensions in Jaén itself, and a resurgent enemy in Granada.

The key textual source for our knowledge of Iranzo's tenure as Constable of Castile and the elaborate pageants he produced in Jaén is the contemporary chronicle *Relaçión de los hechos del muy magnífico e más virtuoso señor, el señor don Miguel Lucas, muy digno Condestable de Castilla* (see Cuevas Mata et al. 2001), a title that reveals its author's partisan attitude toward the Constable. The identity of this author is not known, but we can say with confidence that it was an intimate of the Constable and one who supported him in the factional disputes that had led to his exile from court politics. This biographer was not merely the recorder of the Constable's deeds but a person who likely participated in many of the events described. The chronicle begins with Iranzo's investiture as Constable and ends in 1471, just two years before the Constable's assassination. The intervening years cover nearly the whole of Iranzo's rule in Jaén.

The chronicler explicitly modeled his depiction of Iranzo on that of El Cid, Rodrigo Díaz de Vivar, in the epic *Cantar de Meo Cid*. Just as the Cid was exiled by intriguers at court, so too did the Constable suffer from the depredations of the "*malos mestureros*." Both heroes won great victories against the Muslims only to see their gains squandered by royal truces and strife within Castile. Finally, both heroes remained fiercely loyal to their kings, despite repeated royal failures to honor the faithful vassals in appropriate ways (Clare and García 1991). This story is told through a recounting of the Constable's struggles with his rivals, his daring feats against Granada, and his careful governance of Jaén. The chronicle revolves around detailed descriptions of the numerous feasts, pageants, and rituals that Iranzo arranged to commemorate nearly every significant day on the calendar, descriptions that serve to establish the Constable's generosity, piety, and courtly manners. The chronicler did not base his account solely on his personal recollections and authority. Instead, he offered an array of evidence—documents, eyewitness accounts, and so on—to lend veracity to his telling. Placing Iranzo against the backdrop of chaos in Castile and ceaseless frontier warfare, the *Hechos del Condestable* depicts him as a champion in a world sorely in need of such figures.

The chronicler's account of December 26, 1462 takes care to emphasize those aspects of the festivities that highlighted Iranzo's virtues. Special attention is given to his movements, his words, and his rich attire. The description of the *carta bermeja* festival centers on the letter delivered to the Constable by Muslim knights accompanying the "king of Morocco," whose text clarifies that their surrender was the direct result of Iranzo's character and actions. Beginning with a salute to the "valiant, strong, and noble knight, Don Miguel

Lucas, Constable of Castile," the "king" goes on to say, "I have heard of the great destruction and shedding of blood that you, honored knight, have inflicted on the Moors of the king of Granada, my uncle" (Carriazo 1940:99 [translation by author]). While the delivery and reading of the letter comprise nearly half the text of the account, the *juego de cañas* merits only a few perfunctory words. Much of the description mentions only the key players, leaving the actions of the rest of the crowd of two hundred knights to be revealed only indirectly. Thus, after the tournament: "And with much joy and shouting, and with many trumpets and drums, he [the "king"] went with the said Lord Constable across the whole city to the [Church of the] Magdalena" (Carriazo 1940:99 [translation by author]). This emphasis on Iranzo is perhaps not surprising to modern observers familiar with the practice of "celebrity-watching." It reveals the intent of the production in ways that a description focused on the action of the tournament or the movements of the closing procession could not. At the same time, it presents a perspective likely shared only by the town's elites, telling us little about how the majority of people in Jaén experienced and understood the festivities.

This elite perspective has been adopted by a number of scholars whose representations of the Constable's festivities focus on their intended political utility. The continuing influence of this written record on modern scholars can be seen in a brief examination of the most influential interpretations of civic spectacle in medieval Jaén. Lucien Clare (1996), in his study of court spectacle under Iranzo, contends that the various pageants, tournaments and games had a dual purpose. First, they were designed to promote and maintain a high level of physical fitness and skill. Second, they sustained the religious beliefs of the community while also promoting a frontier ideology through theatrical representations of key themes.

The two dominant socio-political groupings in medieval Castile were the *bando*, a clan-like familial structure, and the local community (see MacKay 1991; Quintanilla Rosa 1982). While structured around a dominant lineage, the *bando* included not only *parientes* (relatives), but also *deudos* (blood and adopted kin), *vasallos* (supporters), and *criados* (servants). In the absence of formal schools and universities, the *bando* took responsibility for the practical and cultural training of its members. The physical games of the Constable's festivities comprised an important part of this practical education for his *parientes*, *deudos*, and *criados*. The *juego de cañas*, an excellent example of this kind of training, played a role in a variety of annual festivals (Clare compiles an impressive list from the *Hechos del Condestable*). The game required the knights to charge in formation at a full gallop, while aiming their nine to twelve foot lance at an opponent's shield and defending with their own shield. After successfully breaking their canes, the knights wheeled and returned to the starting points, again at a full gallop. All of this had to be done within the confines of the Plaza de Santa María and without trampling the spectators. In using such entertainments to drill the knights in horsemanship and the use of their weapons, the Constable ensured that he would have a fit, skilled, and cheerful fighting force. At the same time, he neatly reminded all present that the object of this martial skill was the defeat of the enemy in Granada (Carriazo 1940:170–176; Clare 1996:25–29).

By linking the military struggle with Islam to religious devotion and to his personal rule, Clare argues, Iranzo used civic spectacles to forge and maintain a frontier ideology within the local community. Often tournament mêlées were held on or near major holidays; examples of this include the December 26 mock battle or the even less orthodox *combate de hueves* presented on Easter Monday in 1461 and 1463 (Carriazo 1940:63–64, 123). The latter, in which three or four thousand eggs were expended in a battle between the Constable's home and a wooden castle constructed nearby, was followed by a meal of eggs and cheese, served to all present. The party therefore combined martial and religious themes with a demonstration of the city's wealth and the Constable's generosity. The ensemble of events at the 1462 *carta bermeja* tournament made these connections even more explicit. By inserting himself into an eschatological story of Christianity's ultimate triumph over Islam, dramatized by the Christian knight's victory in the *juego de cañas*, the humiliation of Mohammed, and the "baptism" of the King of Morocco and his knights, Iranzo linked martial and religious success to his personal rule (Clare 1996:29–30).

Angus MacKay (1989) builds on Clare's arguments in a wide-ranging discussion that examines the Constable's theatrical productions within the broad context of frontier culture. He identifies several functions played by these spectacles. In addition to the physical training and frontier ideology posited by Clare, MacKay argues that they influenced popular perceptions of kingship, indelibly marked key events on the collective memory of the community, and placed local happenings into the larger context of *reconquista*. In briefly recounting the content of the burlesque *carta bermeja* tournament, MacKay, while acknowledging that Iranzo "consciously exploited" the medium to get his message across, does not place undue emphasis on the figure of the Constable. Instead, he reconstructs the spectacle as a narrative, listing its events in chronological order without the detailed description provided by the chronicler. For MacKay, the message matters, not its manner of presentation. He presents the *carta bermeja* battle as a "frontier fantasy," which transcended the local and *bando* context in which it was cultivated to speak about universal issues: the roles of kings and vassals and the imminent victory of Christianity (MacKay 1989:235, 239).

Teofilo Ruiz has, in a series of articles, developed an understanding of the ways in which public ceremony in Castile provided a locus for the expression of power, either through elite appropriation of popular symbols or through ritualized violence, and a means for Castilian elites to define themselves. In "Unsacred Monarchy" (Ruiz 1985), he argues that Castilian kings rejected the sacral trappings of power, preferring rituals that defined royal legitimacy through martial prowess and heredity to those that linked their power to institutionalized religion. He later examines the ensemble of symbols displayed during royal festivals held in Valladolid in 1428 to uncover a "symbolic language" expressed through clothing and gestures (Ruiz 1991). This language appropriated motifs of popular culture for political purposes.

Ruiz expands this discussion to explore the links between "high" and "low" culture in the city of Jaén in a detailed analysis of Iranzo's festivals (Ruiz 1994). He roots his argument in the long-running debate about the functions of Carnivalesque inversion in medieval and early modern European cities to reject the prevalent argument that such inversion was a form of popular resistance to the established order (such as Bakhtin 1984). Instead, he contends that Iranzo appropriated elements of popular culture in civic spectacles intended to diffuse social tensions by directing lower-class unrest toward external enemies: both the Muslims and the Constable's noble rivals. Ruiz describes only a couple of festivals in detail, instead using the *Hechos del Condestable* to develop a typology of the various spectacles. First, however, he recasts the city of Jaén as a theater, a distinction that highlights the staged—as opposed to spontaneous—nature of these spectacles. He isolates three themes central to Iranzo's spectacles: (1) the blending of urban and rural space; (2) the mixture of sacred and secular motifs; and (3) a blurring of the boundaries between high and low culture. Each of these aspects, he argues, served to confirm and augment the Constable's status. Civic festivals placed Iranzo in the public eye to remind the populace of his role as defender against the Muslim hordes close to the city. They adapted popular motifs and symbols to accomplish this most effectively.

Ruiz opens his essay with a detailed representation of the *carta bermeja* tournament and the Epiphany festival that followed shortly thereafter. In using this representation to "gain an entry into the rich and complex world" of Castilian festivals, Ruiz emphasizes the theatrical nature of the events, limiting his gaze to those who were "on stage" (Ruiz 1994:297, 304). In doing so, he is faithful to the chronicler's portrayal, paraphrasing it extensively. The figure of the Constable looms large in both depictions:

> on a "beautiful and graceful horse," rode the constable, Don Miguel Lucas
> de Iranzo. The chronicler describes his appearance in detail. He was dressed

in blue damask with silver and gold adornments and wore rich furs. His face was covered with a mask, a crown adorned his head, and in his hands he carried the sword of justice (Ruiz 1994:296–297; cf. Carriazo 1940:102).

While the spotlight shines on Iranzo, the audience in this urban "theater" fades into the shadows.

While Ruiz's contention that Iranzo arranged, staged, and funded the festivals to further his control over the city is convincing, the absence of any competing spectacles is problematic. He notes that the "entire urban population" of Jaén participated in the festival, implying widespread complicity in Don Miguel's agenda (Ruiz 1994:303). The conclusion here is that the common people of Jaén were the Constable's dupes, that "those above continuously appropriate and transform popular unrest and culture for their own benefit" (Ruiz 1994:315). Is it reasonable to suppose that Don Miguel had a hand in every civic spectacle in Jaén (the author of the *Hechos* wants us to think so, but can we trust this?)? While Ruiz is interested in the vertical relations between those above and those below, he does not seek non-elite perspectives for Jaén's festivals. Instead, he gives voice to the resistance of the oppressed by exposing the strategies of the powerful.

Ruiz limits himself to recreating the elite perspectives found in the *Hechos del Condestable* because popular culture "cannot be recaptured in its original form." He argues, following Roger Chartier (1988), that festivals are culturally neutral artifacts: each group in society understands them according to their own values and perspective and takes from them what is most relevant. Although the meaning of such cultural artifacts was created by participants and spectators, the written records of festivals and rituals are always mediated by their (usually elite) author. Therefore, popular culture has been twice appropriated and transformed. First, the Constable integrated popular and Carnivalesque motifs into his court dramas to better bind the people to his authority. Later, the chronicler "claimed and transformed" these symbols to exalt the Constable's deeds (Ruiz 1994:309).

Philippe Buc (2001) has taken Ruiz's point further to argue that there are strict limits to modern readings of medieval rituals. Countering earlier understandings of ritual, such as that of Geoffrey Koziol (1992), in which they were seen to shape beliefs about power and therefore its actual exercise, Buc argues that medieval authority and legitimacy lay not in the performance of rituals, but in controlling their interpretation. The texts describing them, not the dramas themselves, were the forces in the practice of power (Buc 2001:259). He traces the intellectual genealogy of ideas about rituals and their underlying "reality" from the seventeenth century onwards to argue that Durkheimian views of ritual functioning as the "envelope" for deeper spiritual, social, or political truths are based in modern, not medieval, experi-ence. The medievalist should therefore exercise great caution in attempting a hermeneutics of ritual: "one should master a culture's grammar, but not think thoughts none of its members ever thought" (Buc 2001:226–227).

Buc is particularly critical of the influence of Geertzian anthropology, arguing that medieval historians have been seduced by the apparent analo-gies between their work and Clifford Geertz's understanding of the ways in which ceremony shaped society in a modern Balinese society "still suffused, putatively, with religiosity, and the lost world of archaic medieval political culture" (Geertz 1980:13). On closer scrutiny, Buc argues, the seeming kin-ship of societies far removed in time and place results not from an underlying reality, but from a long-standing hermeneutic tradition. Ideas about the social functions of ritual developed by earlier generations of scholars were applied by Geertz to new settings, and were then returned to the study of medieval ceremony in a distorted form. Ultimately, Buc concludes that anthropologi-cal models that focus on the performance of a ritual unearth meaning at the expense of displacing or effacing the structures of contemporary belief.

Although Buc provides an important caution about the risks of misin-terpreting medieval rituals, he underestimates the possibility of identifying mediating factors in a text when he argues that comparative approaches are complexly inapplicable. Max Harris (2000), in his study of the origins of early modern and modern festivals of *moros y cristianos*, attempts to move be-yond the descriptions in the *Hechos del Condestable* to clarify meanings only implicitly presented in the rituals. His points of reference include modern versions of such festivals, and his analysis is influenced throughout by the experiences of people who even now participate in such productions. This approach effectively allows the reader to visualize the events. In agreeing with other scholars that the tournament functioned in part as military training, Harris relates "the general pattern of such games" as drawn from much later sources (some from Latin America) to demonstrate that the *juego de cañas* was a game of Muslim origin and to clarify the precise skills practiced and the degree of difficulty of the performance (Harris 2000:57). Similarly, he includes the chronicler's version of Mohammed's dunking, but goes beyond previous treatments to note that the Church of the Magdalena was a particu-larly poignant location for such a ritual, as it had been built on the site of a mosque demolished during the Christian conquest of the city (M. Harris 2000:58–59). While he cannot point to specific evidence to demonstrate that this location bore such symbolic overtones in Iranzo's Jaén, other scholars have commented on the triumphalist connotations of converted mosques in contemporary Iberia (Burns 1989:326; J. Harris 1997).

Perhaps because he is himself willing to draw on sources from different times and places, Harris is sensitive to the myriad ways in which the *carta bermeja* tournament blurred the boundaries between different places and times and between reality and fantasy: "In a city from which, earlier in that year, fatal raids had been launched into Moorish territory, real Christians beat fictional Moors (played by real Christians) at their own game of canes… Then, the fictional seventh-century Mohammed was unceremoniously dunked and the fictional fifteenth-century king mimetically baptized outside a church, which had colonized a mosque, in a pool once used by real Moors for ritual washing" (M. Harris 2000:59–60). He argues that this was not a simple representation of Christianity's victory over Islam. In producing such vision, Christians had to master the Islamic game of canes, to dress like Muslims, and to consecrate their victory at the site of a former mosque. The fictional enemy was not driven out, but converted and embraced. Harris suggests that the *carta bermeja* tournament was an attempt to imagine a golden age of *convivencia* in which Christian and Muslim knights competed on the tournament ground rather than the battlefield, where all would follow the word of God, and where Christians and Muslims would adopt the best of each other's culture. While Harris acknowledges that this is an ethnocentric vision, he argues that it was still a hopeful one in the context of a "breakdown in *convivencia*" that culminated in the expulsion of Muslims and Jews from Spain in 1492 (M. Harris 2000:59–60).

While Harris builds his interpretation of the festival from a variety of sources, the most significant in the context of his larger work is the evidence provided by modern manifestations of *moros y cristianos* festivals. Thus, in considering the Christian knights dressed as Muslims, he posits that a preference for exotic costumes is the most likely explanation, noting that today's revelers prefer to play the role of Muslims because "the Moors get the better costumes" (M. Harris 2000:56). His conclusions here echo his interpretation of Iranzo's *carta bermeja* spectacle. Now, as then, participants weave a complex path between reality and fantasy as they struggle to articulate the "simultaneous tensions and mutual accommodations of *convivencia*." Although the conquest was completed centuries ago, one participant tells Harris, "The Moors are not a symbol, they are something in us" (M. Harris 2000:216–226).

A subtler, but no less powerful, approach is the inclusion, throughout the book, of photographs of the modern festivals intended to bring the reader into the experience (see Figure 8.1). Although Harris does not directly link these images to his discussion of Iranzo's festival, he does do so when examining late sixteenth-century versions of the *moros y cristianos* ritual by presenting his own experiences as a spectator of the modern games interwoven with testimony from participants. Yet, in considering such photographs and interview testimony as valuable forms of evidence that can enhance our

Figure 8.1   Converted Moorish warriors leave the church. Villena, 1992. By permission of the University of Texas Press.

understanding of earlier events, he neglects to discuss the differences in function between a medieval festival and its modern manifestation driven in part by tourism. The modern spectacle is no longer intended as a tool for elite control over the populace, nor is the story it tells related to an ongoing struggle between Christianity and Islam. The advantages of applying evidence from modern festivals to their earlier incarnations cannot be overstated. Harris can see the costumes, hear the cannon, and interview the participants on the symbolism and significance of the rites. His images provide a helpful reminder that the texts we read refer to actual, enacted events. But such an approach requires caution to avoid the very dangers against which Buc has warned us.

Even if we can assume that modern *moros y cristianos* festivals contain the same visual elements as did Iranzo's *carta bermeja* tournament, we must ask if contemporaries saw them in the same way. One obvious consideration is physical perspective. Harris's photograph of Muslim knights leaving the church (Figure 8.1) shows his subjects in great detail; it was taken either from a short distance or with a telephoto lens. Can we assume that medieval spectators had a comparable view of the participants? While it ultimately might be possible to present images based on medieval sight-lines and spectator distance, attempts to reconstruct the cultural forces that defined ways of seeing the pageants pose more difficult problems. To note just one example, Harris argues that modern revelers prefer to play Muslims because of their costumes. We might posit that modern academics might focus on the accuracy and detail of their garb while participants and tourists value these costumes for their aesthetic and exotic appeal. It is more difficult to accept without evidence the notion that the medieval residents of Jaén, in the midst of an ongoing war with Granada, would have viewed Muslim knights with such romantic notions.

Harris's representation of Iranzo's spectacles is one attempt to move beyond the limited evidence provided by a partisan chronicle. Although it includes more detail, it does not fundamentally differ from those of earlier scholars relying solely on the *Hechos del Condestable* in that he focuses on the intent behind the spectacles, on the Constable's attempt to present a particular vision of society. The question of the reception of that message remains mostly unasked and unanswered because that is not the subject of the chronicle. In the following paragraphs, I apply GIS analysis to several narrow questions about the movements of participants during the *carta bermeja* festival. In this limited application of the tool, my intention is more to suggest new ways of examining medieval ritual outside of a text-based paradigm than it is to offer a completely new interpretation of this particular event.

Although the influence of architecture on ritual activities has been noted by a number of scholars, no systematic attempt has yet been made to con-

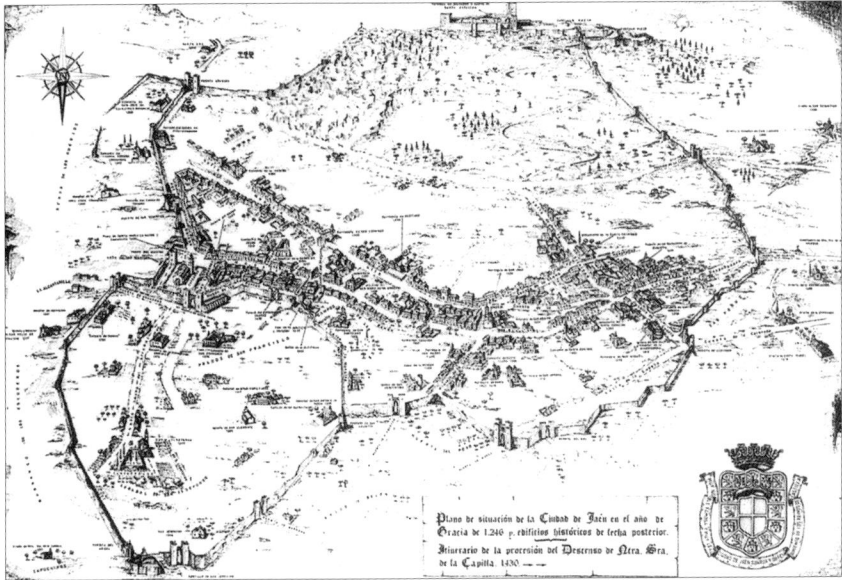

Figure 8.2   A reconstruction of an early map of Jaén. By permission of Oxford University
Press.

sider the implications of the spaces in which the *carta bermeja* tournament
and other festivals in Jaén were conducted (Ruiz [1994:301–304] introduces
such issues but develops them only in general terms). The architecture and
urban spaces of Jaén, however, were more than just the backdrop for pageants; they played an active role in shaping people's behavior and experiences.
A number of scholars, such as Crouzet-Pavan (1992), have demonstrated the
symbolic significance of urban spaces and procession routes. For example,
Sheila Bonde and Clark Maines (Bonde and Maines 2003) have, in their
study of the abbey of Saint-Jean-des-Vignes, articulated an understanding
of the relationship between the material remains of spaces and the meaning
of the rituals conducted in them to conclude that architecture is meaning-
fully constituted. Further, they describe the ways in which documentary and
material evidence should be considered equally and independently to develop a more complete reconstruction of ritual activity. While their approach
cannot be directly applied to Jaén—since Iranzo did not embark on a major building program in Jaén, we cannot assume that the architecture was
designed to enhance the experience of these rituals—it does allow us to
address the ways in which existing structures influenced the conduct and
experience of festivals (Bonde and Maines 2003).

   A first step is to consider the city as a whole. While several scholars have examined the social and economic life of Jaén in the late fifteenth century, con-

temporary images of the city as a whole are relatively rare (see Díez Bedmar 2000; Lázaro Demas 1988; Rodríguez Molina 1996). Two sixteenth-century views of Jaén, Anton van den Wyngaerde's sixteenth-century engraving (Kagan 1989:263–265) and the anonymous view seen in Figure 8.2, show a small city with little or no development outside its high walls. Many of the key landmarks seen here, such as the cathedral, were constructed long after Iranzo's death in 1473. If they are removed from the image, the viewer is left with a heavily-fortified frontier town whose architectural character reflects the overwhelming priority of defense. Working from these near-contemporary views of Jaén as well as those surviving structures that were present in the fifteenth-century, I have developed a bird's-eye plan of the town that includes the major ecclesiastic, civic and defensive buildings (Figure 8.3). This plan emphasizes spatial accuracy over detail with the goal of determining, with a

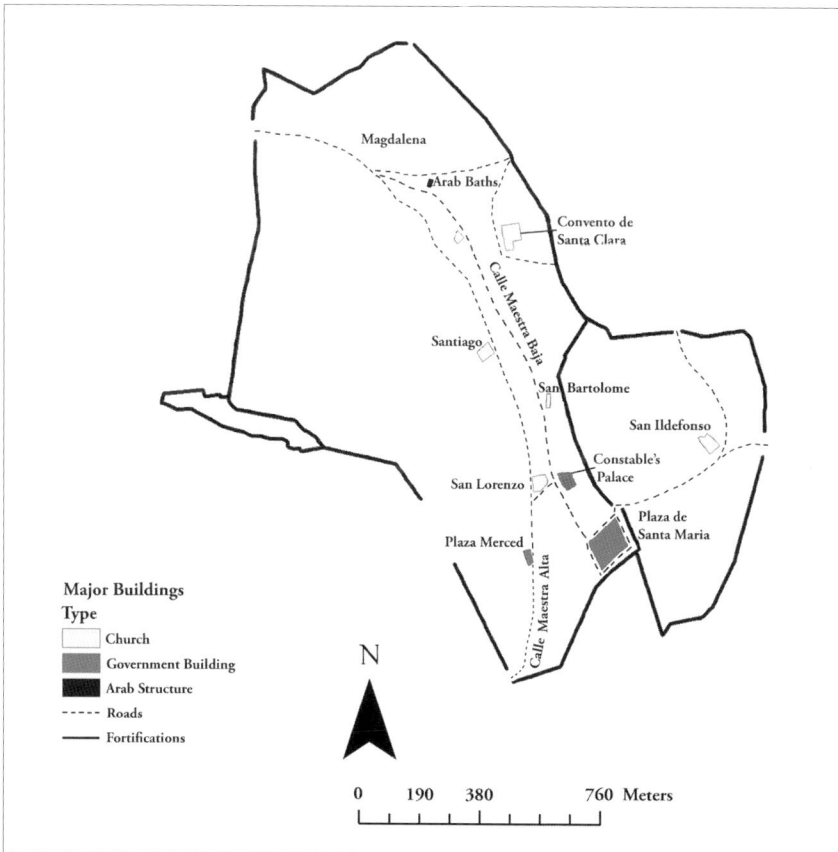

Figure 8.3   Plan of Jaén in the fifteenth century, with major buildings and defensive structures highlighted. Created in ArcGIS (Version 9.1).

reasonable degree of precision, the distances and spaces included in Iranzo's *carta bermeja* play. It begins the study of the ways in which the city's layout and architecture influenced the presentation of public rituals.

Once the likely route of the participants is plotted on this plan (Figure 8.4), two initial observations can be made about the *carta bermeja* play. The first is that the participants covered roughly two miles in the course of entering the city, moving first to the Plaza Santa María and then to the Magdalena, and finally returning to the Constable's palace. Contemporary Corpus Christi processions proceeded at one to two miles per hour (Rubio García 1987:21–22). Hypothesizing a comparable speed for this spectacle, it seems safe to estimate that the processions lasted more than an hour, perhaps ninety minutes. This

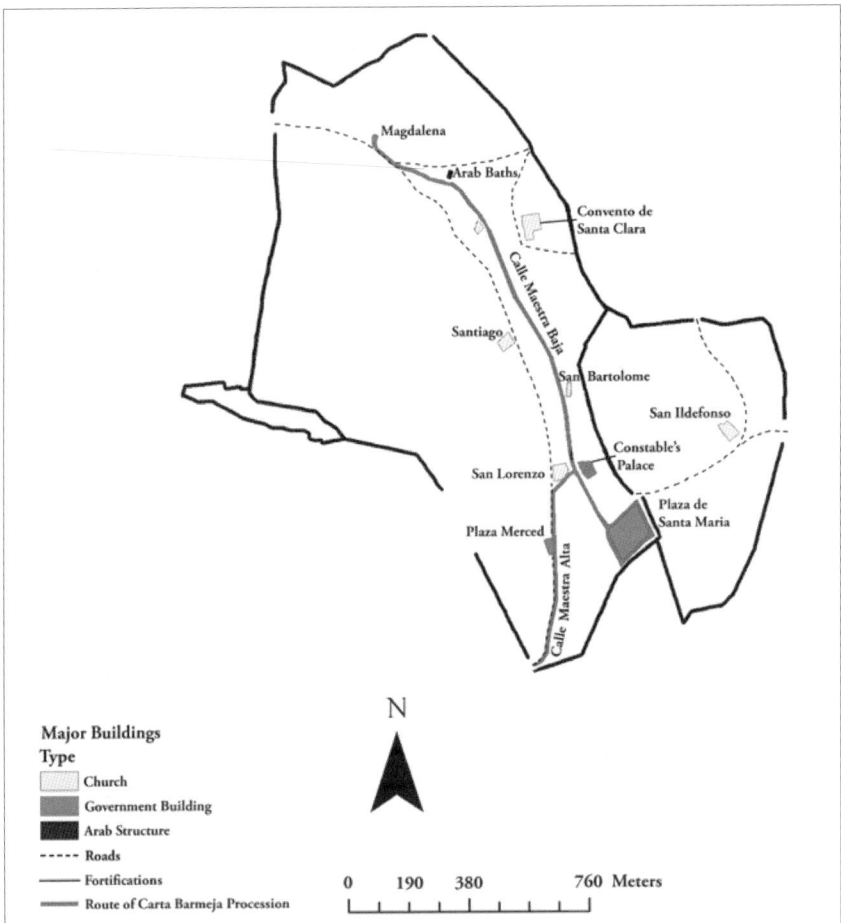

Figure 8.4   Movements of participants during the carta bermeja festival of 26 December 1462. Created in ArcGIS (Version 9.1).

does not include the time spent in presenting the *carta bermeja* to the constable, the three hours or more of the tournament, or the theatrical baptisms of the vanquished Muslims. The closing revelries in Iranzo's palace took place behind closed doors and, as such, were not part of the public festival. We can therefore conclude that the ensemble of events lasted more than five hours and was, for those viewing all or most of it, the primary event of the day. Although answers may prove elusive, the length of the spectacle raises questions regarding who comprised such a group of dedicated spectators and challenges Ruiz's argument that the "entire urban population" was involved. Even on a holiday, for instance, there would be those whose occupations or domestic duties prevented them from enjoying the lengthy show.

Yet the route of the procession also indicates that multiple parishes throughout Jaén were included and that at least a glimpse of the costumed participants was possible for much of the population. The ritual itinerary, which moved along the north-south axis around which much of the town's population dwelled, missed only one of Jaén's main quarters, the parish of San Ildefonso. Indeed, it passed within a hundred meters of nearly every significant religious structure and centered on the key political locales of the Constable's palace and the Plaza Santa María (Figure 8.5). Aided by geography, Iranzo planned his pageant in a way that would integrate the city and ensure that few could fail to notice its occurrence. Prior work on Jaén, notably that of Ruiz (1994:302–305), has demonstrated the ways in which the movements of Iranzo's civic spectacles linked rural and urban as well as public and private spaces. GIS mapping permits the scholar to examine those connections in relation to the actual plan of the city and the demographic distribution of its citizens. It makes it possible to move beyond the confines of an elite representation to a more inclusive understanding of the festival.

The above analysis is but a beginning. The next step is a more intensive examination of Iranzo's festivals that permits a comparison of multiple pageants and includes more detailed data sets including perhaps local population estimates and the distribution of ethnic, occupational, or religious enclaves within the city. This would result in a spatially-oriented understanding of the ways in which particular messages were disseminated. Did procession routes avoid or gravitate toward certain populations? Did they cut across social or cultural divisions? Did they encircle the whole polity or just a part of it? Three-dimensional models can enhance this picture by raising other questions. Though it might be impossible to develop a model of an entire city with existing evidence, even a model limited to the most significant structures can establish viewscapes from different vantage points. What could people actually see? How much of the route of a procession was visible from any one place? What architectural, religious, or artistic sights were linked

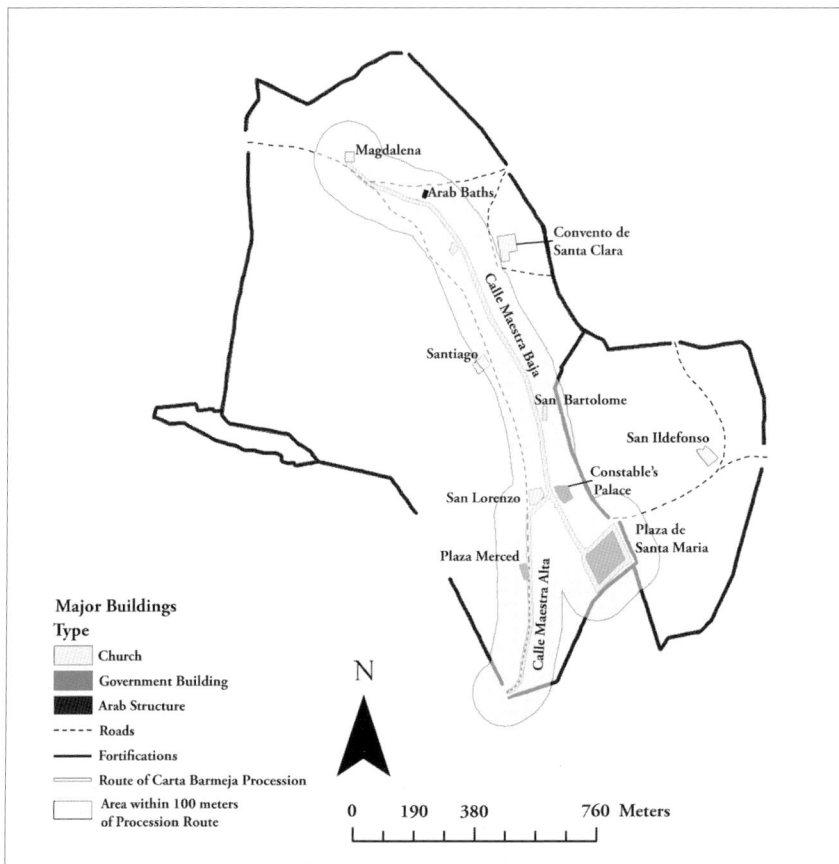

Figure 8.5   Area within 100m of processions during the *carta bermeja* festival of 26 December 1462. Created in ArcGIS (Version 9.1).

with what ritual performances? What groups had the best access? Where were the most advantageous viewing sites? Did people tend to view the festivities at a remove (from their windows, for instance, or rooftops) or were they more likely to crowd near participants? Such questions may not ultimately be answerable, but asking them will remind us that medieval rituals were enacted and bore meaning in dynamic space. Although the manuscript page is our sole witness to these events, it is not the event itself.

9

The World on a Flat Surface:
Maps from The Archaeology of Greece and Beyond

Christopher L. Witmore

On the Properties of Maps: Some Notes on how to Unpack a Thing

Maps. Where do we begin with something so practical, so pervasive, so mundane? As is often the case, that which is close at hand and utterly familiar is that which recedes most readily from our attention. Expressly emphasized by both Martin Heidegger (1971) and Marshal McLuhan (1994), this is the paradox of our immediate material world: in short, despite the proximity of things, many of their qualities and much of their richness remain distant. One way forward with regard to the question of where to begin with maps is to remove oneself just enough as to get a sense of their properties and to gain a handle on the work they do. However, to play upon the paradox, this exercise also involves drawing a map even closer to our attention. We need to create the right amount of distance.

As archaeologists let us consider a map, not as a representation, not as data, not even as information; let us consider a map *as a thing*. Here, we should underline a distinction: *a thing is no mere object*. If we trace the etymology of thing we will arrive at the German word *ding*, which carries connotations of "gathering" or "assembly" (Heidegger 1971). Our point of departure, then, is in asking what is gathered into a thing, in this case, a foldout map of the Pikrodhafni-Potokia coastline, Greece from the rear pocket of *A Greek Countryside* (Jameson et al. 1994; Figure 9.1). This line of treating a map as a thing, I suggest, will help us to better understand the characteristics and actions of a map. So, with an aim to unpacking a map as a thing, let us consider questions related to space, time, materiality/matter, and action/force. These

Figure 9.1   A 1:25,000 foldout map of the Pikrodhafni-Potokia Coastline published by the Argolid Exploration Project (Jameson et al. 1994) in the hands of an archaeologist (photo taken by author).

may seem like strange ingredients to question at the outset, but they will help us begin to wrap our eyes and hands around the properties of this map (after Latour 1986; also Ingold 2007).

Space—where is this map? The map, at a scale of 1:25,000, is of a coastline surveyed by the Argolid Exploration Project (AEP). It projects the shape and topography of a small portion of the Southern Argolid. It depicts the head-land, bays, and shores south of the Hermione peninsula. It presents the letter-number referents assigned to the sites documented by the AEP. Likewise, the map pictured in Figure 9.1 can also *be somewhere*. It is held in the hands, but it could just as easily rest on a desk. It can be placed in a book. It can be placed in a box. It may even be digitized and brought up on a computer screen. In each case, this map has the quality of being portable, of being *mobile*. Of course, a map-in-a-book is not the same as the foldout-map-in-the-hands of an archaeologist, which is not the same as a map-on-a-screen-encapsulating-a-spatial-database. This is because each map has relational specificity, each map enters into an exchange with other elements in a given situation. Yet it is precisely the ability of a map to move between these contexts while retaining consistent qualities that is of interest here.

The property of portability brings us to the question of its materiality—of what is a map made? While the map can be inscribed on a floor, into sand or stone, mobile maps can be made of parchment, paper, cloth, pixels, and so on. These portable materials can be easily folded, rolled up or projected. So, what qualities do all these constituents share? They are all flat. They all have two dimensions.

Time—when is this map? We may slightly rephrase this to ask when was the map produced? Published in 1994, the map translates something of a place at a specific time. But the map is not wholly datable to its moment of production. Many temporalities are simultaneously folded into the map: some are as "distant" as the Chinese development of paper in the second century CE or the assembly of the printing press in the fifteenth century; others are more "proximate," including the latest of a number of geodesic surveys undertaken by the Hellenic Army Geodesic Survey in the 1960s or the initial archaeological survey of the Pikrodhafni in July of 1981. Such diverse temporalities account for the effectiveness of this map (such also could be said of space as well). Moreover, this map can be placed in a sequence with later maps of the area such as the one produced by the AEP Modern Sites Survey (Murray and Kardulias 2000:144, Figure 8.2). As a thing, a map gathers disparate attributes, activities and achievements from various eras—more of this heterogeneous temporal quality will be taken up shortly.

All these properties bring us to the question of action/force—what does this map do? As paper, our map can deliver a paper cut; it can soak up spilled coffee; it can fly across the room as a paper airplane. Its properties will vary with each situation, but for our purposes let us say that this map can also help us navigate between archaeological sites in a valley that we may never have visited. Why is it able to do this? Because this map translates the material world: it translates the 3-dimensional space of the Pikrodhafni-Potokia coastal area into two dimensions. In so doing, it retains something of the visual qualities of this coastal area as seen from above just as other maps may do for the Roman agora of Argos or the citadel walls of Tiryns.

The "action" of maps is always transformed when situated within different networks of relation. As such, issues of power are specific to various practical communities (compare potentially dangerous military strategists to seemingly harmless Classical topographers). Maps may be but one component of these communities, and this diversity cannot be accounted for with superficial glosses offered by hegemonic, all-encompassing, over-dramatized interpretations whereby the panoptic, "lord's view" of the world is always at the expense of another (Harley 1992; Monmonier 1991). We could just as easily discount these glosses of a western gaze as a form of counter-imperialism, but that would get us nowhere. And, far more often than not, an action of a map is to transport a locale elsewhere and, in so doing, to "convey" those viewing somewhere.

After having briefly taken into account these basic questions relating to space, time, materiality, and agency, we can say that: our map translates something of a coastal area at a specific time; like other maps it is flat; it is easily foldable and therefore portable. To sum up (this exercise), a map allows someone to represent a place, to transfer it to somewhere else while maintaining something of its reality in two dimensions (Latour 1986). Such an observation seems obvious enough. However, this point speaks to our very ability to overcome distance with respect to an optical fidelity to certain visual properties of the material world—the importance of this achievement is difficult to overstate.

Locating Maps in Archaeology

Translate the material world onto a flat surface while maintaining something of its qualities without distortion and we have a key ingredient necessary not only for archaeology but also for modern science. Stratigraphic profiles, artifact distribution plans, architectural diagrams, regional maps: the effectiveness of all such media is rooted in our ability to visually transport aspects of the material world. So much rests upon our flat projections. This article takes a closer look at maps through select cases from two centuries of archaeology in the making, both in Greece and beyond. Its aim is to gain a critical distance in order to lend perspective on both the properties and powers of maps in specific locations.

It is remarkable, given the necessity of maps for the work of archaeology, that so little has been written on what it is they *actually do* in the context of archaeological knowledge production (however see Bender 1999 and 2006; Smith 2005; Webmoor 2005; Witmore 2004, 2006a). Then again, it is so very easy to take our own imaging infrastructures and craftsmanship for granted. This ease is partially due to the fact that maps do their jobs so well. Whether one looks at a map-in-a-book, a map-on-the-screen, or a map-in-the-hand, as an observer, one's attention is drawn elsewhere—an affective passage to the scene that is made manifest. With the far made near, an act of locating the features of a coastline in Greece removes our attention from the immediate setting, an ocular engagement with a flat, two-dimensional projection in the hands of an archaeologist outside an Institute in Providence, Rhode Island (Figure 9.1). Clearly there is much more to maps. So how might we better locate them in archaeology? How might we better understand what work maps perform? In recognizing what work maps do, might we be better situated to improve upon them?

This article does not approach these questions by treating flat projections as meaningful records of a Greek coastline, of the city of Athens, or the whole Greek Peloponnesus; rather, in regarding maps as *things*, it places emphasis on how these flat and light ensembles came to facilitate the transportation of select properties of these locales. We are warranted in going so far as to underline how this angle of treating maps as things relates to a particular understanding of *representation*. On the one hand, precautions should be taken with any notion of representation where maps are *summed up* as objective facts, social relations, or power effects. Weighed down by the epistemological baggage associated with a false "bifurcation of nature" (after Whitehead 1920) into ostensibly separate realms—society and nature, subjectivity and objectivity—such representation results in an unfair reductionism where one realm is taken as primary and the other secondary. These realms can never exist in such a relationship for they were never separate in the first place; such a gloss is actually a particular form of *mis*representation.

On the other hand, we have much to gain from an alternative meaning of representation where maps are many things, but what they are in different settings is a consequence of utterly specific map-relations. Maps translate many things, but what are translated can never be entirely contained within a map. If, to say it in yet another way, with the former connotation of representation, maps "stand for" the regions, locales, areas and features they convey, then with the latter, maps "stand in for" them by translating or mobilizing pertinent aspects of the material world and myriad relations with it; maps, as do other media, may *act as surrogates* but can never wholly sum up or subsume. Grounded as an irreductionism, here we encounter representation in its political sense. Such is the definition taken in what follows.

Black boxes engulf maps. In other words, the trials and tribulations implicated in the making of maps are cloaked in darkness. There are very good reasons for this, to be sure. Without black boxes, it would be difficult to get on with the work they help facilitate. At the same time, by prying open select boxes, this article aims to re-member why we should regard maps as tremendous collective achievements. A map is a crowded and busy place, a heterogeneous assemblage. Gathered into maps like the one pictured in Figure 9.1 are hundreds of man-hours, numerous engagements with instruments, negotiations with maquis-covered hillsides, copious mathematical calculations for triangulation and squaring on plane tables, and myriad other contributors. Although we could understand maps as built upon a sequence of labor, this pile-up need not take the form of a linear progression. Though multi-temporal, as was pointed out in the exercise at the start, these accreted achievements are nonetheless simultaneously present in the map. It is through our flat projections that we are able to mobilize events that took place at a distance in space and time. Indeed, because these events were effective acts of delegation (Latour 1994:792), whereby labor was distributed to things (lists of bearings, tabulations, and coordinates, survey notebooks and the final maps), we may now get on with the other work necessary for archaeology.

In pursuing these considerations of maps as collective achievements further, this article will trace the paths of sociotechnical transformation that come together to facilitate an optimal fidelity with respect to the things shown. Once established, maps, as flat projections of the world, gain the qualities of optical consistency, fungiblity and combinability (Latour 1986). From here they come to be arranged in long cascades where subsequent work is built upon (and conditioned by) the outcomes of previous labor. In this, there are major lessons to be drawn for the profession. This article will address five:

1. At key historical junctures, flat projections of the material world played a large role in creating the conditions for the possibility of generating particular forms of archaeological knowledge in Greece and elsewhere.

2. In terms of information design, infrastructure, and possibility, these achievements continue to shape archaeological knowledge production.

3. The qualities of archaeological maps allow them to be built upon, thus forming a kind of media cascade as subsequent maps are compiled out of former ones.

4. The traceability of these cascades is a mainspring of accuracy.

5. Unpacking our media, or rather opening up these black boxes, reveals how *archaeological data are collective achievements.*

All five points, in turn, enrich our understandings of archaeological information infrastructures and knowledge craftsmanship.

Rescuing from obscurity the work that went into our media complicates the oversimplified bifurcation of data and interpretation to the degree that such a dualistic scheme, like others, can never be regarded as a starting point for the production of archaeological knowledge (Witmore 2004). Whether translated into skilled labor, instruments, methods, or media, our knowledge production—better termed "co-production"—is always impacted by achievements which take us beyond any immediate situation at the edge of the trowel, the heel of the boot or the screen of a MacBook Pro (for other assessments emphasizing how interpretation lies behind all aspects of archaeological work, see: Andrews et al. 2000; Edgeworth 1990; Gero 1996; Hodder 1997, 1999; Lucas 2001; Tilley 1989; Thomas 2004a). Whether our engagements with the material world transpire in square holes, in demarcated wheat fields or within the coordinate range of a GIS, they are always prefigured and shaped by the dislocated actions of myriad predecessors through mundane things (cf. Olsen 2003).

Having begun with an ontological inquiry into the map pictured here as Figure 9.1, we may now move on to examine the powers of maps through a comparison of two radically different mappings of Athens, Greece: seventeenth-century pictorial maps-in-books by George Wheler (1682) and Jacob Spon(1678) and a more normative example from Ernst Curtius and J.A. Kaupert's *Atlas von Athen* (1878). With the properties of maps in view, we will touch on further questions concerning the achievements gathered together in, and the roles delegated to, maps. By appealing to historical examples, this article also aims to connect geographical sensibilities to the professionalization of archaeology. To this end, a second historical case study details the compilation and subsequent enrollment of the *Carte de la Morée* (1832), a 1:200.000 map of a region that creates the information grounds for further lines of inquiry. The fact that this map is still with us through long chains of metamorphosis and refinement speaks to the power of such maps as infrastructural bases. It is simultaneously because of these most necessary qualities that maps also harbor certain dangers.

Maps, like all media, are sieves. To translate and mobilize pertinent qualities of the material world is inevitably to relegate others to oblivion. In all too briefly underlining this concern, this article concludes in an altogether different setting with a "deep map" of the San Andreas Fault (on "deep maps" refer to Pearson 2006:15–16; Pearson and Shanks 2001:64–65; after Heat-Moon 1991). If through the flat projection in the hands of an archaeologist *we see and only see* (Witmore 2006a), then with a 42 by 8 foot map-on-a-wall as an event we may draw some lessons of how we may live *through* these projections in a rich and purposefully localized manner. Our goal in this exercise is to aspire to what the artist behind this map-installation hoped for: to recognize how maps can be a conversation.

From the Properties to the Powers of Maps

As an exemplification of some of the foregoing remarks, let us consider a map as drawing together relations between, and forging connections with, various people, things, locales, forms, and experiences—all of which are themselves disparate and heterogeneous in nature. Maps hold on to something of the achievements that contributed to their making: as things, maps gather. To get at the concept of "gathering" let us return to the question: what properties, what qualities allow my thing, this map, to perform in the way that it does? One way to tease out these qualities is through the exercise of comparison.

Consider a seventeenth-century map of Athens in relation to a late nineteenth-century example (Figures 9.2 and 9.3). Of Figure 9.2, a map of Athens extracted from Sir George Wheler's *A Journey through Greece* (1682), we may note several details. The buildings, field boundaries, roads, and mountains are inconsistently sketched: their angle of view varies between vertical, oblique

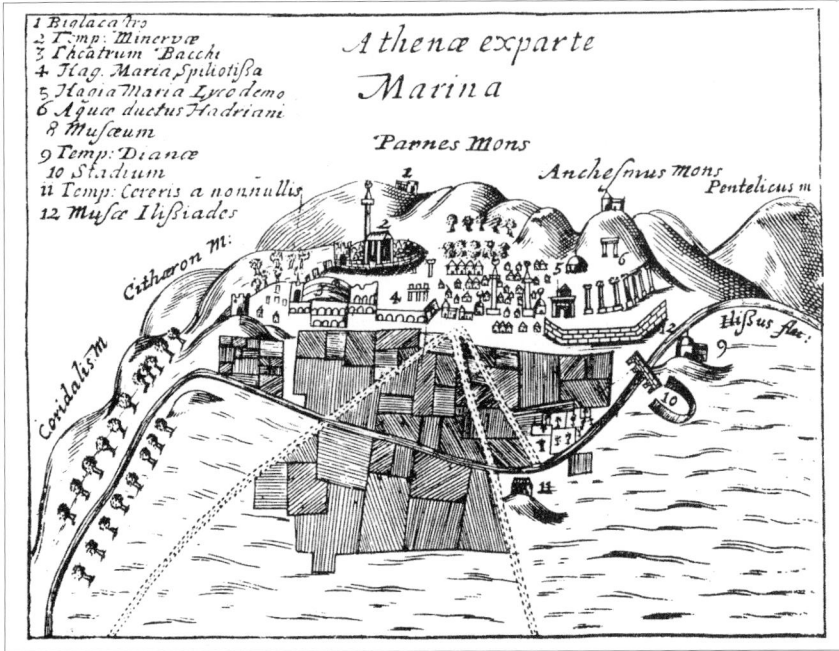

Figure 9.2   The late seventeenth-century map of Athens Greece by Sir George Wheler (1651–
            1724) published in 1682 (Wheler 1682).

and horizontal. Other features too seem haphazard: for example, columns are not so easily differentiated from minarets. Distances between features are inconsistent, not only in relation to each other, but also to any point of view. If the visual elements of Wheler's map are arbitrary and disproportionate, then what purposes did Wheler's map serve?

First, a word of caution: we should be careful of any claim that the map in Figure 9.3 is "more accurate." David Turnbull put it well when he argued that, "accuracy can only be assessed in the light of the purposes for which the map was intended" (1994:41). If one looks closely at Wheler's map, one will note how visual elements are accompanied by numbers. These numbers correspond with a list at the upper left. 1 Biglacastro; 2 Temp. Minervæ; 3 Theatrum Bacchi: the list registers the various monuments of Athens (known in the seventeenth century as "Setines"). As such, Wheler's map is perhaps best described as an inventory of what could be seen, or rather what was dubbed worthy of observation, during the winter 1676–1677. Indeed, Wheler's travel companion Jacob Spon also compiled a map of Athens. It too was an inventory; where Wheler had 12, Spon listed fifty features worthy of note.

Turnbull also argues that maps are more profitably compared in terms of their range and degree of *workability* (1994:54). To understand the workability of a map one cannot treat it as if it were a totally discrete medium. Furthermore, one should be careful with the delicate task of comparison on the basis of contemporary maps. This is because we are so accustomed to a system of representation where accuracy rests upon a faithful and detailed relationship to the things *shown*. Both Wheler's map (like Spon's) and the contemporary map of Athens are faithful; the difference is in *where the faith is placed*.

In the mid-seventeenth century, the topography of Athens was largely unknown to Western Europeans. Wheler and Spon wrote travelogues of their journeys throughout the Mediterranean: *A Journey into Greece* (1682) and *Voyage d'Italie, de Dalmatie, de Grèce et du Levant* (1678), respectively. The mode of registering, of referencing, things seen on the ground was well suited to these travelogues. In both, ancient authors such as Strabo and Pausanias figured prominently—so much so, that the indexicality of both maps was built upon associations with them. What was left of what the ancient authors discussed? How did this compare with the work of other travelers? Such questions were

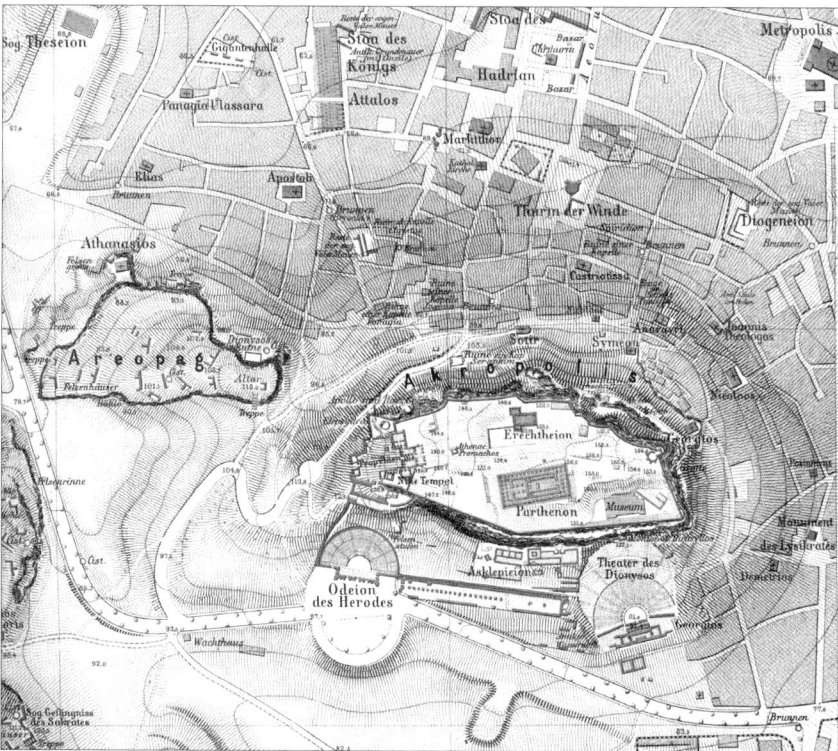

Figure 9.3   A portion of E. Curtius and J.A. Kaupert's 1:4000 map of Athens, published in 1878.

mediated as much by what was written as by what was to be observed (Stoneman 1987:70–83; for a complementary argument in relation to Pausanias, see Cherry 2001:250–51). Of course, Wheler and Spon's maps did more than simply provide checklists. As pictorial statements, both maps also entered into an exchange *with other illustrations* published in their travelogues.

Both Wheler and Spon published detailed images of buildings in Athens such as the Parthenon and Hephaisteion. Whether the lines and angles of buildings were irregular; whether the heights and lengths of architectural features were variable was not necessary for the work these maps performed. While it is worth noting that Wheler was aware of the "mathematical abstraction" necessary for the projection of a region as evidenced by his map of Attica which accompanied his *Journey*, both Wheler and Spon were interested in verifying what of Pausanias, Strabo or other ancient authors was still there, rather than necessarily transporting the things verified back with them. Indeed, we must remember that pictorial maps in the seventeenth century were often inscribed in situations such as legal disputes or land surveys and those who compiled them were often already familiar with the layout of a city or an estate (Turnbull 2000:101–105). With Wheler and Spon such conventions were enacted at a distance. It was on the basis of these associations that we understand the practical utility of such maps. So both Wheler and Spon's maps are better understood in terms of a textual fidelity to ancient authors rather than a visual fidelity to what remained on the ground. Meanwhile, for an eighteenth-century military strategist in Paris or London, the inconsistencies between the two maps are immediately visible once juxtaposed synoptically.

With Curtius and Kaupert's map of Athens (Figure 9.3), the qualities of the visual elements are neither rough nor arbitrary. They are, following William Ivins (1973), visually coherent; they are optically consistent. Given these qualities, we can now *see* how their accuracy rests upon different sets of relations to the things shown. The scale of the map can be modified without transforming its internal properties. For engineers, architects and military officers, much less archaeologists, in order to generate reliable (convincing) knowledge, measurements on the ground must translate into measurements on the page. To attain this quality, one must have linear perspective (a quality which connects with Dutch Art, the *camera obscura*, geometry, optics, and much more [see Alpers 1983]). Maps based upon linear perspective can be superimposed, reformed and combined (something one could not do with Wheler and Spons' maps). One can build upon them.

So what gets us from George Wheler in the late seventeenth century to this late nineteenth-century map? While it is easy to draw radical distinctions between two such disparate imaging practices, it is important to point out that maps are assembled within a scaffolding of other media, whether lists of compass-bearings, trigonometric calculations, or other maps. If we are to understand what lies between Wheler and Spon and our contemporary mapping practices then we must trace the iterative relations, the building of the cascades, the many subtle refinements and shifts that get us to a optimal vantage point in maps.

From Wheler to Curtius and Kaupert, it is only after the return trip is made, so to speak, that other details become apparent (Latour 1987:219–223). For architects in London looking at different plans, for military geographers in Paris gazing at various maps, inconsistencies proliferated, different questions arose, and new trips to Greece had to be undertaken—e.g., the Society of Dilettanti dispatched James Stuart and Nicholas Revett to Greece to undertake more detailed studies of the ancient monuments and to return with the precisely measured plans necessary for Neoclassical architecture in England (Shanks 1996:66; Stoneman 1987:110–130). But, how is it that all these groups are able to look at the same images and trust that they are the same? Once again, it warrants asking: What else is assembled here and what else is gathered into these flat ensembles?

A Further Inquiry into the Powers of Maps

For a map to operate effectively and in exchange with different people in different locations, it has to be multiplied. It is now all too easy to take the act of copying for granted, with our abilities to efficiently, effectively and exactly (or *almost* exactly) reproduce images by scanning, photocopying, and so on. We might say that consistent, repeatable and reliable multiplication is the most important difference between post-Gutenburg European maps and others.

For Bruno Latour (1986), building on the work of William Ivins (1953, 1973) and Elizabeth Eisenstein (1979), the printing press (with graven images) was a way of irreversibly capturing accuracy. The printing press "conserves and spreads everything no matter how wrong, strange or wild" (Latour 1986:12). Copy a map by hand and the adulterations immediately begin to manifest themselves, distortion enters into the process, and by the time it travels via replication a copied map becomes very different from the original. With scriptoria, the transmission of a certain visual culture, of pictorial statements—maps or illustrations—largely remained a local affair. Because the two maps were *never synoptically present* after transcription, discrepancies, errors, corruptions, and deviations by and large went unrecognized (Eisenstein 1979; though, for an example showing that this was not necessarily the case with non-pictorial visual science in the ancient world, see Netz and Noel 2007).

Rather than appeal to some over-dramatized explanation of differences between past and present, Latour suggests we look at much more mundane explanations in our very imaging (and writing) craftsmanship. In so doing, we find that the very combination of linear perspective and replication of imagery on a flat surface without corruption provides a basis for the so-called scientific revolution. The differences rest not with the birth of a more rational mind but with a shift "of the *sight*" (Latour 1986:7); they rest with a transformation in how people *looked* at the world both from a distance and, in turn, up close. (This argument may be contrasted with the more standard belief that modernity came about through a philosophical revolution in how people thought of themselves in relation to the world [refer to Thomas 2004b; also see Witmore 2006b].) For Latour, when it comes to science, archaeology, or history, "books can now carry around with them the realistic images of what they talk about" (1986:11). These realistic images retain the internal qualities of that which they manifest. With the optically consistent and standardized translation of the material world onto a flat surface we find a regular path through space; we gain a repeatable mode of engagement for dealing with landscapes, sites, and features in the archaeology of Greece and beyond (Witmore 2004).

Between the work of figures like Wheler and Spon and the professionalization of archaeology, many intrepid travelers, military men, and diplomats journeyed to Greece. In this interim, we find a slow drift from verifying the presence of things in texts to obtaining reliable translations of the things seen and returning with them (Latour 1987:223). Once back, the ability to arrange various accounts, maps, and measures simultaneously on the same few square meters of wooden table created a situation where differences between maps and plans proliferated and new questions ensued. Debates occurred as to what to observe and how to properly observe it. Instructional literature was produced—from *Instructions to Travellers* (Tucher 1757) to *Hints to Travellers* (Fitzroy and Raper 1854). As inconsistencies proliferated, new initiatives began to correct them (see Latour 1987:215–257 on centers of calculation; for a cautious assessment of the London Royal Geographical Society as a center of calculation see Driver 2001). New trips were planned and undertaken. Such cycles of accumulation and debate, which are conditioned by circumstances of trust, authority, credibility, and influence (Shapin 1998; Witmore and Buttrey 2008), give rise to templates to standardization for dealing with regions, sites and features (Witmore 2004, 2006a).

This terse treatment of the gulf that separates Figure 9.2 and 9.3 threatens to outweigh both the idiosyncrasies of location and the issue of scale—both play major roles. When compared with areas of the Greek interior, Athens is located on the coast and more or less easy to visit. Even by the turn of the nineteenth century, relatively few Western European travelers like Wheler and Spon had journeyed to the inner regions of Greece. Moreover, there was no secure basis for locating towns, roads, or rivers, much less ancient sites, relative to landmasses such as the Peloponnesus or Northern Greece. If, as we now understand, the powers of a map are consequences of association (Law 1986; Turnbull 1994:54), what advantages does translating several thousand square kilometers into several hundred square centimeters of flat, optically consistent, and standardized projection provide?

La Carte de la Morée

The shape of a coastline, the location of safe harbors, the presence of potential hazards (reefs, capes and bays): maps are critical as navigational aids in foreign waters. Until the turn of the nineteenth century, regional maps of the Greek Peloponnesus were often published on the basis of admiralty surveys undertaken from the relative safety of deck and shore. While coastal features were well mapped, these surveys could not securely locate features of the interior (Figure 9.4). During the Napoleonic wars Britain and France spent huge sums of money to standardize geographical knowledge and improve the fidelity of maps relative to roads, streams, the location of villages, fortified areas of defense, and ancient sites in the interiors of key regions. Given the strategic importance of southern Greece in the eastern Mediterranean, by the early nineteenth century both countries had dispatched agents to the Morea (as the Peloponnesus was formerly known). The British sent the military geographer and Classical topographer, William Martin Leake (1777–1860), and the French dispatched the cartographer Jean-Denis Barbié du Bocage (1760–1825). Both figures were tasked with documenting and mapping the region. Leake's map, published in 1830 to accompany his *Travels in the Morea*, was based on over 1500 measurements and enjoyed a brief period as the most detailed map of the Peloponnesus. Still, despite both Leake and du Bocage's best efforts at compiling maps, there was a need for an even more precise regional map, not only in the context of military geography, but also for engaging questions of classical topography. This map was realized under the French *Expédition Scientifique de Morée*.

Modeled upon the collaborative body behind the *Description de l'Egypte*, the French *Expédition* was a large, state-sponsored mission that involved the intense scrutiny of Greece through the Dépôt de la Guerre (Bourguet 1998; Bracken 1975; Lepetit 1998; Wagstaff 2004). From 1829 to 1831, under the leadership of the naturalist, physical geographer and Colonel Jean Baptiste Geneviève Marcellin Bory de Saint-Vincent (1778–1846), a large collaborative body of artists, antiquarians, botanists, draftsmen, geologists, and epigraphers carried out a geographic survey of the Peloponnesus. With the *Expédition*, crossovers between the military and science occurred in the context of

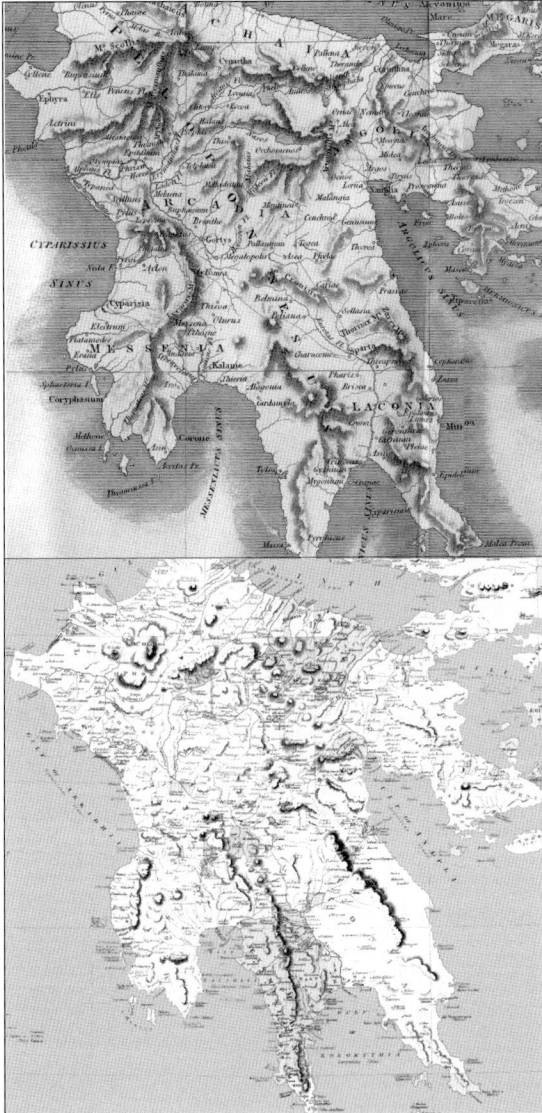

Figure 9.4 A juxtaposition of areas of the Peloponnesus from two maps published in the early nineteenth century. The map on the top accompanied Edward Dodwell's *A Classical and Topographical Tour Through Greece During the Years 1801, 1805, and 1806* (Dodwell 1819) and the one on the bottom is extracted from a map insert with William Martin Leake's *Travels in the Morea* (1830). Note the differences in detail between the areas of the interior. Unlike Leake's, which is based on over 1500 points, Dodwell's map was compiled from admiralty surveys alone. As such, the interior details do not rest on any secure measures.

geographical description and particularly in aspects of discipline, precision, measurement, and observation. The mission was originally divided into three sections: one dealt with the physical sciences, the second with archaeology, and the third with architecture and sculpture. Ironically, the major contribution to archaeology lay not with the work of the art and architecture section, but with that of Puillon de Boblaye in the section concerning the physical sciences and, in particular, descriptive geography and cartography (for this assessment, see Curtius 1851–1852:135–136).

It is with the physical sciences section, and specifically the work of geodesy and triangulation performed during the *Expédition* between 1829 and 1831, that the most detailed and exact, "scientifically-derived" map of the Morea was formulated. For the expedition leader, Bory de Saint-Vincent, the map was no less exact and detailed than those generated for the immediate environs of Paris (1836:iv). With this map, thousands of man-hours of wayfinding, geodesy, triangulation, trigonometry, squaring, and measurement with theodolites, sextants, and plane tables were delegated to a flat projection. Not only were the precise coordinates for ancient sites, monuments, and landscape features calculated relative to the whole of the Peloponnesus, but also, with the incorporation of the geodesic survey, to the globe. In this way, the map provided an exact and globally accurate, three-dimensional (established by X, Y, and Z coordinates) comparative basis against which ancient measurements and distances could be rendered. Moreover, this work was accomplished with the aid of far more refined instruments than Leake or civilian geographers such as Barbié du Bocage had at their disposal.

The *Carte de la Morée* was first published in 1832 in six sheets at a scale of 1:200,000 (Figure 9.5). It was subsequently reduced to a scale of 1:600,000 to accompany the *Physical Science* publication volumes of the *Expédition*. This version excludes many of the topographical details of the smaller-scale, larger-format map in six sheets. In its condensed form the map encompasses the Cycladic islands, the details for which were derived from work by Colonel M. Lapie and further augmented according to charts produced by the British Admiralty and Bory de Saint-Vincent (Puillon de Boblaye 1836:2). The *Carte* was later republished in 1852 as the *Carte de la Grèce* (in 20 sheets at a scale of 1:200,000). Here we may emphasize how this map could be reshuffled in different ensembles while retaining its internal qualities because of the powers of linear perspective—a quality obtained through many long hours of triangulation. Through its various versions, the map would come to rest in the many hands of various groups with diverse interests. But splayed out on an observation table at the Dépôt de la Guerre in Paris of 1832, one would imagine that this map took on an almost incomparable potency.

By the nineteenth century maps had become the most powerful articula-

Figure 9.5   Detail of the Argolid and Corinthia extracted from the 1:200,000 version of the
Carte de la Morée.

tion of power possible (Latour 1986). An officer attentively stooped over the
Carte in Paris now had a reliable and hence "accurate" basis for planning how
to deploy troops on the ground in the Peloponnesus. He could strategize the
movement of his squadrons, all the while knowing what lies at the top of
the pass, over the next hill, or around the next bend where there may be a
bottleneck suitable for a potential ambush. Combined with a topographical
memoir—in effect, a new genre of descriptive geography—one knew how
deep a crossing point was; where the sources of freshwater were to be found;
how many potential combatants were located in a given family, village or
region (also see Godlewska 1999:157–164). It is so much easier to dominate
several thousand square kilometers when they can be manipulated on a few
square meters of tabletop.

A 1:200,000 regional map with its descriptive geography provides a footing from which ancient scholars may focus on different questions. Unlike Sir

William Gell or William Martin Leake, subsequent travelers did not have to rely upon local guides or undertake many tedious hours of wayfinding, measuring angles with compasses and calculating distances with pocket watches on their own. All such ambulatory relations and practices have now been delegated to a map and the associated descriptive geography. With the French map in hand, subsequent scholars could now undertake regional archaeologies or more specific site work. In the mid-nineteenth century, new scholarly concerns shifted to the location of ancient towns; to the paths of ancient routes between Megalopolis—Tegea—Sparta; or to the layout of a battle described in Thucydides. With an installed base for a knowledge infrastructure, new sets of relations were possible; of course, they were also simultaneously limited by such infrastructures (see Bowker 2007:253–254).

The French map would mediate the engagements with, and the knowledge constitution of, the landscapes and sites of the Peloponnesus by subsequent classical topographers, including W.G. Clark (1858:viii), E. Curtius (1851:1852), W.M. Leake (1846), and W. Loring (1895:25). It should be underlined that in this work there was often an overt priority for periods covered by ancient texts, and especially the Classical. And, indeed, similar questions had been raised prior to the publication of the *Carte de la Morée* by earlier travelers to the Peloponnesus. Connecting features of the land with ancient toponyms on the basis of ancient texts was a common characteristic of earlier scholarly work (W. Gell 1817; Leake 1830; Pouqueville 1805). Such work eventually played a role in the linguistic engineering of Ottoman place names: for example, villages such as Kastri and Damala take on their ancient toponyms, Ermioni and Trizína. The difference was that, after the map, the composition of what it was to be a classical topographer had shifted. The groundwork was now laid for subsequent cartographic labor.

Also published as the *Carte Trigonométrique de la Morée* (1832), the survey conducted by *Expédition* formed the basis for the 1880 *Austrian Staff Map* at 1:200,000 scale, published by the Military Geographical Institute of Vienna (*K.u.K. Militärgeographisches Institut*) (British Naval Intelligence Division 1944:397). It provided the template for the 1:300,000, 11-sheet *Greek Ordinance Map* of the Peloponnesus compiled by Major J. Kokides, the first president of the Hellenic Geographical Society. This map was also published by the Military Geographical Institute of Vienna in 1885 (Lolling 1889:cxvi). Kokides' map (Χάρτης του Βασιλείου της Ελλάδος) was enlisted as a basis by German mapmaker H. Kiepert for his *General-Karte des Königreiches Griechenland* also crafted in 1885 in Vienna (French 2003). Kiepert's map was in turn utilized as the 1:300,000 general map of the Argolid in Bernhard Steffen's (1844-1891) *Karten von Mykenai*, 1884 (Figure 9.6). Likewise, Steffen's map was employed by archaeologists such as Christos Tsountas

Figure 9.6   Detail of the Argolid and Corinthia extracted from Bernhard Steffen's *Übersichtskarte von Argolis* in the *Karten von Mykenai* 1884. Steffen's annotations to Kiepert's map, which was based on the *Carte de la Morée*, include the locations of ancient sites and routes indicating the routes of Mycenaean roads.

(Tsountas and Manatt 1903), Alan Wace (1949) and Richard Hope Simpson and D. K. Hagel (2006). Alfred Philippson, a German geographer, compiled his map, the *Pelopónnisos* (1:300,000), on the basis of the *Carte*; so too did Antonios Miliarakis (1886). In this way the results of the French labors were further refined, reshuffled, and combined in order to generate other maps of Greece. The *Carte* is set as a base in a chain of iterative relation.

Need soon arose for maps at a variety of scales. By the turn of the twentieth century the inconsistencies in the maps based upon the French survey became too great to be corrected by wrestling with its constraints in the resulting projections. Such limitations were pointed out in the 1944 *Geographical Handbook* for the British Naval Intelligence Division: the hachuring of the physical topography, for example, was sometimes inaccurate—the French maps were neither contoured nor shaded (compare Figures 9.5 and 9.6)—and the roads and settlements were said to be "obviously out of date" (1944:397).

While scholars would continue to recruit maps built directly upon *Expédition* labor (e.g., Hope Simpson and Hagel 2006), for most, it was no longer sufficient to *re-present* on the basis of the French map or others for that matter. Limitations are inherited in each chain of maps. Accumulated inconsistencies and restrictions eventually justify the need for new cartographic endeavors. Another cycle of survey, geodesy, and triangulation was begun under the Hellenic Military Geographical Service (HMGS). New infrastructural bases and iterative chains were set. At the same time, this subsequent work would be unimaginable without the previous links in these chains. And from the HMGS we may trace the chains associated with its maps at various scales to EuroGeographics (http://www.eurogeographics.org), the company which provides the coverage for Greece in Google Maps (http://maps.google.com/)—a now obligatory passage point, not only for locating the weekend farmer's market, but also for scholarly presentations on everything from sacred Maya caves to Hittite rock reliefs.

Why should we expend so much effort in liberating these details from obscurity? Two reasons should suffice for our purposes here. First, more than historical veracity lies behind our endeavors. Instead of claiming the French map is out of date, like the authors of the British Naval Intelligence *Handbook*, we might say that its fidelity provided sufficient grounds for classical topography and its constraints necessitated return survey trips (national politics and the need for a Greek mapping service also converge upon this new work [see Peckham 2000]). Second, the sheer importance of an accurate portrayal of the material world for archaeology provides a sufficient rationale for rich "sociotechnical" genealogies of our media (Wylie 2013).

In considering the first reason, Michel Serres' distinction between scenography and ichnography is helpful (1995). Set in a relationship of signal and noise, the scenography may on some level be understood as the representation, the ichnography is the pile-up, the cascade that traces the path from the local to the global. When I pull up a Google street map of Athens (something I now manipulate with a single finger), it is routine for me remain at the level of the scenography by, say, plotting out my route from Chalandri to Monastiraki. The ichnography, by contrast, as Serres pointed out, is the "complete chain of metamorphoses" (1995:19) that links up EuroGeographics to the labors of Curtius and Kaupert. *Ichnos* is the Greek word for the trace of the step, the footprint. By tracing the paths of the metamorphoses between these maps we expose the invisible labor and situated practices buried in this same view; in so doing, we localize a global. In the movement from the French *Carte* to the *Austrian Staff Map* to Kokides' *Greek Ordinance Map* to Kiepert's to Steffen's, these chains of transmutation are not severed from the new mapping projects they spawn. On the contrary, they provided a basis for new definitions of accuracy to be accessed in the context of new demands upon maps. As such, they are folded into the maps of various scales published throughout countless archaeological volumes on into the twentieth century and beyond. They contribute to further work and map production. As with GPS or satellite imagery, such military endeavors, we might say, are part of the composition of Greek archaeology.

Returning to the second reason, to trace out these chains is also to provide grounds for an accurate portrayal. We have seen how accuracy is not a virtue of modern, western or scientific maps, as opposed to "ancient," "nonwestern," or "pre-scientific" ones; the difference, it was demonstrated, is in the associations. Different groups have particular object orientations and maps, whether in the hands of travelers, military strategists, or classical topographers, take on different roles as navigation devices, administrative and strategic planning aids, or bases for regional archaeology (on maps in practical navigation see A. Gell 1985; Ingold 2000:219–242). Maps may even become different things in distinct locales (this is why appealing to any one melodramatic critique of maps will simply not do).

For archaeologists, accuracy rests with a faithfulness to the things shown. Features of the material world translated into a map should not be exclusively thought of as existing in a relationship based upon direct correspondence with the things out there. A map of the Athenian Acropolis stands in for the Erectheion, Parthenon, and Propylaea, but its accuracy cannot be located solely with a correspondence between the length of foundations and lines on the page; rather it connects with insuring the verifiability of those measurements and the traceability of how they were mobilized across the "series of transformations" (Latour 1999:123) that exist between cut stone features on the acropolis and the resulting map. In other words, accuracy depends on the ability to maintain conduits through reference between related events that occur in trench, along transect, or through other located practices, in the laboratory, the archive, the study, and the final publication (for this work, see Witmore 2004). In addition to maps, these references often involve cascades of other media—tables of calculation, notebooks, plans, and their various iterations.

What is true of our own practice is true for our ichnographies. The traceability of the chain of metamorphoses has to be insured, should the need ever arise that the validity of archaeological work is challenged. The possibility remains for reiterative work, for retroactive certification, in the future. If we are to leave open the paths, the conduits for the work of verifiability and hence, an accurate portrayal, then full disclosure is requisite. When was the map compiled? Who paid for its production? What instruments, equipment and personnel were involved in its production? What projection was it based upon? No matter how long or short, these media trails ("metamedia") need to be preserved, for they provide the paths between the material world and our very particular media.

Looking for the San Andreas Fault

Thus far, the thrust of matters has been with demonstrating what lies behind the ability of maps to translate the local into mobile, transferable, compatible and, therefore, global terms. By exposing the ichnography of the *Carte de la Morée*, we demonstrated how the "universal" attributes of maps are highly localized (the so-called "view from nowhere" has a place, even a few, but this view cannot speak for all [Bowker 2007; Law and Mol 2001; Shapin 1998]). Before closing, let us continue with this shift to the idiosyncratic possibilities for maps and consider a radically different map-space. From the differential spaces offered by pictorial-maps-in-books or fold-out-maps-on-desks under the gaze of military geographers or classical topographers, we now move to an installation-map-on-a-wall assembled by a performance artist. In making this turn, a secondary aim is to detail how maps are profitably understood as modes of engagement (Shanks 2007; Ryzewski 2009). As modes of engagement, maps may either impact how an archaeologist approaches a valley in Greece, or they may, as with the deep map detailed here, demand a very particular bodily performance along an office corridor.

Over the course of 2001, Cliff McLucas compiled a large graphic map of the San Andreas Fault as a component of the Three Landscapes Project (Shanks 2006). Thirteen panels, each 7 feet high by 3 feet wide, were arranged side by side to form a huge cartographic composition that, with the lighting included, measured 42 feet by 8 feet in all (Figure 9.7). Affixed with mousetraps and thumbtacks to a wall, the panels hung along the second floor corridor outside a studio (what would eventually become the first home for the Stanford Metamedia Lab: http://metamedia.stanford.edu/) in Building 60, the former location of the Stanford Archaeology Center.

As a deep map, *Looking for the San Andreas Fault* conflated diverse sets of information about the places concerned. For McLucas, these sets included: a standard California roadmap, an aerial survey of the complete fault line undertaken in the late 1960s, LANDSAT imagery, 360° vertical panoramas at 11 points along the line (the vertical panorama was a means of breaking with the convention of landscape photography as horizontal), the various languages spoken in the region, journal entries and more. After the first three layers—the roadmap, the aerial survey and LANDSAT imagery—McLucas took leave of such optically consistent and fungible media (maintaining this convention in GIS provides the basis for information design). The subsequent collage of information sets worked against consistent combinability.

Figure 9.7 *Looking for the San Andreas Fault* 2001 (photo by Michael Shanks).

Deep maps manifest contingency—an exchange captured in the competing grids whether Cartesian or linguistic. The latter were generated in various
ways. Tipai, Gabrieleño, Chumasa, Salinon, Costanean, and Pomo; Native
American languages were registered by the length of their supposed territorial
coverage along the line. This metric grid was juxtaposed with a Spanish text
documenting the final journey of Jesus Christ (a connection to the Spanish
missions along the line), a notebook in English and a journal in Welsh compiled by Dorian Llywelyn, a fellow researcher on the project. In this, McLucas played upon tensions between universality and deep locality, between the
cartographer and the spaces associated with the fault.

McLucas made no attempt to extract his presence from this work. Instead,
he wove people, including himself as a co-producer, into the map as figures
who intervene along the fault. Door open, McLucas was often present in the
studio. With artist in residence, the map was "informed;" it possessed the
capability of being responsive to its audience. Eventually, the map presents a
conundrum that in looking for the fault, one gets lost in the multiplicities of
places that coexist along the line. McLucas recognized that there are myriad
other spaces besides that of mapmakers (also Sloterdijk and Latour 2009).

For McLucas, deep maps are necessarily big; the large size was the only way
to combine the complex layers. It was also a means (and end) to design a very
different transaction from those facilitated by maps in other spaces. Maps are
often taken to be an archetype of control; standing over a desk, shuffling back

and forth to a map in a book or moving the tip of your finger in sync with a cursor on screen, it is easy to manipulate distant lands with one's hands. A map as an installation-corridor provides an altogether different angle on this archetype.

From south to north, from the Salton Sea to Shelter Cove, the 13 panels became 13 steps evocative of a journey undertaken by McLucas and Llywelyn along the length of the line. This notion of a journey is more than evocative; the map was designed as lived. "Unstable, fragile and temporary" McLucas' deep map of the San Andreas was a dynamic installation (Shanks 2008). As an event, one cannot construe its function as that of archival documentation— it no longer exists and we are left with traces: a video diary, a reduced scale version on a wall in the Stanford Humanities Center, notes on a wiki page, a photographic gallery of the deep map. Because of this, we should recall its immersive, iterative, and performative character.

Unlike computer-screens-on-tables and books-on-desks where a very particular exchange relegates a largely passive role to our bodies—bums on seats, working with eyes and hands—McLucas' large deep, map-on-a-corridor-wall was an invitation for the viewer to become a participant. In order to follow the full length of the line or to address resolution (by stepping forward or back), the deep map demanded a moving, peripatetic engagement on the part of the viewer. Move closer, look left, look right, step back, continue to the right; such were its operational demands. If, for those who attentively encountered the work on a recurrent basis, the repetition of these pedestrian relationships established a familiarity with the work, then such effects were short lived. Each layer—from the simple road map to the final scans of McLucas' journal—appeared over a protracted period as a new panel overlaying the previous one. In this, each new panel retained the previous layers within its overall composition. As each new layer was added, the sedimentation of different orders of accumulating material increased. Encountering a new panel compelled an observer to enter the work. Living, kinetic, even spontaneous, McLucas' deep map choreographed an iterative experience that broke with the standard signal of our flat projections as we often confront them in a site report or GIS. Something of what maps-in-books or maps-on-screens cannot convey was evoked in the (visceral) engagement. The deep map was designed to appeal to more than a visual interplay between eyes and hands, as it operated in a corporeal exchange with a walking, attentive participant-observer.

Looking at the San Andreas Fault poses a different answer to the questions with which this chapter began: How might we better locate maps? What work do they perform? Through maps the local may be translated into the global, but this global is always located, it is localized through specific spaces of articulation and exchange. While maps transport something of the material world at a distance, this may not be the only work they do. They may indeed break with this ease of circulation (an attribute of the global) and invite other relations. A 42 x 8 foot map on a wall along a corridor may *enact* very different effects by prompting radically different experiences. As an installation *Looking at the San Andreas Fault* offered a different take on maps, mobility, and manipulation: it was what McLucas hoped for—a conversation, not a final statement.

Conclusion

Jorge Luis Borges encapsulated the image "of exactitude in science" in a short parable of an Empire where the craft of cartography attained such a degree of perfection that the very map of that Empire coincided with the physical territory of the Empire "point for point" (1972). Having attained what was believed to be the greatest possible fidelity to the world, subsequent generations lost interest in the pursuit of cartography. Eventually, the map proves so cumbersome that it is abandoned to sun, wind, and rain. Later, in the time of the author, all that remains of the map are "a few tattered fragments" in the Western Desert. Apart from these remnants, "no other relic is left of the Discipline of Geography" (1972:141).

Borges presents readers with the pursuit of an unmediated, objective "view from nowhere" that breaks down when its locus is everywhere. For our purposes, we may take the liberty to go so far as to claim that the cartographers' map, based on a misplaced wish for one-for-one correspondence to the whole of this land, is rendered unworkable because it no longer circulates aspects of the Empire at a distance. Borges' cartographers aimed at a transcendent level of truth, which denied the fragile, costly, iterative, political, and located nature of its co-production. There was no place for the labor, events, and "life supports" that were involved at each and every level of the map's making (Sloterdijk and Latour 2009; also see Shapin 1998). No transits, no surveyors' chains, no plane tables, no copper plates, no archives containing lists of bearings and tabulations or any previous maps remain. Having expanded the gridded space of the drafting table into the land, the cartographers of this Empire also impressed this table on the variable spaces of the territory. In so doing, they reduced many spaces to one by appealing to a universal (the associated work was kept invisible): such are dominative actions worthy of the label "Empire."

What the cartographers in Borges' parable failed to *realize* while they expanded their flatlands to the point of blotting out the sun was that an accurate portrayal does not rest upon a total, transcendent fidelity to the visible;

what counts is a recognition that something, somewhere, and someone is missing. Every material past engaged by normative archaeology is blanketed by the mapmaker's space. While this is most necessary for archaeology, this space is also rife with peril. If we are to be cautious of final statements like those of Borges' cartographers, conduits must exist to reveal how and why this one view was arrived at, despite the myriad other possibilities. And, no doubt, from time to time these conduits need to be inspected, retraced and rearticulated.

Acknowledgments

While Bruno Latour's 1986 article "Visualization and Cognition: Thinking with the Eyes and the Hands" (later republished as "Drawing things together" [Latour 1990]) provides both model and inspiration for this chapter, the subsequent critiques by scholars including John Law and Annemarie Mol (2001) and Steven Shapin (1998) have also contributed to its formation. I am indebted to Michael Shanks for generously sharing materials from the Three Landscapes Project. I thank Sheila Bonde, John F. Cherry, Steve Houston, Matt Ratto, Krysta Ryzewski, and Tim Webmoor for their invaluable insights. Any remaining defects are mine.

10

To be or not to be in Past Spaces:
Thoughts on Roman Immersive Reconstructions

Diane Favro

Most ancient buildings stand in mute silence; the chasm between their operational life and modern academic inquiries is wide and deep. Only a few structures speak to us across the centuries. At the enormous Temple of Artemis at Sardis, a column bears an inscription (mid-second century CE) boasting: "My torus and my foundation block are each a single stone, and of all [the columns] I was the first to rise" (Buckler and Robinson 1932:143–144). Miles away and centuries later, the fifth-century church of St. Theodore recalls former rituals at Gerasa, "I have been made at once an amazement and marvel to those passing by, …[Here] formerly [in pagan times] so many four-footed toiling beasts fell down here that a stomach-turning stench arose. And often someone nearby pinched his nose and gave up the desire of breathing to avoid the bad smell" (Crowfoot 1929:21–22). These first-person accounts by ancient buildings underscore Roman esteem for construction expertise and the power of building experience to define and shape human rituals. Sadly, most ancient architecture is known only through mute fragments; how then can we study the process of building or the experience of the great Roman spaces?

Reconstructions provide one means.[1] Through drawings, paintings, models, and recreations scholars attempt to complete the incomplete, to fashion windows into history. All reconstructions are intellectually arrogant (Jameson 2004:1). We can never be in the past, despite our dreams of time travel, me-

---

1. Terminology in this field is notoriously ill-defined, with the four R's (recreation, reconstruction, replication, restoration) often conflated or confused with other terms (anastylosis, reassembly, simulation, evocation; Golvin 2008:2-4). The emphasis here is on pictorial and physical reconstructions, not written (Molyneaux 1997:1–9; for a prose reconstruction of ancient Rome see Favro 1996).

ticulous simulations or recaptured memories à la Freud (Freud 1989:17–18). Architectural critic Martin Filler noted, "It's not what we don't know about the past that dooms…re-creations, but rather what we do know, raising false hopes that no amount of painstaking research can fulfill" (Filler 2006). Traditionally, the discipline of archaeology focused on physical objects, ignoring or denigrating unquantifiable sensorial aspects of historical places. In recent decades the proliferation of immersive digital environments—from gaming to Second Life to pervasive computing—has directed attention to the experience of past spaces. Scholars studying Roman environments today exploit high-tech immersive virtual reality digital simulations replete with interactivity, multisensory stimuli, human characters, and non-linear narratives. As ways of seeing and researching change in response, a paradigm shift is in process (Gillings 2002:10). Practitioners grapple with ways to conduct and theorize the experiential and environmental depth of digital historical recreations. An initial step is to contextualize such efforts within a broader historical continuum of immersive reconstructions situated on-site, off-site, and in the virtual realm. To be or not to be in past spaces, that is the question. Do immersive architectural reconstructions promote the scholarly agenda? Or subvert, convert, and divert knowledge production?

Subversion

All Roman reconstructions derive and emanate from archaeological sites. The most potent allow for bodily engagement with the physical remains and actual places where Roman life was lived. *Anastylosis* (from the ancient Greek "erect again") uses architectural remains for *in situ* rebuilding. International guidelines clarify appropriate representational conventions such as the visual distinction between original and added elements, though notably the Venice Charter specifically argues for a ban on physical reconstructions (Gazzola 1964; Vacharopoulou 2005). Costly and potentially politically charged, *anastylosis* usually involves only segments of an excavation, with primary attention given to relatively fast and inexpensive projects. Typical is the raising of columns along streets as at Apamea (Figure 10.1). The imagery is powerful, yet viewers must keep in mind that even the most detailed on-site reconstructions are incomplete and thus misleading. The architectural, topographic, and cultural context is not just absent, it is subverted. Though lauded as tourist attractions, on-site reconstructions are academically controversial. During rebuilding, original pieces may be reworked or damaged. The quest to use original materials may compromise valuable archaeological evidence at ancient quarries. Stabilization techniques, including the use of rebars and concrete, can result in unforeseen physical degradation as documented at

Figure 10.1 *Anastylosis* of main street in Apamea, Syria (photograph by author).

Assos (Rose 2008). *Anastylosis* imprisons the original documentary information, complicating future alterations in response to new techniques or theories.

Equally problematic, essential elements of rich architectural and urban experiences are altered or missing, including portable and ephemeral features (sculptures, painted color, banners, garlands, landscaping, and of course the sounds and smells of the original human occupants). In most cases the re-erected colonnades lack the roofs that once provided cooling shade and individual reconstructed buildings ache for the embrace of a surrounding urban context. Visually, the homogeneity and purity of *anastylosis* environments is a fiction. The highly colored palette of antiquity has faded from view and memory, the rich hues of polished marbles and painted surfaces muted by exposure and lack of maintenance. Large in scale and permanent, the concretized results at their best present a selected moment in the life of a site; at their worst they ignore international guidelines and blend components from different periods, and even different buildings, subverting the specificity of historical time. Experiential engagement is mediated by tourisitic agendas which address safety issues, bus schedules, and photo-opportunities rather than the emulation of realistic historical habitation.

The simulation of constructing provides a more directed experience. The ten-

ets of Experimental Archaeology focus on fabrication using actual or recreated
ancient tools and techniques (Renfrew and Bahn 2005:110–115). Though usually associated with small objects it can also be applied to on-site architectural
projects. The replication of original building techniques provides invaluable
information about construction, statics, and the interplay between tool and
design. Such an approach, however, is costly and time consuming, necessitat-
ing the recreation not only of architectural components, but also ancient tools
and machinery, and creates problems regarding modern safety. Yet the direct
engagement with ancient construction, even when using modern techniques,
compels researchers to consider the materiality, statics, and processes in a way
significantly different from reconstruction on paper or computer.

Being on site also prompts consideration of the potent, if intangible, phe-
nomenological power of place. To "walk in the footsteps" of the ancients is a
vicarious pleasure, yet not without scholarly merit. The Romans revered the
spirit of each place, the *genius loci,* that combined the memory and meaning of every event that had occurred at the spot (Norberg-Schulz 1980). In
the first century BCE Cicero noted, "I cannot say whether it is a natural
instinct or a kind of illusion, but when we see the places where we are told
that the notables of the past spent their time, it is far more moving than
when we hear about their achievements or read their writings" (Cicero, *de
Finibus,* 5.2). Indeed, the engagement of the body with a place reconnects
researchers with the hard-to-verify actions and meanings associated with a
locus. Simultaneously, on-site analyses put the scholar in direct contact with
the sensory experience of an original location: breezes filled with aromas of
wild sage and sheep droppings, the glare of strong Mediterranean sunlight
bouncing off polished stone faces, the smooth surfaces of stairs worn through
generations of use, and so on. Individualistic, subjective, and transformed
over the centuries, the sensorial and perceptual responses to such stimuli have
not been critically or fully theorized (Gillings 2002). Trained to document
hard evidence, archaeologists do not have a scholarly apparatus with which to
evaluate smells, sounds, or haptic responses, nor to access ancient moods and
memories. Even Pompeii, the gold standard of archaeological urban remains
(many extensively reconstructed), has prompted only a handful of experiential analyses (Ellis 2004; Ling 1990). Complex sensorial and spatial explorations are often distilled into unisensory studies, minimizing the importance
of multisensory interaction in shaping human response. Sight dominates
research, largely because it can be documented in photographs and presented
as two-dimensional viewing cones on plans (Favro 1993; Figure 10.2). In
reaction, initial experiments are underway investigating multisensorial
experiences at ancient sites using videowalks, podcasts, audio recordings, and
interviews of remembered sensations (Tringham et al. 2007).

The fourth-dimension remains particularly understudied. Though an essential factor of history, time is undefined, distorted, or simply subverted in most immersive on-site settings. Re-erected structures are given broad chronological labels ("Imperial" or "Constantinian") with no finer temporal granulation. *Anastylosis* projects appear in an unrealistic partial state (half ruined/half restored) or, even more disturbing, as impossibly "new" with no aging, no graffiti, no moss. The architectural moment recreated is selective and fossilized, countering the Roman belief that buildings and cities, like people, grow

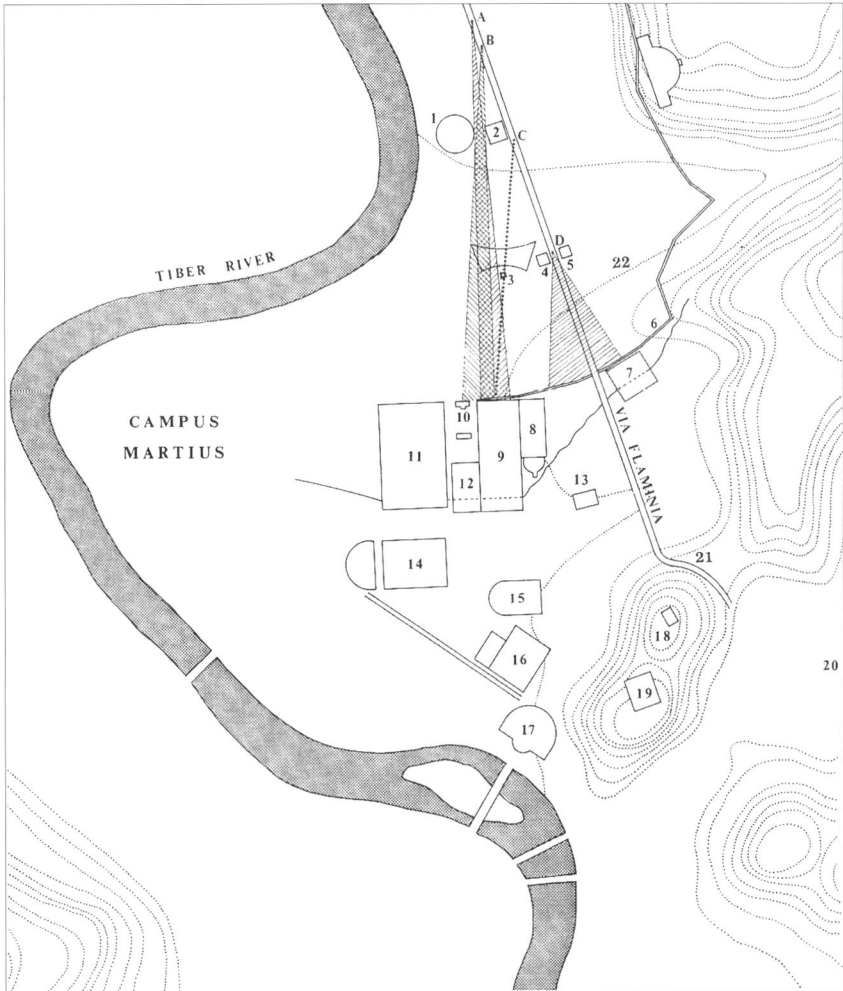

Figure 10.2 Plan of Northern Campus Martius in Augustan Rome with viewing cones (drawing by author).

old and show their age (Plutarch, *Moralia* 599). The complex interaction of time and sensory stimuli is ignored. In antiquity the days spent lurching on camelback across vast, waterless desert affected perception of the great city of Palmyra with its flowing fountains and cool shadowy porticos, an experience very different from arriving in a speeding, air-conditioned car.

Initial attempts to acquire multisensory data at on-site reconstructions have focused on quantifiable scientific data such as the measurement of temperatures and humidity in Roman baths or acoustics in theaters (Faretani et al. 2001; Yegül with Couch 2003). William L. MacDonald assumed a more dynamic role, walking the partially reconstructed streets of numerous Roman cities to develop his perceptive definition of Roman urban armatures based on the choreographed interplay of eye-catching features, spatial variety, the play of light and shade, visual rhythms, and imagined sounds (MacDonald 1988). Such immersive involvement with the physical remains changes the researcher-data interface, compelling scholars to consider the physical environment as operative in shaping and reinforcing ancient daily rituals and overall communal cohesion.

Caution, however, is required. No matter how accurate, *anastylosis* remains a hollow shell without the original human interaction. Fikret Yegül (1976:172) argues, "[i]nstitutions of a past culture are meaningful to us only as embodiments of the human spirit and ideal within their full cultural context; they cannot be cut out, isolated, and transferred up and down the historical scale." Presenting the magnificent re-erected Marble Court at the Sardis Bath Gymnasium complex, he distinguished between reconstructing an institution and reconstructing a building. Modern sightseers craning their necks to watch the light play over spiral columns, stepping down into the now dry pools, or listening to the babble of languages spoken by tourists may feel in tune with ancient users, yet clearly the specifics are significantly different from those of Roman *flâneurs*. Archaeologists Michael Shanks and Christopher Tilley wrote, "Empathy cannot achieve truly historical creation which relates past and present, holding them together in their difference, in the instant of the historic present" (Shanks and Tilley 1993:15). Physiological uniformitarianism, the assumption that processes observed today also occurred in the past, is easily dismissed (Houston and Taube 2000; Shanks and Tilley 1993). A full-scale reconstruction on site is indeed subversive; it lives a modern life for modern occupants. Yet the empathetic and rigorous study of immersive experiences can stimulate and enrich architectural and archaeological inquiries, redirecting attention to the analysis of historical environments as occupied by human users.

Conversion

In comparison to on-site reconstructions, Roman buildings erected off-site undergo significant conversion. For example, the Ara Pacis originally rose along the ancient Via Flaminia, forming an ensemble with the great Augustan sundial (Horologium Augusti) to the west and the Mausoleum of Augustus to the north. Excavators in the 1930s surgically removed the remains buried under later buildings, and reconstructed them with a different orientation adjacent to the Mausoleum, adding casts of far flung pieces (Van Buren 1949). The relocation severed the altar from its original topographic significance and forged new historical and political meanings. The carved figures of the procession no longer enticed pedestrians to move west from the Via Flaminia toward the Horologium (Favro 1993). Encased within a modernist box in the 1930s, the Ara Pacis was sequestered in the rarified realm of the collected art work, a status maintained in the controversial new enclosure by Richard Meier.

Large-scale reconstructions of ancient buildings literally entered museums during the halcyon days of cultural appropriation. In 1908, the Market Gate (120 CE) from Miletus was transported from Asia Minor to Berlin and reconstructed in the Pergamon Museum (Bilsel 2003). The transferral necessitated significant physical interventions (including the insertion of iron girders), as well as conceptual recontextualization. Tamed, sheltered and protected, the reconstructed structure no longer celebrates entry into a bustling agora. The Miletus gate rises in the museum's "Roman Architecture" room adjacent to that housing Hellenistic architectural exhibits, thus affirming historical and stylistic evolution. Its central opening leads not into a market, but into a display room holding the relocated Babylonian Ishtar gate, disrupting chronological ordering, but articulating German artistic and political hegemony. Extracted from their original locations and functional life, these reconstructed structures are converted from living buildings into representative types, categorized into artistic, cultural, chronological, and stylistic taxonomies.

The cost and technical difficulty of moving entire Roman buildings are of course daunting. Furthermore, such transferals are rightly prohibited today by modern laws protecting cultural patrimony. In lieu of the actual buildings, three-dimensional physical architectural exhibits in museums can showcase models either of building segments or scaled-down maquettes (Figure 10.3).[2]

---

2. Recent repatriation of museum pieces centers on portable objects, not large architectural pieces even when there are viable claims. In a new book James Cuno argues for the revival of archaeological partage, the division of finds among parties, which could result in further removal of architectural elements from sites (Cuno 2008).

Figure 10.3 Reconstructed Imperial library based on those in the Forum of Trajan and Hadrian's Villa, Museo della Civiltà Romana (photograph by author).

These surrogates facilitate the ready comparison of various structures, emphasizing their relativised places in historical and artistic continua. The creation of the first museums of architecture in late-eighteenth-century France sparked on-going arguments about whether such reconstructions should be treated as artworks or as didactic specimens like the displays found in natural history museums (Szambien 1988). In both cases the architecture became a highly mediated object of study isolated from human experience.

Though small in scale, physical reconstruction models have the potential to advance immersive research inquiries, promoting analysis of tectonics and construction. Those depicting larger environments, such as the model of Constantinian Rome (*Plastico*) by Italo Gismondi, allow exploration of building distribution and sightlines in urban space (Figure 10.4; Filippi 2007). Unfortunately, in most cases museum models do not distinguish hypothetical additions from the documented remains as is now common with restored sculptures. In fact, source data is generally omitted. In some instances physical models have been manipulated to facilitate viewing, or to satisfy aesthetic or political agendas. The topography of the Rome model was selectively altered to accentuate the height of hills and select monuments were increased in scale by 15–20%. Despite ahistorical adjustments, such physical models readily become concretized and iconic. Their visual power coupled with the imprimatur of a museum implies a standard of scholarly accuracy that requires considered assessment (Hinard 1991).

Reconstruction models are also useful in laboratory contexts where researchers conduct various experiments including the evaluation of lighting and structural stability (Smith 2004). Yet the necessary miniaturization brings challenges. Reduced-scale models present a totalizing, omniscient viewpoint that tends to devalue the content and consideration of experiential engagement. Model-scopes "place" observers in recreated spaces, but are monocular and thus compromise stereoscopic veracity. Individual experiments can be isolating and misleading. Data gathered from a small reconstruction placed on a light-table do not consider topography, illumination reflected from other structures, or sequential experiences. Tectonic experiments on small models are not directly scalable (Frischer 2008:ix). In addition, one-of-a-kind lab models are not easily transported and are infrequently archived; thus they are not available for comparative experiments by scholars.

Two-dimensional reconstructions are more easily distributed, replicated, and up-dated, yet they raise other issues, from the symbolic connotations of various media to the impact of selective viewing angles, scales, experiential presentation, and access to underlying data. Artists and set design-

Figure 10.4 Plaster model of Constantinian Rome (*Plastico*) created under the direction of Italo Gismondi (photograph by author).

ers have for centuries recreated non-academic, emotionalized renderings of
Roman environments. Accessible to a broad range of viewers, these evocative
representations imply that the complexities of history can be readily understood by non-experts. As archaeology began to professionalize in the nineteenth century, researchers spurned lush imagery that might be construed as
unscholarly, emotional (feminine), and unserious. In directed contrast they
employed measured drawings (preferably with pristine lines and no shading,
color, or sensorial data) to underscore the work as academic, rational (male),
and serious (Arnold 2005:92). While the restricted reproduction capabilities
of publishing were also a factor, archaeologists clearly sought to solidify their
status as members of an academic elite responsible for the creation and stewardship of scientific knowledge. The sanitized elevations, sections, and axonometric drawings conveyed a clinical air of documented, quantified scientific
data (Bois 1981). Difficult to read, these drawing types highlighted the need
for expertise. Examples abound, as with the encyclopedic "printed museums" of the early nineteenth century. In page after page of J.N.L. Durand's
famous anthology of architecture, *Recueil et parallèle des edifices de tout genre*
(1799–1800), black-and-white reconstruction drawings categorized restored
buildings according to culture, function, and form (Durand 1799; Madrazo
1994). The depictions are carefully measured, but regularized and stripped
of color and physical setting, thereby minimizing consideration of space and
immersive experiences. Presented as types, the crisply rendered Roman buildings are not sullied by information about reconstruction data, process, or use.
They stand not as once-occupied structures, but isolated formal objects.

In academia, three-dimensional representations of reconstructed architecture were likewise sanitized and stripped of sensorial information. Early
researchers favored axonometric projections which appear distorted, but
maintain uniform scaled measurements. In *L'art de bâtir chez les Romains*
the engineer François Auguste Choisy represented a perspective view displaying a reconstructed Roman arch like a lab specimen with "frog's-eye-view"
that showed plan, elevation, section, and interior in one engraving (Figure
10.5; Choisy 1873). In general, he privileged sight over all other senses in
his images, yet took care to provide supporting scientific documentation and
validating, meticulously measured two-dimensional plans. A generation later
Constantinos Doxiadis built upon Choisy's work in his book *Raumordnung
im griechischen Stadtebau* (Doxiadis 1937). Following scientific methodology,
he gathered empirical data on-site and made numerous "lab" sketches to help
argue that the Greeks designed major religious sites as stereometric wholes to
be viewed from specific polar coordinates. Trained as an architect, Doxiadis
considered the reconstruction drawings as operative tools in the testing and
validation of research hypotheses.

Today, scientific reconstruction images and models stand separate from more emotive renderings of reconstructed environments replete with color, plantings, people, atmospheric qualities, and textures. In general the latter

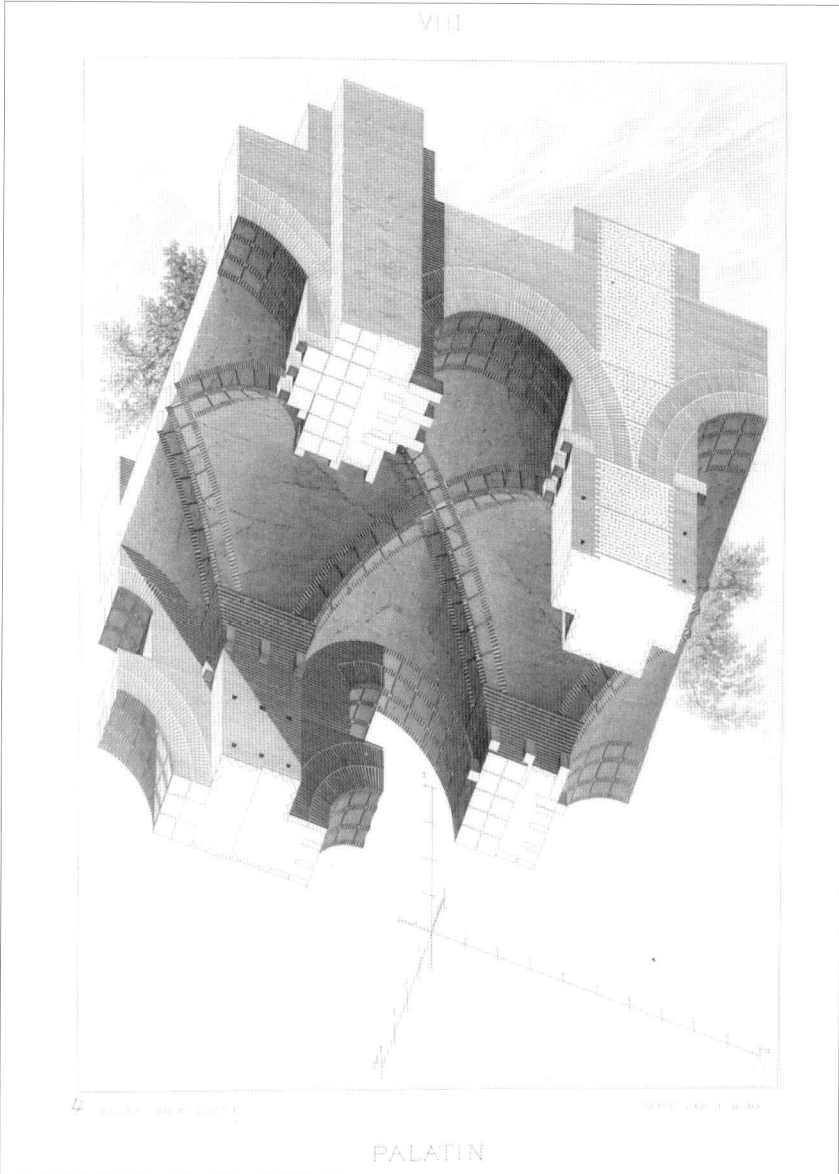

Figure 10.5 "Frog's-eye-view" axonometric of reconstructed vaults from the Imperial Palace on the Palatine, Rome, by Choisy (1873); etching by G. Baranger.

(including digital depictions) are assigned to the secondary realm of "educational images," appropriate for the eyes and minds of untrained students and the general public. Whether created by independent cartoonists, illustrators working closely with experts or by respected academics, colorful holistic reconstruction renderings are rarely reviewed in scholarly journals (Chaillet 2004; Connolly and Dodge 1998; Coulon and Golvin 2002; Forte 2008). Such separation reaffirms the interpretation of immersive, reconstructions as fostering knowledge transfer, not knowledge production. Yet the act of creating these works generates valuable interpretations and raises significant questions. The visual power of the images, in turn, impacts analysis and interpretation. Whether physical or pictorial, fixed or interactive, well-researched secondary reconstructions are transformative. Static and impossible to enter, they tend to convert the original Roman buildings into art objects, types, or tools removed from bodily engagement.

Diversion

Sensory responses from antiquity cannot be easily quantified, compared, or placed within a rigorous scientific mold. Feelings, fragrances, and sounds all waft away, leaving only memories cited in ancient texts which are often elitist and personal. Empirical data seem too loose, too personal, too tainted by our modern sensibilities. Populist presentations such as *son et lumière* shows, reenactments, circus events, and 3-D films (as well as sensurround and smellavision) divert scholarly interest away from sensory studies. Even recent attempts to recolorize ancient remains using projected light emphasize performance rather than sensorial analysis (Broccoli et al. 2008). Yet the senses are valid subjects of investigation (Rodaway 1994). Joy in perceptual pleasures is arguably an innate human trait, though mediated by specific environmental and cultural contexts. The Romans overtly valued positive sensorial pleasures as indications of status. Pliny the Elder described the pleasure of fragrances as a luxury that is "among the most elegant and also the most honorable enjoyments in life" (Pliny, *Naturalis Historia* 13.1). In the first century CE, his nephew Pliny the Younger wrote numerous letters carefully enumerating the sensorial diversions offered at his country residences. He sought not merely to entice his readers to visit, but also to affirm his own sophistication, discrimination, and wealth. There were so many modulated sensory experiences at his Laurentine villa that Pliny felt obliged to provide a dark, soundproof room as a counterpoint (Pliny, *Epistulae* 23).

Comprehensive sensory engagement occurs in full-scale recreations of Roman environments, yet is seldom evaluated. In the 1970s, oil baron J. Paul Getty recreated the form and sensory experiences of a Roman country residence to affirm his own elite status. Modeled after the Villa of the Papyri at Herculaneum, the Getty Museum at Malibu was among the first great art institutions to be inspired by a domestic, not monumental, ancient work of architecture, a shift that facilitated inclusion of sensorially rich environments. Though touted as a scientifically accurate reconstruction, the project is inconsistent. Programmatic, legal, and topographic restraints, as well as the patron's preferences, dictated significant changes to the original villa's DNA. Elements from various Roman villas were incorporated to substitute for incomplete information and enhance the overall appearance. Other adjustments were more arbitrary. Historical consultant Norman Neuerburg noted that the colors of the reconstructed wall paintings were subdued from Roman garishness to address contemporary taste, making a semantic distinction that the Getty Villa is, "a recreation rather than a reproduction" (Filler 2006; *New York Times* 1974). The result was negatively described as a misleading *bricolage* of ancient components which were neither labeled nor analyzed, underscoring that a building cannot be easily footnoted or considered a hypothesis (Yegül 1976:173). Anthropologist George E. Marcus noted, "[the Getty Villa] lives the dialectic of fake and authenticity, but it does not reflect upon it" (Marcus 1990:329). All visitors acknowledged the sensory pleasures of splashing fountains, aromatic plants, shiny marbles, golden light, and views of the glistening sea, yet academic critics did so with obvious guilt, denigrating the importance of sensory reception in ancient villa design.

The high costs of recreating habitable Roman environments promote non-academic collaborations, as for example with the edutainment industry. In 1998 the *NOVA* PBS series funded the building of a Roman bath for the *Secrets of Lost Empires* series. The reconstruction was not of an actual structure, but a "generic" provincial imperial Roman bath in Asia Minor (*NOVA/PBS* 2000). The scholarly team headed by Fikret Yegül followed the practices of experimental archaeology; they researched analogues and building techniques, meticulously documented construction, and conducted scientific experiments on thermal properties (Figure 10.6). Practical limits, such as the forty-six day film schedule, compromised the experiment. The concrete was not allowed to dry fully, nor the bricks to age a year as recommended by Vitruvius. Even so, the researchers acquired invaluable data about building methods, heating duration, intensity, and distribution. Yet more than quantifiable scientific facts were learned. At the end of construction the researchers took a bath together, an experience that reaffirmed the highly subjective nature of sensorial responses (how hot is too hot?) and underscored the importance of ranges rather than fixed measurements. Splashing together like school boys, the experts forgot their scholarly disagreements while gaining new appreciation for the sensual and social pleasures of ancient bathing and (Yegül 2003:168). Other experiments, such as the Roman farm at Butser, remain in continuous operation, monitoring responses to climate changes and aging over time (Evans 2003).

In the twenty-first century immersive interactive, real-time digital models are attracting new attention to experiential aspects of historical reconstructions (Frischer 2008; Gillings 2005; Sylaiou et al. 2004). On a base level, the use of computers imparts an imprimatur of scientific validity that must be constantly challenged as any reconstruction is only as good as the data and methods used. At their best, digital architectural reconstructions follow rigorous protocols now being articulated in international charters (Frischer and Stinson 2007). Constructed on a Cartesian grid, digital reconstructions impose a rigorous, uniform measurement system; documented GPS coordinates provide granular accuracy and increase consideration of the vertical z-axis both above and below ground. Computer models require extensive and precise information, equivalent to that necessary for constructing the original structure. In effect, the medium compels modelers and scholars to develop greater technical architectural knowledge than required for making a drawing or small physical model. Many original findings occur during the process of creation. For example, a UCLA team creating a three-dimensional digital model of the Basilica Aemilia had to make adjustments to the two-dimensional reconstruction drawings by Heinrich Bauer which had misconstrued some interrelationships between parts, including access to the interior gallery (Figure 10.7; Digital Roman Forum 2005). Computer models allow the entire creation process to be transparent, visually coding extant remains from hypothetical components with tools such as veracity sliders (Kensek 2007).

Figure 10.6 Generic Imperial Bath in Asia Minor created for 2000 *NOVA Builds a Bath* television show, Turkey (photograph by Fikret Yegül).

Figure 10.7 Cutaway view, virtual reality model of the Basilica Aemilia, Roman Forum, Rome
UCLA Cultural VR Lab 2003 © Regents University of California.

Every element can instantaneously be linked with documenting sources and rationales for modeling decisions, irrevocably intertwining the evidence trail with the representation.[3]

The scientific associations and capabilities of digital reconstruction models have stimulated the adoption of scientific protocols. Researchers treat the recreated digital historical environments as laboratories for testing not only alternative reconstructions, but also more quantifiable experiments. For example, UCLA teams have conducted day-lighting studies based on extensive astronomical data calibrated for the specific site location and times of day and historical year (Figure 10.8; Frischer and Stinson 2007). Other researchers have used puzzle theory to recombine fragments of an ancient marble map of Rome, and algorithms to plot building distributions in a digital model based on a scan of the *Plastico* (Figure 10.9; Guidi et al. 2005; Trimble and Levoy 2002). The emphasis on knowledge production minimizes the need for hyper-realistic representation, redefining the traditional character of historical reconstructions (Gillings 2002). For example, Chris Johanson created a diagrammatic rather than realistic model to test Pliny's claim that the

---

3. The ICOMOS Charter of 2007 recommends that all secondary reconstructions, including computer models, provide direct access to information sources (ICOMOS 2007).

Figure 10.8 Digital reconstruction and lighting analysis of the Basilica of Maxentius, Rome;
UCLA Experiential Technologies Center 2007 © Regents University of California.

Romans identified the noon hour by observing the sun's position in relation to specific monuments in the Roman Forum (Pliny, *Naturalis Historia*
7.212). In contrast to other reconstruction media, digital models are easily distributed, promoting retesting and assessment of experiments by other
scholars and interaction with experts from many fields, from computer scien-
tists to acousticians and structural engineers (Favro 2006).

Digital reconstruction models are reshaping the narrative of knowledge production, moving away from a linear narrative to an iterative, more dynamic
exchange between bottom-up data and top-down interpretations (Forte and
Siliotti 1997:12–13). At the same time, the readers' roles are being redefined;
they become operators able to move through the recreated environments at
will and select whether to show (or hide) associated data, negotiating as well
as evaluating the specific reconstruction (Forte 2008; Gillings 2002:22). This
non-linear engagement highlights immersion as a means to gain and create
knowledge. While Choisy's images or the *NOVA* Bath remain relatively static, the digital Roman Forum model is constantly changing as new evidence
and interpretations are incorporated and technologies evolve. The presentation and evaluation of findings are likewise becoming more mobile as the
fixed, individually-authored reconstruction and accompanying monograph is
replaced by an evolving, collaboratively-created digital knowledge platform.
This shift creates the need for critical version control, archiving, and the
assessment of research products as non-static and open-ended.

Robust digital technologies enable and legitimize multisensory analysis. Notably, real-time computer models forefront spatio-temporal, kinetic concerns (Favro 2006). Observers move in and through the recreated environments at will, yet too often without any historical contextualization. Evaluation of spaces is enhanced when perceived at a human-viewing level, yet the ability to "fly" entices people to experience unrealistic viewpoints and action. The actual pace of a pedestrian is slow and unbearably frustrating for generations raised on the hyper-speed of gaming. Most presenters accelerate movement, distorting the historical experience. The addition of localized sound and navigation maps in the UCLA real-time simulation model of the Roman Forum allows observers to both situate themselves in space and calibrate their speed of movement (Experiental Technologies Center 2006). Time is also warped by privileging the moment of building completion; digital reconstructions too often depict structures with an assembly-line, hyper-real freshness as if all were constructed at the same historical moment and perpetually freed from the ravages of time (Gray 1995; Vacharopoulou 2005). Few depict building construction in progress. On the positive side, time sliders and urban evolution programs, when done well, replace periodization with more fluid, evolutionary depictions emphasizing the *longue durée*. Such broad temporal swaths, however, divert researchers from considering more nuanced evolutionary changes experienced at ground level.

Figure 10.9 Digital model of Constantinian Rome based on the *Plastico* model, UCLA CVR-Lab © Regents University of California; image © The Board of Visitors of the University of Virginia

The coupling of sensory information in digital environments is imperfect. Ocular centrism still dominates, minimizing tactility, olfaction, and other responses experienced by what the architect Juhani Pallasmaa calls "the eyes of the skin" (Pallasmaa 2005:9). The situation is further exacerbated by the segregation of research into sense-specific fields of study (Barbara and Perliss 2006; Blesser and Salter 2006). Most importantly, quantified data on sensory research has to be considered in a specific social context. All sensory interpretation is culturally constituted, shaped by occupants' status, background, and other factors (Houston and Taube 2000). While scholars have explored the cultural constitution of vision, the Roman interpretation of other senses has yet to be fully examined (Elsner 2007). Digital human figures have been employed to determine crowd distributions in Roman spaces, not sensory reception; interactive avatars such as those in the Via Flaminia Virtual Museum operate as actors not analytical apparati (Forte 2008; Frischer et al. 2007; Gutierrez 2007). Effective psycho-environmental analyses are impossible without human subjects. The Romans are long dead. For all the talk of "moving through" digital reconstruction models, modern observers interact vicariously, prevented from true sensorial engagement by the fourth wall of the computer screen, their own static positions and overwhelming cultural differences. Experiential depth in digital reconstruction models remains shallow. Imperfect as surrogates, these immersive recreations should be valued as effective and flexible interpretive devices (Gillings 2002:27). They successfully divert attention from the quest for the authentic form and refocus it on scientific methodology, multisensory analysis, interdisciplinary engagement, and enriched process.

Traditionally, reconstructions were evaluated as objects held up to an unachievable standard of authenticity. If, as Baudrillard argues, authenticity is not attainable in our contemporary world, should we seek it in historical recreations whether *anastylosis*, physical or digital models, or images (Dovey 1985; Gillings 2002:20–23)? Recreated immersions reaffirm the significance of sensory experiences, broadening the research agenda and redefining how we engage with the historical subject. Scholars today are slowly reconceptualizing reconstructions from attempts *to be* in the past as to more holistic and experientially rich investigations of *being* in historical environments.

Acknowledgments

I would like to thank Sheila Bonde and Stephen Houston for their support and encouragement throughout.

References

Adams, Richard E. W.

1971 *The Ceramics of Altar de Sacrificios*. Papers of the Peabody Museum of Archaeology and Ethnology, vol. 63, no. 1. Cambridge, MA: Harvard University.

1999 *Rio Azul: An Ancient Maya City*. Norman: University of Oklahoma Press.

Adams, Richard E. W., and Aubrey S. Trik

1961 *Temple I (Str. 5D-1): Post-Constructional Activities*. Tikal Report No. 7. University Museum, University of Pennsylvania, Philadelphia.

Addington, Lucille R.

1986 *Lithic Illustration: Drawing Flaked Stone Artifacts for Publication*. Chicago, IL: University of Chicago Press.

Adkins, Lesley and Roy Adkins

1989 *Archaeological Illustration*. Cambridge: Cambridge University Press.

Allen, Kathleen M.S., Stanton W. Green, and Ezra B.W. Zubrow (editors)

1990 *Interpreting Space: GIS and Archaeology*. London: Taylor and Francis.

Alpers, Svetlana

1983 *The Art of Describing: Dutch Art in the Seventeenth Century*. Chicago, IL: The University of Chicago Press.

Ancien, Bernard

1983 La chronique tourmentée de l'église et des bâtiments de l'abbaye de Saint-Crépin-le-Grand de Soissons. *Abbayes et prieures de l'Aisne; Mémoires de la Fédération des Sociétés d'Histoire et d'Archéologie de l'Aisne* XXVIII: 201–225.

Andrews, Gill, John C. Barrett, and John S.C. Lewis

2000 Interpretation Not Record. The Practice of Archaeology. *Antiquity* 74: 525–530.

Andrews, Malcom

1999 *Landscape and Western Art*. Oxford: Oxford University Press.

Ankersmit, Frank R.

2001 *Historical Representation*. Stanford, CA: Stanford University Press.

Agurcia, Ricardo and Barbara Fash

2006 The Evolution of Structure 10L-16, Heart of the Copán Acropolis. In *Copán: The History of an Ancient Maya Kingdom*, edited by E. Wyllys Andrews and William L. Fash, 201–237. Santa Fe, NM: School of American Research.

Ardren, Traci

2006 Mending the Past: Ix Chel and the Invention of a Modern Pop Goddess. *Antiquity* 80: 25–37.

Arnold, Dana

2005 Unlearning the Images of Archaeology. In *Envisioning the Past: Archaeology and the Image*, edited by Sam Smiles and Stephanie Moser, 92–114. Oxford: Blackwell.

Arreola, José María

 1922   Códices y documentos en mexicano. In *La Población del Valle de Teotihuacan, Volume 2*, edited by Manuel Gamio, 549–594. Instituto Nacional Indigenista, Mexico City, Mexico.

Bahktin, Mikhail

 1984   *Rabelais and His World*. Bloomington: Indiana University Press.

Baigrie, Brian (ed.)

 1996   *Picturing Knowledge: Historical and Philosophical Problems Concerning the Use of Art in Science*. Toronto: University of Toronto Press.

Baltard P.-L.

 1806   Galerie Française des Productions de tous les arts. *Athénaeum* 1.

Barbara, Anna and Anthony Perliss

 2006   *Invisible Architecture: Experiencing Places Through the Sense of Smell*. Milan: Skira Editore.

Barber, Bruno and Christopher Thomas

 2002   *The London Charterhouse*. Museum of London Archaeology Service Monograph 10. London: Museum of London Archaeology Service.

Barceló, Juan A.

 2000   Visualizing What Might Be: An Introduction to Virtual Reality Techniques in Archaeology. In *Virtual Reality in Archaeology*, edited by Juan A. Barceló, Maurizio Forte, and Donald H. Sanders, 9–35. BAR International Series No. 843. Oxford: Archaeopress.

Barceló, Juan A., Maurizio Forte, and Donald H. Sanders (eds.)

 2000   *Virtual Reality in Archaeology*. BAR International Series No. 843. Oxford: Archaeopress.

Barnhart, Edwin L.

 2001a   The Palenque Mapping Project, 1998–2000 Final Report. Electronic document, http://www.famsi.org/reports/99101/, last accessed August 8, 2010.

 2001b   The Palenque Mapping Project: Settlement and Urbanism at an Ancient Maya City. Unpublished Ph. D. dissertation, Department of Anthropology, University of Texas at Austin.

Barratt, Glynn, Vince Gaffney, Helen Goodchild, and Stephen Wilkes

 2000   Survey at Wroxeter using Carrier Phase, Differential GPS Surveying Techniques. *Archaeological Prospection* 7(2): 133–143.

Barrett, John

 1988   Fields of Discourse. Reconstituting a Social Archaeology? *Critique of Anthropology* 7: 5–16.

Barthes, Roland

 1986   *The Rustle of Language*. Translated by Richard Howard. Oxford: Blackwell.

Baud, Anne

 2003   *Cluny: un grand chantier medieval au coeur de l'Europe*. Paris: Librairie Picard.

Baudez, Claude-François

  1993   *Jean-Frédéric Waldeck, peintre: le premier explorateur des ruines mayas.* Paris: Editions Hazan.

  1994   *Maya Sculpture of Copan: The Iconography.* Norman: University of Oklahoma Press.

Bedos-Rezak, Brigitte Miriam

  2000   Medieval Identity: A Sign and a Concept. *American Historical Review* 105(5): 1489–1533.

  2005   Signes d'identité et principes d'altérité au XIIe siècle: L'individu, c'est l'autre. In *L'indivi-du au moyen âge: Individuation et individualisation avant la modernité*, edited by Brigitte Miriam Bedos-Rezak and Dominique Iogna-Prat, 43–57. Paris: Aubier-Flammarion.

Bejune, Matthew and Jana Ronan.

  2008   Social Software in Libraries. Washington, DC: Association of Research Libraries.

Bender, Barbara

  1999   Subverting the Western Gaze: Mapping Alternative Worlds. In *The Archaeology and Anthropology of Landscape: Shaping Your Landscape*, edited by Peter J. Ucko and Robert Layton, 31–45. London: Routledge.

  2006   Place and Landscape. In *Handbook of Material Culture*, edited by Christopher Tilley, Webb Keane, Susanne Kuechler-Fogden, Mike Rowlands, and Patricia Spyer, 303–314. London: SAGE Publishers.

Berger, John

  1984   *Ways of Seeing.* London: BBC.

Berggren, Asa and Ian Hodder

  2003   Social Practice, Method and Some Problems in Field Archaeology. *American Antiquity* 68: 421–434.

Berlin, Heinrich

  1967   The Destruction of Structure 5D-33-1st at Tikal. *American Antiquity* 32: 241–242.

Berman, Judith C.

  1999   Bad Hair Days in the Paleolithic: Modern (Re)Constructions of the Cave Man. *American Anthropologist* 101: 288–304.

Bibliothèque nationale de France (BnF)

  Est., Ve 20, "Receuil de plans et d'élévations des abbayes de chanoines réguliers de France." Archival material at BnF, Paris, France.

Bibliothèque Sainte Geneviève (BSG)

  Est., Cartons 74, 75, 147, and 148. Archival material at BSG, Paris.

Bilsel, S. M. Can

  2003   *Architecture in the Museum: Displacement, Reconstruction and Reproduction of the Monuments of Antiquity in Berlin's Pergamon Museum.* Unpublished Ph.D dissertation, Department of History and Theory of Architecture, Princeton University.

Binford, Lewis

  1977   General Introduction. In *For Theory Building in Archaeology*, edited by Lewis Binford, 1–10. New York: Academic Press.

1981   Behavioural Archaeology and the Pompeii Premise. *Journal of Anthropological Research* 37(3): 195–208.

1989   *Debating Archaeology*. New York: Academic Press.

Black, Stephen L.

1990   The Carnegie Uaxactun Project and the Development of Maya Archaeology. *Ancient Mesoamerica* 1: 257–276.

Blesser, Barry and Linda-Ruth Salter

2006   *Spaces Speak, Are You Listening? Experiencing Aural Architecture*. Cambridge, MA: MIT Press.

Blumenfeld-Kosinski, Renate

1990   *Not of Woman Born: Representations of Caesarean Birth in Medieval and Renaissance Culture*. Ithaca, NY: Cornell University Press.

Bohrer, Frederick N.

2005   Photography and Archaeology: The Image as Object. In *Envisioning the Past: Archaeology and the Image,* edited by Sam Smiles and Stephanie Moser, 180–191. Oxford: Blackwell.

Bois, Yve-Alain

1981   Metamorphosis of Axonometry. *Daidalos* 1: 41–58.

Bolly, Jean-Jacques, Jean-Marie, Duvosquel, Jean-Baptiste Lefevre, and Daniel Misonne

1990   *Monastères bénédictins et cisterciens dans les albums de Croÿ (1596–1611).* Revue bénédictine, vol. 100 (1990). Brussels: Crédit Communal De Belgique.

Bond, C. James

2004   *Monastic Landscapes*. Stroud: Tempus.

Bonde, Sheila and Clark Maines

2004   The Archaeology of Monasticism in France: The State of the Question. In *Bilan et perspectives des études médiévales (1993–1999); Actes du IIe Congrés européen d'Études Médiévales, Barcelona, 8–12 juin, 1999*, edited by Jacquelin Hamesse, 715–718. Textes et Études du Moyen Age 22. Turnhout: Brepols.

Bonde, Sheila, and Clark Maines (eds.)

2003   *Saint-Jean-des-Vignes in Soissons: Approaches to its Architecture, Archaeology, and History*. Bibilotheca Victorina XV. Turnhout: Brepols.

Borges, Jorge Louis

1972   Of Exactitude in Science. In *A Universal History of Infamy*, 141. Translated and compiled by Norman Thomas di Giovanni. New York: Dutton.

Bory de Saint-Vincent, M. (Jean Baptiste)

1836   *Expédition Scientifique de Morée. Section des sciences physiques: Relation.* Paris: F.G. Levrault.

Bourguet, Marie Noëlle (ed.)

1998   *L'invention scientifique de la Méditerranée. Égypte, Morée, Algérie*. Paris: École des Hautes Études en Sciences Sociales.

Bowker, Geoffrey C.

2007   Localizing Global Technoscience. In *The Postcolonial and the Global*, edited by Revathy Kishnaswamy and John Charles Hawley, 252–259. Minneapolis: University of Minnesota Press.

Bracken, C.P.

1975   *Antiquities Acquired: The Spoliation of Greece*. Newton Abbot: David and Charles.

Bradley, Richard

1997   "To See is to Have Seen": Craft Traditions in British Field Archaeology. In *The Cultural Life of Images: Visual Representation in Archaeology*, edited by Brian Leigh Molyneaux, 62–71. London: Routledge.

2003   Seeing Things: Perception, Experience and the Constraints of Excavation. *Journal of Social Archaeology* 3: 151–168.

2006   The Excavation Report as a Literary Genre: Traditional Practice in Britain. *World Archaeology* 38: 664–671.

Brasseur de Bourbourg, Charles-Étienne

1865   Rapport sur les ruines de Mayapan et d'Uxmal au Yucatan (Mexique). In *Archives de la Commission Scientifique du Méxique*, vol. 2, 234–288. Paris: Imprimerie Impériale.

Braunfels, Wolfgang

1972   *Monasteries of Western Europe: The Architecture of the Orders*. 3rd ed. Princeton, NJ: Princeton University Press.

Brigman, Daniel

1996   Computers and Architectural Pastiche: Watching Architecture Reconstruct Itself at CAA. *Architronic*. Electronic document, http://corbu2.caed.kent.edu/architronic/v5n1/v5n1.06d.html, last accessed August 8, 2010.

British Naval Intelligence Division

1944   *Greece: Vol. 1. Physical Geography, History, Administration and Peoples*. Geographical Handbook Series.

Broccoli, Umberto, Umberto Croppi, Antonio Paolucci, and Michael Hill

2008   *I colori dell'Ara Pacis*, exhibition, Museo dell'Ara Pacis, Rome, December 26–January 6, 2009.

Bryant, David J. and Barbara Tversky.

1999   Mental Representations of Perspective and Spatial Relations from Diagrams and Models. Journal of Experimental Psychology: learning, memory, and cognition 25(1): 137–156.

Bryson, Norman

1988   The Gaze in the Expanded Field. In *Vision and Visuality*, edited by Hal Foster, 87–114. Seattle: Bay Press.

Buc, Philippe

2001   *The Dangers of Ritual: Between Early Medieval Texts and Social Scientific Theory*. Princeton, NJ: Princeton University Press.

Buckler W. H. and David M. Robinson (eds.)

1932   *Greek and Latin inscriptions*. Publications of the American Society for the Excavation of Sardis vol. 7, no. 1. Leiden: Brill.

Burns, Robert I.

1989   The Significance of the Frontier in the Middle Ages. In *Medieval Frontier Societies*, edited by Robert Bartlett and Angus MacKay, 307–330. Oxford: Oxford University Press.

Bynum, Caroline W.

1982   *Jesus as Mother: Studies in the Spirituality of the High Middle Ages*. Berkeley: University of California Press.

Carr, Robert F. and James E. Hazard

1961   *Map of the Ruins of Tikal, El Peten, Guatemala*. Tikal Reports no. 11. Philadelphia: University Museum, University of Pennsylvania.

Carriazo, Juan de Mata (ed.)

1940   *Hechos del Condestable don Miguel Lucas de Iranzo (Crónica del siglo XV), edición y estudio por Juan de Mata Carriazo*. Madrid: Espasa Calpe.

Carter, John

1780–1786, 1787–194 *Specimens of the Ancient Sculpture and Painting, now remaining in this kingdom*. London: John Carter.

1786–1793 *Views of Ancient Buildings in England: Drawn in different tours and engrav'd*. London: John Carter.

1795   *The Ancient Architecture of England*. Reprinted in 1814. H.G. Bohn, London.

1803   Publication of Cathedrals by the Antiquarian Society. *Gentleman's Magazine* 73(1): 106–107.

1805   The Pursuits of Architectural Innovation, no. 88. Windsor Castle, Cont. *Gentleman's Magazine*, 75(2): 818–819

Castañeda, Quetzil

1996   *In the Museum of Maya Culture: Touring Chichen Itza*. Minneapolis: University of Minnesota Press.

Catherwood, Frederick

1844   *Views of Ancient Monuments in Central America, Chiapas, and Yucatan*. London: F. Catherwood.

Cazort, Mimi, Monique Kornell, and K.B. Roberts

1997   *The Ingenious Machine of Nature: Four Centuries of Art and Anatomy*. Ottawa: National Gallery of Canada.

Chaillet, Gilles

2004   *Dans la Rome des Césars*. Grenoble: Editions Glénat.

Chaplin, Willy

n.d.   Modern Surrealistic Art. Electronic document, http://www.dreamagic.com/captn/terry.html, last accessed August 8, 2010.

Charnay, Désiré

1887   *The Ancient Cities of the New World; Being Travels and Explorations exic and Central America From 1857–1882*. London: Chapman and Hall.

Charnay, Désiré, and Eugène-Emmanuel Viollet-le-Duc

1863   *Cités et Ruines Américaines: Mitla, Palenqué, Izamal, Chichen-Itza, Uxmal*. Paris: A. Morel.

Chartier,Roger

1988 *Cultural History: Between Practices and Representations*. Translated by Lydia Cochrane. Ithaca, NY: Cornell University Press.

Chase, Diane, and Arlen F. Chase (eds.)

1994 *Studies in the Archaeology of Caracol, Belize*. Pre-Columbian Art Research Institute Monograph 7. San Francisco, CA: Pre-Columbian Art Research Institute.

Chassel, Jean-Luc (ed.)

2003 *Sceaux et usages de sceaux: Images de la Champagne médiévale*. Paris: Somogy.

Cherry, J.F.

2001 Travel, nostalgia and Pausanias's giant. In *Pausanias: Travel and Memory in Roman Greece*, edited by S.E. Alcock, J.F. Cherry, and J. Elsner, 247–255. Oxford: Oxford University Press.

Choisy, Auguste

1873 *L'Art de bâtir chez les Romains*. Paris: Ducher et cie.

Clack, Timothy and Marcus Brittain (eds.)

2007 *Archaeology and the Media*. Walnut Creek, CA: Left Coast Press.

Clare, Lucien

1996 Fêtes, jeux et divertissements à la cour du connétable de Castille, Miguel Lucas de Iranzo (1460–1470): les exercices physiques. Reprinted in *Frontières andalouses la vie à Jaén entre 1460 et 1471, d'après Los hechos del condestable Miguel Lucas de Iranzo*, edited by Jacques Heers, 15–4. *Iberica* n.s. 6. UFR D'études Ibériques, Paris. Originally published 1987 in *La fête et l'écriture : théatre de cour, cour-théâtre en Espagne et Italie, 1450–1530*, Centre aixois de recherches hispaniques, 5–32. Aix-en-Provence: Université de Provence.

Clare, Lucien, and Michel García

1991 La guerre entre factions ou clientèles dans la Crónica de Miguel Lucas de Iranzo. In *Bandos y querellas dinásticas al final en España al final de la Edad Media. Actas del Coloquio celebrado en la Biblioteca Española de París los días 15 y 16 de mayo de 1987*, edited by Lucien Clare and Jacques Heers, 59–77. Paris: Biblioteca Española de París.

Clark, John W.

1897 *The Observances in Use at the Augustinian Priory of S. Giles and S. Andrew at Barnwell, Cambridgeshire*. Cambridge: Macmillan and Bowes.

Clark, William George

1858 *Peloponnesus: Notes of Study and Travel*. London: J.W. Parker and Son.

"Cluny dans le monde scientifique," Institut für Frühmittelalterforschung, http://www.uni-muenster.de/Fruehmittelalter/Projekte/Cluny/links_cluny.htm#I, last accessed August 8, 2010.

Coe, Michael D.

1973 *The Maya Scribe and His World*. New York: Grolier Club.

Coe, William R.

1959 *Piedras Negras Archaeology: Artifacts, Caches, and Burials*. Philadelphia: University Museum, University of Pennsylvania.

1990   *Excavations in the Great Plaza, North Terrace and North Acropolis of Tikal.* Tikal Report No. 14. Philadelphia: University Museum, University of Pennsylvania.

Coe, William R., and Vivian L. Broman

1958   *Excavations in the Stela 23 Group.* Tikal Report No. 2. Philadelphia: University Museum, University of Pennsylvania.

Coe, William R., and William A. Haviland

1982   *Introduction to the Archaeology of Tikal, Guatemala.* Tikal Report No. 12. Philadelphia: University Museum, University of Pennsylvania.

Conant, Kenneth John

1954   Mediaeval Academy Excavations at Cluny VIII, Final Stages of the Project. *Speculum* 29: 1–43.

1968   *Cluny: les églises et la maison du chef d'ordre.* Mâcon: Protat Frères.

1970   Mediaeval Academy Excavations at Cluny 8. *Speculum* 45: 1–39.

Connolly, Peter and Hazel Dodge

1998   *The Ancient City.* Oxford: Oxford University Press.

Constable, Giles

1974   The Study of Monastic History Today. In *Essays on the Reconstruction of Medieval History,* edited by Vaclav Mudroch and G. S. Couse, 19–51. Montreal/Kingston: McGill-Queen's University Press.

Coppack, Glyn

1991   *Mount Grace Priory (North Yorkshire).* London: English Heritage.

Coulon, Gérard and Jean-Claude Golvin

2002   *Voyage en Gaule romaine.* Errance: Actes Sud.

Courajod, Louis

1869   *Études iconographiques sur la topographie ecclésiastique de la France aux XVIIe et XVIIe siècles/le Monasticon Gallicanum.* Paris: Liepmannssohn et Dufour.

Crook, J. Mordaunt

1995   *John Carter and the Mind of the Gothic Revival.* London: Maney.

Crouzet-Pavan, Élisabeth.

1992   *"Sopra le acque salse". Espaces, pouvoir et société à Venise à la fin du Moyen Age,* 2 vols. Rome: L'école française de Rome.

Crowfoot, J. W.

1929   The Church of S. Theodore at Jerash. Translated by A.H.M. Jones. *Quarterly Statement of the Palestine Exploration Fund* 61: 17–36.

Cuevas Mata, Juan, Juan del Arco Moya, and José del Arco Moya (eds.)

2001   *Relación de los hechos del muy magnífico e más virtuoso señor, el señor don Miguel Lucas, muy digno condestable de Castilla.* Jaén: Ayuntamiento de Jaén and Universidad de Jaén.

Cunliffe, Barry

1985   *Heywood Sumner's Wessex.* Roy Gasson Associates, Wimborne, England.

Cuno, James

2008 *Who Owns Antiquity? Museums and the Battle over Our Ancient Heritage.* Princeton, NJ: Princeton University Press.

Curtius, E.

1851–52: *Peloponnesos, eine historisch-geographische Beschreibung der Halbinsel.* Volume 1 and 2. Gotha: Verlag von Justus Perthes.

Curtius, Ernst and Johann August Kaupert

1878 *Atlas von Athen.* Berlin: Verlag von Dietrich Reimer.

Daston, Lorraine and Peter Galison

1992 The Image of Objectivity. *Representations* 40: 81–128.

Delingette, Hervé

2002 Bridging the Gap between Archeological Datasets and Digital Representations. In *Three-Dimensional Imaging in Paleoanthropology and Prehistoric Archaeology*, edited by Bertrand Mafart and Hervé Delingette, 89–92. BAR International Series No. 1049. Oxford: Archaeopress.

Derrida, Jacques

1976 *Of Grammatology.* Translated by Gayatri Chakravorty Spivak. Baltimore, MA: Johns Hopkins University Press.

Desmond, Lawrence G. and P. M. Messenger

1988 *A Dream of Maya: Augustus and Alice Le Plongeon in Nineteenth-Century Yucatan.* Albuquerque: University of New Mexico Press.

Dickenson, Victoria

1998 *Drawn from Life: Science and Art in the Portrayal of the New World.* Toronto: University of Toronto Press.

Die Zisterzienserabtei Cluny, IKA: Informations- und Kommunikationstechnologie in der Architektur, http://www.cad.architektur.tu-darmstadt.de/, last accessed August 8, 2010.

Dietler, Michael

1994 "Our Ancestors the Gauls": Archaeology, Ethnic Nationalism, and the Manipulation of Celtic Identity in Modern Europe. *American Anthropologist* 96: 584–605.

Díez Bedmar, María del Consuelo

2000 El Urbanismo Medieval de Jaén a través del documento escrito: La aplicación "Base de Datos." In *La Historia en una Nueva Frontera: XIII Congreso Internacional de la Asociación History & Computing*, edited by Francisco José Aranda Pérez, Francisco Fernández Izquierdo, and Porfirio Sanz Camañes. From CD-ROM accompanying printed volume. La Mancha: Ediciones de la Universidad de Castilla-La Mancha.

Di Grazia, Vicenzo

1991 *Rilievo e disegno nell'archeologia e nell'architettura: tecniche, opinioni e teorie.* Rome: Edizione Kappa.

Digital Roman Forum, UCLA

2005 Electronic document, http://dlib.etc.ucla.edu/projects/Forum/reconstructions/BasilicaFulvia_1/issues, last accessed August 8, 2010.

Dillon, Brian (ed.)

  1985   *A Student's Guide to Archaeological Illustration*. Los Angeles: Institute of Archaeology, University of California Los Angeles.

Dodwell, Edward

  1819   *A Classical and Topographical Tour Through Greece During the Years 1801, 1805, and 1806*. London: Rodwell and Martin.

Doering, Travis and Lori Collins

  2005   Mesoamerican Three-Dimensional Imaging Project. Electronic document, http://research.famsi.org/3D_imaging/index.php, last accessed August 8, 2010.

Douglas, James

  1793   *Nenia Britannica*. London: John Nichols.

Dovey, Kimberly

  1985   The Quest for Authenticity and the Replication of Environmental Meaning. In *Dwelling, Place and Environment: Towards a Phenomenology of Person and World*, edited by D. Seamon and R. Mugerauer, 33–48. Dordrecht: Martinus Nijhoff Publishers.

Doxiadis, K.A.

  1937   *Raumordnung im griechischen Stadtebau*. Heidelberg: Kurt Vowinckel Verlag.

Driver, Felix

  2001   *Geography Militant: Cultures of Exploration and Empire*. Oxford: Blackwell Publishers.

Durand, Jean-Nicolas-Louis

  1799–1800 *Recueil et parallèle des édifices en tout genre, anciens et modernes*. Paris: Gille Fils.

Edgeworth, Matt

  1990   Analogy as Practical Reason: The Perception of Objects in Excavation Practice. *Archaeological Review from Cambridge* 9(2): 243–251.

Eisenstein, Elizabeth

  1979   *The Printing Press as an Agent of Change,* 2 vols. Cambridge: Cambridge University Press.

Ellis, Steven J.R.

  2004   The Distribution of Bars at Pompeii: Archaeological, Spatial, and Viewshed Analyses. *Journal of Roman Archaeology* 17: 371–384.

Elsner, Jaś

  2007   *Roman Eyes: Visuality and Subjectivity in Art and Text*. Princeton, NJ: Princeton University Press.

Enwezor, Okwui

  2008   *Archive fever: Uses of the Document in Contemporary Art*. New York: Steidl.

Escobedo, Héctor L. and Stephen D. Houston

  1997a   Introducción: La Primera Temporada de Campo del Proyecto Arqueológico Piedras Negras, 1997. In *Proyecto Arqueológico Piedras Negras: Informe Preliminar No. 1, Primera Temporada, 1997*, edited by Héctor L. Escobedo and Stephen D. Houston, iii–iv. Guatemala: Instituto de Antroplogía e Historia de Guatemala.

Escobedo, Héctor L. and Stephen D. Houston (eds.)

1997b   *Proyecto Arqueológico Piedras Negras: Informe Preliminar No. 1, Primera Temporada, 1997*. Guatemala: Instituto de Antroplogía e Historia de Guatemala.

1998   *Proyecto Arqueológico Piedras Negras: Informe Preliminar No. 2, Segunda Temporada, 1998*. Guatemala: Instituto de Antroplogía e Historia de Guatemala.

1999   *Proyecto Arqueológico Piedras Negras: Informe Preliminar No. 3, Tercera Temporada, 1999*. Guatemala: Instituto de Antroplogía e Historia de Guatemala.

2000   *Proyecto Arqueológico Piedras Negras: Informe Preliminar No. 4, Cuarta Temporada, 2000*. Guatemala: Instituto de Antroplogía e Historia de Guatemala.

Evans, Dai Morgan

2003   *Rebuilding the Past, A Roman Villa*. London: Methuen Publishing Limited.

Evans, Joan

1956   *A History of the Society of Antiquaries*. Oxford: Oxford University Press.

Experiential Technologies Center (ETC)

2006   Electronic document, http://www.etc.ucla.edu/technology/default.htm, last accessed August 2010.

Fagan, Garrett G. and Kenneth L. Feder

2007   Crusading Against Straw Men: An Alternative View of Alternative Archaeologies: Response to Holtorf (2005). *World Archaeology* 38: 718–729.

Fane, Diana

1993   Reproducing the Pre-Columbian Past: Casts and Models in Exhibitions of Ancient America 1824–1935. In *Collecting the Pre-Columbian Past: A Symposium at Dumbarton Oaks, 6 and 7 October 1990*, edited by Elizabeth H. Boone, 141–176. Washington, DC: Dumbarton Oaks.

Farnetani, Andrea, Patrizio Fausti, Roberto Pompoli, and Nicola Prodi

2001   Acoustical Measurements in Ancient Roman Theatres. *Acoustical Society of America Journal* 115(5): 24–77.

Fash, Barbara W.

1992   Late Classic Architectural Sculpture Themes in Copán. *Ancient Mesoamerica* 3: 89–104.

2004   Cast Aside: Revisiting the Plaster Cast Collections form Mesoamerica. *Visual Resources* 20(1): 3–17.

2006   Walking Through a Glass Plate: The Recovery of an Ancient Maya Text. Paper presented at the Peabody Museum Weekend of the Americas, October 13–15, Cambridge, Massachusetts. Paper on file at the Peabody Museum of Archaeology and Ethnology, Harvard University, Cambridge, Massachusetts.

2007   Cross-Cultural Intersections and Museums: The Copan Sculpture Museum and Catalogue. Unpublished Master's thesis, Liberal Arts in Extension Studies, Museum Studies Program. Cambridge, MA: Harvard University.

2011   *The Copan Sculpture Museum: Ancient Maya Artistry in Stucco and Stone*. Cambridge, MA: Peabody Museum Press.

Fash, Jr., William L.

1991   *Scribes, Warriors and Kings: The City of Copan and the Ancient Maya*. London: Thames and Hudson.

2001   *Scribes, Warriors and Kings: The City of Copan and the Ancient Maya.* 2nd edition. London: Thames and Hudson..

2002   Religion and Human Agency in Ancient Maya History: Tales from the Hieroglyphic Stairway. *Cambridge Archaeological Journal* 12(1): 5–19.

2006   Digging into Maya History: Hidden Truths and Contextual Clues about the Hieroglyphic Stairway. Paper presented at the Peabody Museum Weekend of the Americas, October 13–15, Cambridge, Massachusetts. Paper on file at the Peabody Museum of Archaeology and Ethnology, Harvard University, Cambridge, Massachusetts.

Fash, William and Kurt Long

1983   *Introduccion a la arqueología de Copán, Honduras, Vol. III: Mapa Arqueológico del Valle de Copán.* Tegucigalpa: Instituto Hondureño de Antropología e Historia.

Favro, Diane

1993   Reading the Augustan City. In *Narrative and Event in Ancient Art*, edited by Peter Holliday, 230–257. Cambridge: Cambridge University Press.

1996   *The Urban Image of Augustan Rome.* Cambridge: Cambridge University Press.

2006   In the Eyes of the Beholder: Virtual Reality Re-creations and Academia. *Journal of Roman Archaeology* (s.s.) 61: 321–334.

Fergusson, Peter

2008   Prior Wibert's Fountain Houses: Service and Symbolism at Christ Church, Canterbury. In *The Four Modes of Seeing: Approaches to Medieval Imagery in Honor of Madeline Harrison Caviness*, edited by Evelyn S. Lane, Elizabeth Carson Pastan, and Ellen M. Shortell, 53–65. Aldershot: Ashgate.

Filippi, Fedora

2007   *Ricostruire l'Antico prima del virtuale. Italo Gismondi Un architetto per l'archeologia (1887–1974).* Rome: Quasar.

Filler, Martin

2006   The Getty for Better and Worse. *New York Review of Books*, 53(18). Electronic document, http://www.nybooks.com/articles/19603, last accessed August 8, 2010.

Fitzroy, Robert, and Henry Raper (eds.)

1854   Hints to Travellers. *Journal of the Royal Geographical Society* 24: 328–358.

Fitzsimmons, James L., Andrew Scherer, Stephen D. Houston, and Héctor L. Escobedo

2003   Guardian of the Acropolis: The Sacred Space of a Royal Burial at Piedras Negras, Guatemala. *Latin American Antiquity* 14: 449–468.

Folan, William J., Ellen R. Kintz, and Laraine Fletcher

1983   *Coba, A Classic Maya Metropolis.* New York: Academic Press.

Ford, Anabel

1987   *Population Growth and Social Complexity: An Examination of Settlement and Environment in the Central Maya Lowlands.* Arizona State Anthropological Research Papers No. 35. Tempe: Arizona State University.

Forte, Maurizio

1997   Introduction. In *Virtual Archaeology: Recreating Ancient Worlds*, edited by Maurizio Forte and Alberto Siliotti, 8–13. New York: Harry N. Abrams.

2003   Mindscape: Ecological Thinking, Cyber-Anthropology and Virtual Archaeological Landscapes. In *The Reconstruction of Archaeological Landscapes through Digital Technologies*, edited by Maurizio Forte and P. Ryan Williams, 95–108. BAR International Series No. 1151. Oxford: Archaeopress.

2008   *The Virtual Museum of the Ancient via Flaminia*. CNR, Istituto per le Tecnologie Applicate ai Beni Culturali di Roma. Interactive museum display and website , http://www.vhlab.itabc.cnr.it/flaminia/, last accessed August 8, 2010.

Forte, Maurizio and Stephen Kay

2003   Remote Sensing, GIS and Virtual Reconstruction of Archaeological Landscapes. In *The Reconstruction of Archaeological Landscapes through Digital Technologies*, edited by Maurizio Forte and P. Ryan Williams, 109–115. BAR International Series No. 1151. Oxford: Archaeopress.

Forte, Maurizio and Alberto Siliotti (eds.)

1997   *Virtual Archaeology: Re-creating Ancient Worlds*. New York: Abrams.

Foucault, Michel

1990   *The Order of Things: An Archaeology of the Human Sciences*. New York: Vintage Books.

Fowler, William and Stephen Houston

1991   Tikal Report No. 14: A Review Essay. *Latin American Anthropology Review* 3: 61–63.

French, Josephine (ed.), with Valerie Scott and Mary Alice Lowenthal (consulting eds.)

2003   *Tooley's Dictionary of Mapmakers. Revised Edition, K-P*. Riverside, CT: Early World Press.

Freud, Sigmund

1989   *Civilization and Its Discontents*. Translated by James Strachey. New York: W.W. Norton.

Frieling, Rudolf

2008   *The Art of Participation: 1950—Now*. New York: Thames and Hudson.

Frischer, Bernard

2008   From Digital Illustration to Digital Heuristics. In *Beyond Illustration: 2D and 3D Digital Technologies as Tools for Discovery in Archaeology*, edited by Bernard Frischer and Anastasia Dakouri-Hild, v–xxiv. BAR International Series No. 1805. Oxford: Archaeopress.

Frischer, Bernard and Anastasia Dakouri-Hild (eds.)

2008   *Beyond Illustration: 2D and 3D Digital Technologies as Tools for Discovery in Archaeology*. BAR International Series No. 1805. British Archaeological Reports, Oxford: Archaeopress.

Frischer, Bernard and Philip Stinson

2007   The Importance of Scientific Authentication and a Formal Visual Language in Virtual Models of Archaeological Sites: The Case of the House of Augustus and Villa of the Mysteries. In *Interpreting the Past: Heritage, New Technologies and Local Development*, Proceedings of the Conference on Authenticity, Intellectual Integrity and Sustainable Development of the Public Presentation of Archaeological and Historical Sites and Landscapes Ghent. Electronic document, http://www.iath.virginia.edu/~bf3e/revision/pdf/Frischer_Stinson.pdf, last accessed August 8, 2010.

Frischer, Bernard, Diane Favro, Paolo Liverani, Sible De Blaauw, and Dean Abernathy

2000   Virtual Reality and Ancient Rome: The UCLA Cultural VR Lab's Santa Maria Maggiore Project. In *Virtual Reality in Archaeology*, edited by Juan A. Barceló, Maurizio Forte, and Donald H. Sanders, 155–169. BAR International Series No. 843. Oxford: Archaeopress.

Galison, Peter

1997   *Image and Logic: A Material Culture of Microphysics*. Chicago, IL: University of Chicago Press.

Gazzola, Piero

1964   *The Venice Charter*. Electronic document, http://www.international.icomos.org/e_venice.htm#publication, last accessed August 8, 2010.

Gebhard, David

1993   *Robert Stacy-Judd: Maya Architecture and the Creation of a New Style*. Santa Barbara, CA: Capra Press.

Geertz, Clifford

1980   *Negara: The Theatre in Nineteenth-Century Bali*. Princeton, NJ: Princeton University Press.

Gell, Alfred

1985   How to Read a Map: Remarks on the Practical Logic of Navigation. *Man* 20: 271–286.

Gell, William

1817   *Itinerary of the Morea. Being a Description of the Routes of that Peninsula*. London: Rodwell and Martin.

Germain, Dom Michel

1967 [1871] *Monasticon Gallicanum*. Edited by Achille Peigné-Delacourt. 1967 facsimile ed. Brussels: Culture et civilization.

Gero, Joan M.

1996   Archaeological Practice and Gendered Encounters with Field Data. In *Gender and Archaeology*, edited by Rita P. Wright, 251–280. Philadelphia: University of Pennsylvania Press.

Gero, Joan and Doris Root

1990   Public Presentation and Private Concerns: Archaeology in the Pages of National Geographic. In *The Politics of the Past*, edited by Peter Gathercole and David Lowenthal, 342–350. London: Routledge.

Getty Conservation Institute

2006   *The Hieroglyphic Stairway of Copán, Honduras: Study Results and Conservation Proposals, A Project Report*. Los Angeles, CA: Getty Conservation Institute.

Giannachi, Gabriella, Nick Kaye and Michael Shanks (eds.)

2012   *Archaeologies of Presence: Art, Performance and the Persistence of Being*. New York: Routledge.

Gibson, Sheila

1991   *Architecture and Archaeology: The Work of Sheila Gibson*. Rome: British School at Rome.

Gillings, Mark

2000   Plans, Elevations, and Virtual Worlds: The Development of Techniques for the Routine Construction of Hyperreal Simulations. In *Virtual Reality in Archaeology*, edited by Juan A. Barceló, Maurizio Forte, and Donald H. Sanders, 59–69. BAR International Series No. 843. Oxford: Archaeopress.

2002   Virtual Archaeologies and the Hyper-real. Or, What Does it Mean to Describe Something as *Virtually*-real? In *Virtual Reality in Geography*, edited by Peter Fisher and David Unwin, 223–239. London: Taylor and Francis.

2005   The Real, the Virtually Real and the Hyperreal: the Role of VR in Archaeology. In *Envisioning the Past: Archaeology and the Image*, edited by Sam Smiles and Stephanie Moser, 223–239. Oxford: Blackwell.

Godlewska, Anne M.C.

1999   *Geography Unbound: French Geographical Science from Cassini to Humboldt.* Chicago, IL: University of Chicago Press.

Golden, Charles

2002   Bridging the Gap Between Archaeological and Indigenous Chronologies: Investigation of the Early Classic / Late Classic Divide at Piedras Negras, Guatemala. Unpublished Ph.D. dissertation, Department of Anthropology, University of Pennsylvania.

Golvin, Jean-Claude

2008   Signification et problèmes de définition. In *De la restitution en archéologie, Archaeological restitutior.* Editions du Patrimoine Centre des Monuments Nationaux. March 2008. Electronic document, http://editions.monuments-nationaux.fr/fr/les-ouvrages-en-ligne/bdd/livre/9, accessed June 7, 2008.

Gombrich, Ernst Hans

1960   *Art and Illusion.* New York: Pantheon Books.

Gordon, Alexander

1726   *Itinerarium Septentrionale: Or, A Journey Tho' Most of the Counties of Scotland, and Those in the North of England.* London.

Gordon, George Byron

1902   *The Hieroglyphic Stairway, Ruins of Copan: Report on Explorations by the Museum.* Memoirs of the Peabody Museum of American Archaeology and Ethnology Vol. 1, No. 6. Cambridge, MA: Peabody Museum, Harvard University.

Gordon, George B., and John Alden Mason (eds.)

1925–1943 *Examples of Maya Pottery in the Museum and Other Collections.* 3 vols. Philadelphia: University Museum, University of Pennsylvania.

Gough, Richard

1768   *Anecdotes of British Topography: or, An Historical Account of What Has Been Done for Illustrating the Topographical Antiquities of Great Britain and Ireland.* London: W. Richardson and S. Clark.

Graham, Ian

1967   *Archaeological Explorations in El Peten, Guatemala.* Middle American Research Institute Publication No. 33. New Orleans, LA: Tulane University.

1979   *Corpus of Maya Hieroglyphic Inscriptions, Volume 3, Part 2: Yaxchilan*. Peabody Museum of Archaeology and Ethnology, Harvard University, Cambridge, Massachusetts.

2002   *Alfred Maudslay and the Maya: A Biography*. Norman: University of Oklahoma Press.

Gray, Noel

1995   Seeing Nature: The Mathematisation of Experience in Virtual Realities. *History of European Ideas* 20(1–3): 341–348.

Greenblatt, Stephen

1991   Resonance and Wonder. In *Exhibiting Cultures: The Poetics and Politics of Museum Display*, edited by Ivan Karp and Steven Lavine, 42–56. Washington, DC: Smithsonian Institution.

Greene, Merle, Robert L. Rands, and John A. Graham

1972   *Maya Sculpture from the Southern Lowlands, the Highlands and Pacific Piedmont, Guatemala, Mexico, Honduras*. Berkeley, CA: Lederer, Street, and Zeus.

Greenhouse, Wendy

1985   Benjamin West and Edward III: A Neoclassical Painter and Medieval History. *Art History* 8(2): 178–191.

Grewe, Klaus

1991   Der Wasserversorgungsplan des Klosters Christchurch in Canterbury (12 Jahrhundert). In *Die Wasserversorgung im Mittelalter, Geschichte der Wasserversorgung*, Band 4, edited by Klaus Grewe, 229–236. Mainz am Rhein: Philipp von Zabern.

1996   Le monastère de Christchurch à Cantorbéry (Kent, Grande-Bretagne): interprétation et signification du plan du réseau hydraulique (XIIe siècle). In *L'hydraulique monastique: Milieux, reseaux, usages*, edited by Armelle Bonis and Monique Wabont, 123–133. Grâne: Creaphis.

Gröning, Philip

2007   *Into Great Silence*, a film by Philip Gröning. Zeitgeist Video.

Gross, A.G.

1990   *The Rhetoric of Science*. Cambridge, MA: Harvard University Press.

Gugliotta, Guy

2007   The Maya: Glory and Ruin Part I—The Kingmaker. *National Geographic* 212(2): 74–85.

Guidi, Gabriele, Bernard Frischer, and Monica De Simone

2005   3D Digitization of a Large Model of Imperial Rome. Proceedings of the Fifth International Conference on 3-D Digital Imaging and Modeling. Electronic document http://ieeexplore.ieee.org/iel5/9854/31039/01443292.pdf, accessed June 8, 2008.

Gutierrez, Diego, Bernard Frischer, Eva Cerezo, and Francisco Serón

2007   AI and Virtual Crowds: Populating the Colosseum. *Journal of Cultural Heritage* 8(2): 176–185.

Hacking, Ian

1983   *Representing and Intervening: Introductory Topics in the Philosophy of Natural Science*. Cambridge: Cambridge University Press.

Halle, Uta

  2005   Archaeology in the Third Reich: Academic Scholarship and the Rise of the "Lunatic Fringe." *Archaeological Dialogues* 12: 91–102.

Hammond, Norman (ed.)

  1991   Cuello: An Early Maya Community in Belize. Cambridge: Cambridge University Press.

Hammond, Norman, Sheena Howarth, and Richard Wilk

  1999   *The Discovery, Exploration, and Monuments of Nim Li Punit, Belize*. Research Reports on Ancient Maya Writing No. 40. Washington, DC: Center for Maya Research.

Handler, Richard and Eric Gable

  1997   *The New History in an Old Museum: Creating the Past at Colonial Williamsburg*. Durham, NC: Duke University Press.

Hankins, Thomas and Robert Silverman

  1995   *Instruments and the Imagination*. Princeton, NJ: Princeton University Press.

Haraway, Donna

  2003   Cyborgs to Companion Species: Reconfiguring Kinship. In *Chasing Technoscience: Matrix for Materiality*, edited by Don Ihde and Eva Selinger, 58–82. Indianapolis: Indiana University Press.

Harley, John B.

  1992   Deconstructing the Map. In *Writing Worlds: Discourse, Text and Metaphor in the Representation of Landscape*, edited by Trevor J. Barnes and James S. Duncan, 231–247. London: Routledge.

Harley, John B. and David Woodward (eds.)

  1987   *The History of Cartography, Volume I: Cartography in Prehistoric, Ancient, and Medieval Europe and the Mediterranean*. Chicago, IL: University of Chicago Press.

Harris, Julie A.

  1997   Mosque to Church Conversion in the Spanish Reconquest. *Medieval Encounters* 3: 158–172.

Harris, Max

  2000   *Aztecs, Moors, and Christians: Festivals of Reconquest in Mexico and Spain*. Austin: University of Texas Press.

Harris, T.M.

  2002   GIS in archaeology. In *Past Time, Past Place: GIS for History*, edited by A.K. Knowles, 131–143. Redlands, CA: ESRI Press.

Harvey, Philip D. A.

  1991   *Medieval Maps*. Toronto: University of Toronto Press.

Heat-Moon, William Least

  1991   *PrairyErth (A Deep Map): An Epic History of the Tallgrass Prairie Country*. Boston, MA: Houghton Mifflin.

Heidegger, Martin

  1971   *Poetry, Language, Thought*. Translated by Albert Hofstadter. New York: Harper and Row.

Hernández, Xavier, Jordi Ballonga, and Josep Escofet

1992   *San Rafael: A Central American City Through the Ages*. Boston, MA: Houghton Mifflin.

Heslop, T. A.

1982   The Conventual Seals of Canterbury Cathedral. In *Medieval Art and Architecture at Canterbury before 1220* [Conference Proceedings of the British Archaeological Association, 1979], edited by Nicola Coldstream and Peter Draper, 94–100. London: Maney Publishing.

Higgins, Tony, Peter Main, and Janet Lang (eds.)

1994   *Imaging the Past: Electronic Imaging and Computer Graphics in Museums and Archaeology*. British Museum Occasional Paper No. 114. London: British Museum Press.

Hinard, François

1991   La maquette comme objet scientifique. In *Rome. L'espace urbain & ses représentations*, edited by François Hinard and Manuel Royo, 281–286. L'Aigle: Presses del'Université de Paris-Sorbonne.

Hodder, Ian

1989   Writing Archaeology Site Reports in Context. *Antiquity* 63: 268–274.

1994   The Narrative and Rhetoric of Material Culture Sequences. *World Archaeology* 25: 268–282.

1997   "Always Momentary, Fluid and Flexible": Towards a Reflexive Excavation Methodology. *Antiquity* 71: 691–700.

1999   *The Archaeological Process: An Introduction*. Blackwell, Oxford, England.

2003   Archaeological Reflexivity and the "Local" Voice. *Anthropological Quarterly* 76: 55–69.

Hodder, Ian and Scott Hutson

2003   *Reading the Past: Current Approaches to Interpretation in Archaeology*. 3rd ed. Cambridge: Cambridge University Press.

Hohmann, Hasso

1995   *Die Architektur der Sepulturas-Region von Copán in Honduras*. Graz: Academic Publishers.

Holmes, William H.

1895   *Archaeological Studies among the Ancient Cities of Mexico: Monuments of Yucatan*. Anthropological Series vol.1, no.1, part I. Chicago: Field Columbian Museum.

Holtorf, Cornelius

2005 *From Stonehenge to Las Vegas: Archaeology as Popular Culture*. Walnut Creek, CA: Altamira Press, .

Hooke, Robert

1665   *Micrographia or Some physiological descriptions of minute bodies made by magnifying glasses. With observations and inquiries thereupon*. London: Jo. Martyn and Ja. Allestry.

Hope, William H. St John

1902   The London Charterhouse and its Old Water Supply. *Archaeologia* 58(1): 293–312.

Hope Simpson, Robert and D.K. Hagel

2006   *Mycenaean Fortifications, Highways, Dams and Canals*. Sävedalen: Paul Åströms Förlag.

Horn, Walter, and Ernst Born

1979 *The Plan of St-Gall: A Study of the Architecture and Economy of, and Life in a Paradigmatic Carolingian Monastery.* 3 vols. Berkeley: University of California Press.

Horsfield, Peter

2003 The Ethics of Virtual Reality: The Digital and its Predecessors. Electronic document, http://www.wacc.org.uk/wacc/publications/media_development/2003_2/the_ethics_of_virtual_reality_the_digital_and_its_predecessors, accessed April 9, 2008.

Houston, Stephen D.

1998 Classic Maya Depictions of the Built Environment. *In Function and Meaning in Classic Maya Architecture*, edited by Stephen D. Houston, 333–372. Washington, DC: Dumbarton Oaks.

Houston, Stephen, and Karl Taube

2000 An Archaeology of the Senses: Perception and Cultural Expression in Ancient Mesoamerica. *Cambridge Archaeological Journal* 10(2): 261–294.

Houston, Stephen, and John Robertson, and David Stuart

2000 The Language of Classic Maya Inscriptions. *Current Anthropology* 41: 321–356.

Hruby, Zachary X.

2006 "Apocalypto" Does Disservice to its Subjects. *San Francisco Chronicle* 11 December: C-1. San Francisco.

ICOMOS

2007 Charter for the Interpretation and Presentation of Cultural Heritage Sites10. Electronic document, http://www.enamecharter.org/downloads/ICOMOS_Interpretation_Charter_EN_10-04-07.pdf, last accessed August 8, 2010.

Ingle, Marjorie I.

1989 *The Mayan Revival Style: Art Deco Mayan Fantasy.* Albuquerque: University of New Mexico Press.

Ingold, Tim

2000 *The Perception of the Environment: Essays in Livelihood, Dwelling and Skill.* London: Routledge.

2007: Materials against Materiality. *Archaeological Dialogues* 14(1): 1–16.

Inomata, Takeshi, and Stephen Houston

2001 Opening the Royal Maya Court. In *Royal Courts of the Ancient Maya,* Vol. I, edited by Takeshi Inomata and Stephen D. Houston, pp. 3–23. Boulder: Westview Press.

Ivins, William M.

1953 *Prints and Visual Communication.* Cambridge, MA: Harvard University Press.

1973 *On the Rationalization of Sight.* New York: Plenum Press.

Jameson, John H.

2004 Introduction: Archaeology and Reconstructions. In the *The Reconstructed Pas: Reconstructions in the Public Interpretation of Archaeology and History*, edited by John Jameson, Jr., 1–19. Walnut Creek, CA: Altamira Press.

Jameson Jr., John H., John E. Ehrenhard, and Christine A. Finn (eds.)

2003 *Ancient Muses: Archaeology and the Arts.* Tuscaloosa: University of Alabama Press.

Jameson, Michael H., Curtis N. Runnels and Tjeerd H. van Andel

  1994   *A Greek Countryside: The Southern Argolid from Prehistory to the Present Day.* Stanford, CA: Stanford University Press.

Jessup, Ronald

  1975   *Man of Many Talents: An Informal Biography of James Douglas, 1753–1819.* London: Phillimore.

Joyce, Rosemary

  2002   *The Languages of Archaeology: Dialogue, Narrative, and Writing.* Oxford: Blackwell.

Kagan, Richard (ed.)

  1989   *Spanish Cities of the Golden Age: The Views of Anton van den Wyngaerde.* Berkeley: University of California Press.

Kantner, John

  2000   Realism vs. Reality: Creating Virtual Reconstructions of Prehistoric Architecture. In *Virtual Reality in Archaeology*, edited by Juan A. Barceló, Maurizio Forte, and Donald H. Sanders, 47–52. BAR International Series No. 843. Oxford: Archaeopress.

Kaye, Nick

  2000   *Site-Specific Art: Performance, Place and Documentation.* London: Routledge.

Kenderdine, Sarah

  2004   Avatars at the Flying Palace: Stereographic Panoramas of Angkor Cambodia. In *The International Conference on Hypermedia and Interactivity in Museums (ICHIM) 2004*, 1–24. Berlin: Museum Archives and Informatics.

Kensek, Karen M.

  2007   A Survey of Methods for Showing Missing Data, Multiple Alternatives, and Uncertainty in Reconstructions. *CSA Newsletter* 19(3). Electronic document, http://www.csanet.org/newsletter/winter07/nlw0702.html, last accessed August 8, 2010.

Kidder, Alfred V.

  1946   Introduction. In *Excavations at Kaminaljuyu, Guatemala*, edited by Alfred V. Kidder, Jesse D. Jennings, and Edwin M. Shook, 1–9. Carnegie Institution of Washington Publication No. 561. Washington, DC: Carnegie Institution of Washington.

  1950   Sylvanus Griswold Morley 1883–1948. In *Morleyana: A Collection of Writings in Memoriam Sylvanus Griswold Morley 1883-1948*, edited by Arthur J. O. Anderson, 93–102. Santa Fe, NM: School of American Research.

Knighton, Tess

  1997 Spaces and Contexts for Listening in 15th-century Castile: The Case of the Constable's Palace in Jaén. *Early Music* 25: 661–677.

Knowles, David, and J. Kenneth S. Saint Joseph

  1952   *Monastic Sites from the Air.* Cambridge: Cambridge University Press.

Koob, Manfred

  2006   Informations- und Kommunikationstechnologie in der Architektur. Electronic document, http://www.cad.architektur.tu-darmstadt.de/, last accessed August 8, 2010.

Koziol, Geoffrey

    1992   *Begging Pardon and Favor: Ritual and Political Order in Early Medieval France*. Ithaca, NY: Cornell University Press.

Kreps, Christina K.

    2003   *Liberating Culture: Cross-cultural Perspectives on Museums, Curation, and Heritage Preservation*. London: Routledge.

Latour, Bruno

    1986   Visualization and Cognition: Thinking with Eyes and Hands. In *Knowledge and Society: Studies in the Sociology of Culture Past and Present*, 1–40. The Anthropology of Science and Technology, vol. 6. Amsterdam: Elsevier.

    1987   *Science in Action: How to Follow Scientists and Engineers through Society*. Cambridge, MA: Harvard University Press.

    1990   Drawing Things Together. In *Representation in Scientific Practice*, edited by Michael Lynch and Steve Woolgar, 19–68. Cambridge, MA: MIT Press.

    1994   Pragmatogonies. *American Behavioral Scientist* 37(6): 791–808.

    1996   Do Scientific Objects Have a History? Pasteur and Whitehead in a Bath of Lactic Acid. *Common Knowledge* 5(1): 76–91.

    1999   *Pandora's Hope: Essays on the Reality of Science Studies*. Cambridge, MA: Harvard University Press.

Laurence, Ray

    2004   The Uneasy Dialogue Between Ancient History and Archaeology. In *Archaeology and Ancient History: Breaking Down the Boundaries*, edited by Eberhard W. Sauer, 99–113. London: Routledge.

Law, John

    1986   On the Methods of Long Distance Control: Vessels, Navigation and the Portuguese Route to India. In *Power, Action and Belief*, edite by John Law, 236–263. London: Routledge.

Law, John and Annemarie Mol

    2001   Situating Technoscience: An Inquiry into Spatialities. *Environment and Planning D: Society and Space* 19(5): 609–21.

Lawrence, Clifford H.

    2001   *Medieval Monasticism: Forms of Religious Life in Western Europe in the Middle Ages*. 3rd ed. New York: Longman.

Lázaro Demas, María Soledad

    1988   *Desarrollo histórico del casco urbano de Jaén hasta 1600*. Jaén: Colegio Oficial de Aparejadores y Arquitectos Técnicos de Jaén.

Leake, William Martin

    1830   *Travels in the Morea*. 3 vols. London: John Murray.

    1846   *Peloponnesiaca: A Supplement to Travels in the Morea*. London: J. Rodwell.

Leech, Roger H.

    2008   Understanding Nevis: GPS and Archaeological Field Survey in a Postcolonial Landscape. In *Archaeology and Geoinformatics: Case Studies from the Caribbean*, edited by Basil A. Reid, 127–136. Tuscaloosa: University of Alabama Press.

Lenoir, Timothy and Henry Lowood

2005   Theaters of War: The Military-Entertainment Complex. In *Collection—Laboratory—Theater: Scenes of Knowledge in the 17th Century*, edited by Helmar Schramm, Ludger Schwarte, and Jan Lazardzig, 427–456. Berlin: Walter de Gruyter.

Lepetit, Bernard

1998   Missions scientifiques et expeditions militaries: remarques sur leurs modalités d'articulation. In *L'Invention Scienfitique de la Méditerranée. Égypte, Morée, Algérie*, edited by Marie Noëlle Bourguet, 97–116. Paris: École des Hautes Études en Sciences Sociales.

Lessig, Lawrence

2008   *Remix: Making Art and Commerce Thrive in the Hybrid Economy*. New York: Penguin Press.

Lewis, Wilmarth S. (ed.)

1937   *The Yale Edition of the Correspondence of Horace Walpole,* vol. 2. New Haven, CT: Yale University Press.

Libellus de diversis ordinibus et professionibus qui sunt in aecclesia. Edited and translated by Giles Constable and Bernard S. Smith. Rev. ed. 2003. Oxford: Oxford University Press.

Ling, Roger

1990   A Stranger in Town: Finding the Way in an Ancient City. *Greece & Rome*, 2nd Ser. 37(2): 204–214.

Lolling, H.G.

1889   Books and Maps. In *Baedeker's Greece: A Handbook for Travellers*, written and compiled by Karl Baedeker, cxiii–cxvi. Leipzig: Karl Baedeker.

López Camacho, Javier

2006   Prospección arqueológica en el sur de Quintana Roo. In *Investigación, docencia y patrimonio: Memorias de la Jornadas de Arqueología*, edited by Ivonne Schönleger Riusech and Alberto Villa Kamel, 57–76. México: Instituto Nacional de Antropología e Historia (INAH).

Lorenzi, Rossella

2008   Light Beams to Color Rome Column. Electronic document, http://dsc.discovery.com/news/2008/04/10/trajan-column.html, last accessed August 8, 2010.

Loring, W.

1895   Some Ancient Routes in the Peloponnese. *The Journal of Hellenic Studies* 15: 25–89.

Lowenthal, David

1996   *Possessed by the Past: The Heritage Crusade and the Spoils of History*. New York: Free Press.

Lowood, Henry

2009   Virtual Reality. Electronic document from Encyclopædia Britannica Online, http://www.britannica.com/EBchecked/topic/630181/virtual-reality, last accessed August 8, 2010.

Lucas, Gavin

2001   *Critical Approaches to Fieldwork: Contemporary and Historical Archaeological Practice*. London: Routledge.

Lutz, Catherine A., and Jane L. Collins

　1993　*Reading National Geographic.* Chicago, IL: University of Chicago Press.

Lynch, Michael, and Samuel Edgerton.

　1988　"Aesthetics and Digital Image Processing. In *Picturing Power*, eds. G. Fyfe and John Law, 184–220. London: Routledge.

Lynch, Michael and Steve Woolgar (editors)

　1990　*Representation in Scientific Practice.* Cambridge, MA: MIT Press.

MacDonald, William L.

　1988　*The Architecture of the Roman Empire: An Urban Appraisal.* New Haven, CT: Yale University Press.

MacKay, Angus

　1989　Religion, Culture, and Ideology in Late Medieval Castilian-Granadan Frontier Societies. In *Medieval Frontier Societies*, edited by Robert Bartlett and Angus MacKay, 217–243. Oxford: Clarendon Press.

　1991　Los bandos: Aspectos culturales. In *Bandos y querellas dinásticas al final en España al final de la Edad Media. Actas del Coloquio celebrado en la Biblioteca Española de París los días 15 y 16 de mayo de 1987*, edited by Lucien Clare and Jacques Heers, 15–27. Paris: Biblioteca Española de París.

McCluskey, Eileen K.

　1998　A Pathway to the Past: Mayan Staircase Project Seeks to Preserve Ancient History. *Harvard Gazette*, 15 October:2–3. Cambridge, Massachusetts.

McVicker, Mary F.

　2005　*Adela Breton: A Victorian Artist Amid Mexico's Ruins.* Albuquerque: University of New Mexico Press.

McLuhan, Marshall

　1994　*Understanding Media: The Extensions of Man.* Cambridge, MA: MIT Press.

Madrazo, Leandro

　1994　Durand and the Science of Architecture. *Journal of Architectural Education* 48(1): 12–24.

Makarius, Michel

　2004　*Ruins.* Paris: Flammarion.

Maler, Teobert

　1901　*Researches in the Central Portion of the Usumacintla Valley.* Memoirs of the Peabody Museum of Archaeology and Ethnology Vol. 2, No. 1. Peabody Museum of Archaeology and Ethnology. Cambridge, MA: Harvard University.

　1908　*Explorations in the Department of Peten, Guatemala and Adjacent Region: Topoxté, Yaxhá, Benque Viejo, Naranjo.* Memoirs of the Peabody Museum of American Archaeology and Ethnology, vol. 4, no. 2. Cambridge, MA: Harvard University.

Manovich, Lev

　2006　Visual Technologies as Cognitive Prostheses: A Short History of the Externalization of the Mind. In *The Prosthetic Impulse: From a Posthuman to a Biocultural Future*, edited by Marquard Smith and Joanne Morra, 203–219. Cambridge, MA: MIT Press.

Marcus, George E.

1990   The Production of European High Culture in Los Angeles: The J. Paul Getty Trust as Artificial Curiosity. *Cultural Anthropology* 5(1): 314–330.

Martos López, Luis Alberto

2002   *Por las tierras mayas del oriente: Arqueología en el área de Calica, Quintana Roo*. México: Instituto Nacional de Antropología e Historia (INAH).

Maudslay, Alfred P.

1889–1902 *Archaeology: Biologia Centrali Americana, or, Contributions to the Knowledge of the Fauna and Flora of Mexico and Central America*. London: R.H. Porter and Dulau.

Mayer, Brantz

1844   *Mexico, As It Was and As It Is*. 2nd edition. New York: New York and Company.

Meyrick, Samuel Rush and Charles Hamilton Smith

1815   *The Costume of the Original Inhabitants of the British Islands: from the earliest periods to the sixth century; to which is added, that of the Gothic nations on the western coasts of the Baltic, the ancestors of the Anglo-Saxons and Anglo-Danes*. Printed by William Bulmer and Co. Shakspeare Press, published by R. Havell, London.

Miliarakis, A.

1886   *Geographia tou Nomou Argolidos kai Korinthias*. Athens: Bibliopoleion Hestias, Typographeion Korinnes.

Miller, Mary E.

2002   Reconstrucción de los Murales de Bonampak. *Arqueología Mexicana* X(55): 44–55.

Millon, René, Bruce Drewitt, and George Cowgill

1973   *The Teotihuacán Map: Volume 1 Part 2*. Austin: University of Texas Press.

Molyneaux, Brian Leigh

1997   Introduction: The Cultural Life of Images. In *The Cultural Life of Images: Visual Representation in Archaeology*, edited by Brian Leigh Molyneaux, 1–10. London: Routledge.

Monmonier, Mark

1991   *How to Lie with Maps*. Chicago, IL: University of Chicago Press.

Morley, Sylvanus G.

1920   *The Inscriptions at Copan*. Carnegie Institution of Washington Publication No. 219. Washington, DC: The Carnegie Institution of Washington.

1937–1938 *The Inscriptions of the Petén*. Carnegie Institution of Washington Publication No. 437. Washington, DC: Carnegie Institution of Washington.

1955   The Maya of Yucatan. In *National Geographic on Indians of the Americas: A Color-Illustrated Record*, edited by Matthew Stirling, 182–215. Washington, DC: National Geographic Society.

Moscati, Paola (editor)

2007   *Virtual Museums and Archaeology: The Contribution of the Italian National Research Council*. Florence: All'Insegna del Giglio.

Moser, Stephanie

1998   *Ancestral Images: The Iconography of Human Origins*. Ithaca, NY: Cornell University Press.

2001 Archaeological Representation: The Visual Conventions for Constructing Knowledge About the Past. In *Archaeological Theory Today*, edited by Ian Hodder, 262–283. Cambridge: Polity Press.

Muehrcke, Phillip C. and Juliana O. Muehrcke

1998 *Map Use: Reading, Analysis, and Interpretation*. 4th edition. Madison, WI: JP Publications.

Murphy, Kevin D.

2000 *Memory and Modernity: Viollet-le-Duc at Vézelay*. State College: Pennsylvania State University Press.

Murray, Priscilla M. and P. Nick Kardulias

2000 The Present as Past: An Ethnoarchaeological Study of Modern Sites in the Pikrodhafni Valley. In *Contingent Countryside: Settlement, Economy and Land Use in the Southern Argolid Since 1700*, edited by Susan Buck Sutton, 141–168. Stanford, CA: Stanford University Press.

Myrone, Martin

2007 The Society of Antiquaries and the Graphic Arts: George Vertue and his Legacy. In *Visions of Antiquity: the Society of Antiquaries of London, 1707–2007*, edited by Susan Pearce, 99–121. London: Society of Antiquaries of London, .

Nagel, Thomas

1986 *The View From Nowhere*. Oxford: Oxford University Press.

Neiske, Franz

1997 Cluny dans le monde scientifique. Electronic document, http://www.uni-muenster.de/Fruehmittelalter/Projekte/Cluny/links_cluny.htm#I, last accessed August 8, 2010.

Nelson, Robert S.

2000 Descartes's Cow and Other Domestications of the Visual. In *Visuality Before and Beyond the Renaissance: Seeing as Others Saw*, edited by Robert S. Nelson, 1–21. Cambridge: Cambridge University Press.

Nelson, Zachary Nathan

1999 El Mapa Preliminar de Piedras Negras: Temporada de 1999. In *Proyecto Arqueológico Piedras Negras: Informe Preliminar No. 3, Tercera Temporada, 1999*, edited by Héctor L. Escobedo and Stephen D. Houston, 415–426. Guatemala: Instituto de Antroplogía e Historia de Guatemala.

2005 *Settlement and Population at Piedras Negras, Guatemala*. Unpublished Ph.D. dissertation, Department of Anthropology, Pennsylvania State University.

Netz, Reviel, and William Noel

2007 *The Archimedes Codex: How a Medieval Prayer Book is Revealing the True Genius of Antiquity's Greatest Scientist*. Philadelphia: Da Capo Press.

New York Times (NYT)

1974 Roman Villa is Recreated on Coast to House Getty Art Collection. 17 January:41. New York.

Niccolucci, Franco (ed.)

2002 *Virtual Archaeology: Proceedings of the VAST Euroconference, Arezzo 24–25 November 2000*. BAR International Series No. 1075. Oxford: Archaeopress.

Norberg-Schulz, Christian

    1980   *Genius Loci: Towards a Phenomenology of Architecture.* New York: Rizzoli.

NOVA/PBS.

    2000   *Nova Builds a Bath.* Electronic document, http://www.pbs.org/wgbh/nova/lostem-pires/roman/builds.html, last accessed August 8, 2010.

Nurse, Bernard

    2007   The Development of the Library. In *Visions of Antiquity: the Society of Antiquaries of London, 1707–2007,* edited by Susan Pearce, 199–226. London: Society of Antiquaries of London.

Olsen, Bjørnar

    2003   Material Culture after Text: Re-membering Things. *Norwegian Archaeological Review* 36(2): 87–104.

Pacaut, Marcel

    1993   *Les ordres monastiques et religieux au moyen âge.* Rev. ed. Paris: Armand Colin.

Pallasmaa, Juhani

    2005   *The Eyes of the Skin: Architecture and the Senses.* Hoboken, NJ: John Wiley and Sons.

Pastoureau, Michel

    1996   Les sceaux et la fonction sociale des images. In *L'image: Fonctions et usages des images dans l'Occident médiéval,* edited by Jérôme Baschet and Jean-Claude Schmitt, 275–308. Cahiers du Leopard d'Or, Vol. 5. Paris: Leopard d'Or.

Patrik, Linda

    1985   Is There an Archaeological Record? In *Advances in Archaeological Method and Theory: Volume 8,* edited by Michael Schiffer, 27–62. New York: Academic Press.

Peabody Museum of Archaeology and Ethnology

    2007a   Digital Imaging in the Photographic Archives. *Symbols* (Spring):1–2, 8–9. Peabody Museum and the Department of Anthropology. Cambridge, MA: Harvard University.

    2007b   The Hieroglyphic Stairway Conference, Fall 2006. *Symbols* (Spring):1 and 10. Peabody Museum and the Department of Anthropology. Cambridge, MA: Harvard University.

Pearce, Susan (ed.)

    2007   *Visions of Antiquity: the Society of Antiquaries of London, 1707–2007.* London: Society of Antiquaries of London.

Pearson, Mike

    2006   *"In Comes I" Performance, Memory and Landscape.* Exeter: University of Exeter Press.

Pearson, Mike and Michael Shanks

    2001   *Theatre/Archaeology.* London: Routledge.

Peckham, Robert Shannan

    2000   Map Mania: Nationalism and the Politics of Place in Greece, 1870—1922. *Political Geography* 19: 77–95.

Pendergast, David M.

    1979   *Excavations at Altun Ha, Belize, 1964–1970, Vol 1.* Toronto: Royal Ontario Museum.

Percy, Thomas

    1744   *Reliques of Ancient English Pottery.* London.

Petit, Nicholas

    1991   Les abbayes génovéfaines dans l'Oise: vues et plans retrouvés. *Bulletin du Groupe d'étude des monuments et oeuvres d'art du Beauvaisis* 51: 15–35.

Piggott, Stuart

    1965   Archaeological Draughtsmanship; Principles and Practice Part I: Principles and Retrospect. *Antiquity* 39: 165–176.

    1978   *Antiquity Depicted: Aspects of Archaeological Illustration.* London: Thames and Hudson.

Platt, Colin

    1984   *The Abbeys and Priories of Medieval England.* New York: Fordham University Press.

Pluciennik, Mark

    1999   Archaeological Narratives and Other Ways of Telling. *Current Anthropology* 40(5): 653–678.

Pollefeys, Marc, Luc Van Gool, Maarten Vergauwen, Kurt Cornelis, Frank Verbiest, and Jan Tops

    2003   3D Recording for Archaeological Fieldwork. *IEEE Computer Graphics and Applications* 23(3): 20–27.

Pouqueville, François C.H.L.

    1805   *Voyage en Morée, à Constantinople, en Albanie et dans plusieurs autre parties de l'Empire Ottoman pendant les années 1798, 1799, 1800, et 1801.* 3 vols. Paris: Gabon.

Powell, Alvin

    2006   Harvard Collection Turns Historic. *Harvard Gazette*, 7 December. Cambridge, MA.

    2007a   New Technology Heads South. *Harvard Gazette* 12 April. Cambridge, MA.

    2007b   Corpus Team Overcomes Scanning Snags: Ingenuity, Flexibility Helps Corpus Expedition Manage Bumps in Road. Harvard University Gazette Online, electronic document, http://www.hno.harvard.edu/gazette/2007/04.26/99-corpus.html, accessed April 7, 2008.

    2007c   Peabody Teams Will Scan Other Endangered Monuments. *Harvard Gazette* 3 May. Cambridge, MA.

Proskouriakoff, Tatiana

    1946   *An Album of Maya Architecture.* Carnegie Institution of Washington, Publication No. 558. Washington, DC: Carnegie Institution of Washington.

    1962   Civic and Religious Structures of Mayapan. In *Mayapan, Yucatan, Mexico*, edited by H. E. D. Pollock, Ralph L. Roys, Tatiana Proskouriakoff, and A. Ledyard Smith, 86–163. Washington, DC: Carnegie Institution of Washington, Publication 619. Carnegie Institution of Washington.

    1963   *An Album of Maya Architecture.* Reprinted edition. Norman: University of Oklahoma Press.

Puillon de Boblaye, Emile Le

1836   *Expédition Scientifique de Morée: Recherches Géographiques sur les Ruines de la Morée.* Paris: F.G. Levrault.

Putnam, Hilary

1981   *Reason, Truth and History.* Cambridge: Cambridge University Press.

1988   *Representation and Reality.* Cambridge, MA: MIT Press.

Quintanilla Rosa, María Concepción

1982   Estructuras sociales y familiares y papel político de la nobleza cordobesa (siglos XIV–XV). *En la España medieval* 3: 331–352.

Raskin, Jef

2002   *The Human Interface: New Directions for Designing Interactive Systems.* Reading, MA: Addison Wesley.

Reilly, Paul

1991   Towards a Virtual Archaeology. In *Computer Applications and Quantitative Methods in Archaeology 1990*, edited by Kris Lockyear and Sebastian Rahtz, pp. 133–139. BAR International Series No. 565. Oxford: Tempus Reparatum.

Renfrew, Colin and Paul G. Bahn

2005   *Archaeology: The Key Concepts.* London: Routledge.

Rhyne, Charles S.

2006   Clean Art? *Journal of the American Institute for Conservation* 45(3): 168.

Richner, Werner, Horst Cramer, Manfred Koob, and Ulrich Best

1993   *Cluny: Architektur als Vision.* Heidelberg: Braus.

Roberts, K. B. and J.D.W. Tomlinson

1992   *The Fabric of the Body: European Traditions of Anatomical Illustrations.* Oxford: Oxford University Press.

Rodaway, Paul

1994 *Sensuous Geographies: Body, Sense, and Place.* London: Routledge.

Rodríguez Molina, José

1996   *La vida de la ciudad de Jaén en tiempos del Condestable Iranzo.* Jaén: Concejalía de Cultura.

Rorty, Richard

1979   *Philosophy and the Mirror of Nature.* Princeton, NJ: Princeton University Press.

Rose, Mark

2008   New Hope for a Forgotten City. *Archaeology* 61(2): 36–39.

Rubio García, Luis.

1987   *La procesión de Corpus en el Siglo XV en Murcia.* Murcia: Academia Alfonso X El Sabio.

Ruiz, Teofilo F.

1985   Unsacred Monarchy: The Kings of Castile in the Later Middle Ages. In *Rites of Power*, edited by Sean Wilentz, 109–144. Philadelphia: University of Pennsylvania Press.

1991 Festivités, couleurs, et symboles du pouvoir en Castille au XVe siècle. *Annales E.S.C.* 46: 521–546.

1994 Elite and Popular Culture in Late Fifteenth-Century Castilian Festivals: The Case of Jaén. In *City and Spectacle in Medieval Europe*, edited by Barbara A. Hanawalt and Kathryn L. Reyerson, pp. 296–318. Medieval Studies at Minnesota Vol. 6. Minneapolis: University of Minnesota Press.

Rymsdyk, Jan van and Andreas van Rymsdyk

1778 *Museum Britannicum*, Vol. I. London: Moore.

Ryzewski, Krysta (ed.)

2009 Experience, Modes of Engagement, Archaeology. *Archaeologies* 5(3).

Sabloff, Jeremy A.

1975 Excavations at Seibal: Ceramics. In *Excavations at Seibal, Department of Peten, Guatemala*. General Editor, Gordon R. Willey. Memoirs of the Peabody Museum of Archaeology and Ethnology Memoirs vol 13, no. 2. Cambridge, MA: Harvard University.

Satterthwaite, Jr., Linton,

1943 *Piedras Negras Archaeology: Architecture, Part 1, No. 1, Introduction.* Philadelphia: University Museum, University of Pennsylvania.

2005 [1943] Architecture: Introduction. In *Piedras Negras Archaeology, 1931–1939*, edited by John M. Weeks, Jane A. Hill, and Charles Golden, 155–183. Philadelphia: University of Pennsylvania Museum of Archaeology and Anthropology.

Saturno, William A., David Stuart, and Boris Beltrán

2006 Early Maya Writing at San Bartolo, Guatemala. *Science* 311(5765): 1281–1283.

Schiffer, Brian

1976 *Behavioral Archaeology*. New York: Academic Press.

1988 The Structure of Archaeological Theory. *American Antiquity* 53: 461–485.

Schnapp, Jeffrey, Michael Shanks, and Matthew Tiews (eds.)

2004 *Archaeologies of the Modern: A Special Issue of Modernism/Modernity* 11(1).

Schlegel, Gerhard and James Hogg, eds.

2004 *Monasticon Cartusiense* Band II, *Analecta Cartusiana* 185:2. Salzburg: Instutut für Anglistik und Amerikanistik, Universität Salzburg

Scott, Walter Sir

1814 *The Border Antiquities of England and Scotland; Comprising Specimens of Architecture and Sculpture, and Other Vestiges of Former Ages, Accompanied By Descriptions. Together With Illustrations of Remarkable Incidents in Border History and Tradition, and Original Poetry, 2 Volumes.* London: Printed for Longman, Hurst, Rees, Orme, and Brown.

1892 *Waverly, or, 'Tis Sixty Years Since.* London: Adam and Charles Black.

1892 *Guy Mannering, or, The Astrologer.* London: Adam and Charles Black.

1893 *Ivanhoe: A Romance.* London: Adam and Charles Black.

Serres, Michael

1995 *Genesis.* Translated by Genevieve James and James Nielson. Ann Arbor: University of Michigan Press.

Shanks, Michael

1996   *Classical Archaeology of Greece: Experiences of the Discipline*. London: Routledge.

1997   Photography and Archaeology. In *The Cultural Life of Images: Visual Representations in Archaeology*, edited by Brian Leigh Molyneaux, 73–97. London: Routledge.

1999   *Art and the Early Greek City State*. Cambridge: Cambridge University Press.

2004   Three Rooms. *Journal of Social Archaeology* 4: 147–180.

2006   The Three Landscapes Project. Electronic document, http://documents.stanford. edu/MichaelShanks/62, last accessed August 8, 2010.

2007   Digital Media, Agile Design and the Politics of Archaeology. In *Archaeology and the Media*, edited by Timothy Clack and Marcus Brittain, 273–289. Walnut Creek, CA: Left Coast Press.

2008   Deep Mapping. Electronic document, http://documents.stanford.edu/MichaelShanks/51, last accessed August 8, 2010.

2009   *The Archaeological Imagination*. Walnut Creek, CA: Left Coast Press.

Shanks, Michael and Randall McGuire

1996   The Craft of Archaeology. *American Antiquity* 61: 75–88.

Shanks, Michael and Christopher Tilley

1987   *Re-constructing Archaeology: Theory and Practice*. Cambridge: Cambridge University Press.

1993   *Reconstructing Archaeology: Theory and Practice*. New Studies in Archaeology. 2nd edition. London: Routledge.

Shapin, Steven

1984   Pump and Circumstance: Robert Boyle's Literary Technology. *Social Studies of Science* 14: 481–520.

1998   Placing the View from Nowhere: Historical and Sociological Problems in the Location of Science. *Transactions of the Institute of British Geographers* n.s. 23(1): 5–12.

Siewiorek, Dan, Asim Smailagic and Thad Starner

2008   *Application Design for Wearable Computing*. San Rafael, CA: Morgan and Claypool Publishers.

Sloterdijk, Peter and Bruno Latour

2009   Spheres and Networks: Two Ways to Reinterpret Globalization. Paper presented at the Harvard University Graduate School of Design, February 17, 2009, Cambridge, MA.

Smiles, Sam

1994   *The Image of Antiquity: Ancient Britain and the Romantic Imagination*. New Haven, CT: Yale University Press.

2000   *Eye Witness: Artists and Visual Documentation in Britain, 1770–1830*. Aldershot: Ashgate.

Smiles, Sam and Stephanie Moser (eds.)

2005   *Envisioning the Past: Archaeology and the Image*. Oxford: Blackwell.

Smith, Albert C.

2004   *Architectural Model as Machine: A new view of models from antiquity to the present day*. Oxford: Architectural Press.

Smith, A. Ledyard

1950   *Uaxactun Guatemala: Excavations of 1931–1937*. Carnegie Institution of Washington, Publication 588. Washington, DC: Carnegie Institution of Washington.

1962   Residential and Associated Structures at Mayapan. In *Mayapan, Yucatan, Mexico*, edited by H. E. D. Pollock, Ralph L. Roys, Tatiana Proskouriakoff, and A. Ledyard Smith, pp. 165–319. Carnegie Institution of Washington, Publication 619. Washington, DC: Carnegie Institution of Washington.

1972   *Excavations at Altar de Sacrificios: Architecture, Settlement, Burials and Caches*. Papers of the Peabody Museum of Archaeology and Ethnology vol. 62, no. 2. Cambridge, MA: Harvard University.

1982   Major Architecture and Caches. In *Excavations at Seibal, Department of Peten, Guatemala*. General Editor, Gordon R. Willey. Memoirs of the Peabody Museum of Archaeology and Ethnology Memoirs vol 15, no. 1. Cambridge, MA: Harvard University.

Smith, Monica L.

2005   Networks, Territories, and the Cartography of Ancient States. *Annals of the Association of American Geographers* 95(4): 832–849.

Sorrel, Alan

1981   *Reconstructing the Past*. Edited by Martin Sorrel. London: Batsford.

Spier, Jo

1978   *Dat alles heeft mijn Oog gezien: Herinneringen aan het concentratiekamp, Theresienstadt 1942–1945*. Amsterdam: Elsevier.

Spier, Peter

1980   *People*. New York: Doubleday.

1983   *Christmas*. New York: Doubleday.

Spier, Peter, and Alice J. Hall

1975   A Traveler's Tale of Ancient Tikal: A Portfolio of Paintings. *National Geographic* 148(6): 799–811.

Spon, Jacob

1678   *Voyage d'Italie, de Dalmatie, de Grèce et du Levant*. France: Cellier.

Steffen, Bernhard

1884   *Karten von Mykenai*. Berlin: D. Reimer.

Steiner, Melanie

2005   *Approaches to Archaeological Illustration: A Handbook*. London: Council for British Archaeology.

Stewart, Susan

1994   *Crimes of Writing: Problems in the Containment of Representation*. Oxford: Oxford University Press.

Stoneman, Richard

1987   *Land of Lost Gods: The Search for Classical Greece*. Norman: University of Oklahoma Press.

Stuart, David,

 2006   The Story on the Steps: Reconstructing the Text of Copan's Hieroglyphic Stairway. Paper presented at the Peabody Museum Weekend of the Americas, October 13–15. Paper on file at the Peabody Museum of Archaeology and Ethnology. Cambridge, MA: Harvard University.

Sumner, Heywood

 1988   *The Ancient Earthworks of Cranborne Chase*. Stroud: Sutton.

Sylaiou, Stella and Petros Patias

 2004   Virtual Reconstructions in Archaeology and Some Issues for Consideration. *IMEROS* 4. Electronic document, http://www1.fhw.gr/publications/print/imeros/en/04/article01.html#note02, last accessed August 8, 2010.

Szambien, Werner

 1988   *Le Musee d'architecture*. Paris: Picard.

Taylor, Karen T.

 2000   *Forensic Art and Illustration*. Boca Raton, FL: CRC.

Taylor, Rabun M.

      2003 *Roman Builders: A Study in Architectural Process*. Cambridge: Cambridge University Press.

Thomas, Julian

 2004a The Great Dark Book: Archaeology, Experience, and Interpretation. In *A Companion to Archaeology*, edited by John L. Bintliff, 21–36. Oxford: Blackwell.

 2004b *Archaeology and Modernity*. London: Routledge.

Thompson, J. Eric S.

 1962   *A Catalog of Maya Hieroglyphs*. Norman: University of Oklahoma Press.

 1971   Maya Hieroglyphic Writing: An Introduction. Third edition. Norman: University of Oklahoma Press.

Tilley, Christopher

 1989   Excavation as Theatre. *Antiquity* 63: 275–280.

Tokovinine, Alexandre and Barbara Fash

 2008   Scanning History: The Corpus of Maya Hieroglyphic Inscriptions Tests a 3-D Scanner in the Field. *Symbols* (Spring):17–20. Cambridge, MA: Peabody Museum of Archaeology and Ethnology, Harvard University.

Totten, George Oakley

 1926   *Maya Architecture*. Washington, DC: The Maya Press.

Tourtellot, Gair

 1988   Excavations at Seibal, Department of Peten, Guatemala: Peripheral Survey and Excavation—Settlement and Community Patterns. In *Excavations at Seibal, Department of Peten, Guatemala*. Series edited by Gordon R. Willey (general editor). Memoirs of the Peabody Museum of Archaeology and Ethnology, vol. 16. Cambridge, MA: Peabody Museum of Archaeology and Ethnology, Harvard University.

Tozzer, Alfred M.

1911   *A Preliminary Study of the Prehistoric Ruins of Tikal, Guatemala: A Report of the Peabody Museum Expedition, 1909–1910.* Memoirs of the Peabody Museum of American Archaeology and Ethnology, vol. 5, no. 2. Cambridge, MA: Peabody Museum of Archaeology and Ethnology, Harvard University.

1913   *A Preliminary Study of the Prehistoric Ruins of Nakum, Guatemala: A Report of the Peabody Museum Expedition, 1909–1910.* Memoirs of the Peabody Museum of American Archaeology and Ethnology, vol. 5, no. 3. Cambridge, MA: Peabody Museum of Archaeology and Ethnology, Harvard University.

Trimble, Jennifer and Marc Levoy

2002   *Stanford Digital Forma Urbis Romae Project.* Electronic Document, http://formaurbis.stanford.edu/docs/FURproject.html, last accessed August 8, 2010.

Tringham, Ruth, Michael Ashley, and Steve Mills

2007   *Senses of Places: Remediations from text to digital performance.* Electronic Document, http://chimeraspider.wordpress.com/2007/09/19/remediated-places-final-draft/, last accessed August 8, 2010.

Tsountas, Chrēstos [Christos] and John Irving Manatt

1903   *The Mycenaean Age: A Study of the Monuments and Culture of Pre-Homeric Greece.* London: MacMillan.

Tucher, Josiah

1757   *Instructions to Travellers.* Dublin: Printed for William Watson.

Tufte, Edward

1997   *Visual Explanations.* Cheshire, CT: Graphics Press LLC.

2001   *The Visual Display of Quantitative Information.* 2nd edition. Cheshire, CT: Graphics Press LLC.

Turnbull, David

1994   *Maps are Territories: Science is an Atlas.* Chicago. IL: University of Chicago Press.

2000   *Masons, Tricksters and Cartographers: Comparative Studies in the Sociology of Scientific and Indigenous Knowledge.* Amsterdam: Harwood Academic Publishers.

Tversky, Barbara

1999   Spatial Schemes in Depictions. In *Schemas and Abstract Thought*, edited by Merideth Gattis, 9–112. Cambridge, MA: MIT Press.

Vacharopoulou, Kalliopi

2005   Monument Conservation in the Mediterranean: Issues and Aspects of Anastylosis. In *Symposium on Mediterranean Archaeology*, edited by Camilla Briault, Jack Green, Anthi Kaldelis, and Anna Stellatou, 1–10. BAR International Series No. 1391. Oxford: British Archaeological Reports.

van Buren, A. W.

1949   Review of *The Ara Pacis Augustae* by G. Moretti and V. Priestley. *The American Journal of Philology* 70(4): 418–421.

Vingtain, Dominique

1998   *L'abbaye de Cluny: Centre de l'Occident medieval.* Paris: CNRS Editions.

Viollet-le-Duc, Eugène-Emmanuel

   1867–1870 *Dictionnaire raisonné de l'architecture française du XIe au XVIe siècle.* Paris: Morel.

Visualisation in Archaeology

   2009   Visualisation in Archaeology. Electronic document, http://www.viarch.org.uk/, last accessed August 8, 2010.

von Hagen, Victor W.

   1950   *Frerick Catherwood, Architect.* Oxford: Oxford University Press.

Wace, Alan J. B

   1949   *Mycenae: An Archaeological History and Guide.* Princeton, NJ: Princeton University Press.

Wagstaff, Malcolm

   2004   Surveying the Morea: The French Expedition, 1828–1832. In *Travellers in the Near East*, edited by Charles Foster, 167–182. London: Stacey International.

Wark, Robert R.

   1975   *Sir Joshua Reynolds' "Discourses on Art".* New Haven, CT: Yale University Press.

Webmoor, Timothy

   2005   Mediational Techniques and Conceptual Frameworks in Archaeology: A Model in 'Mapwork' at Teotihuacan, Mexico. *Journal of Social Archaeology* 5(1): 52–84.

   2007   What About 'One More Turn After the Social' in Archaeological Reasoning? Taking things seriously. *World Archaeology* 39: 547–562.

   2008   From Silicon Valley to the Valley of Teotihuacan: The 'Yahoo!s' of New Media and Digital Heritage. *Visual Anthropology Review* 24(2): 181–198.

Weeks, John M., Jane A. Hill, and Charles Golden (eds.)

   2005   *Piedras Negras Archaeology, 1931–1939: Piedras Negras Preliminary Papers; Piedras Negras Archaeology: Architecture, by Linton Satterthwaite, Jr., Mary Butler, and J. Alden Mason.* Philadelphia: Museum of Archaeology and Anthropology, University of Pennsylvania.

Wheatley, David and Mark Gillings

   2002   *Spatial Technology and Archaeology: The Archaeological Applications of GIS.* London: Taylor and Francis.

Wheler, George

   1682   *A Journey into Greece.* London: Printed for William Cademan, Robert Kettlewell, and Awnsham Churchill.

White, Gregory G. and Thomas F. King

   2007   *The Archaeological Survey Manual.* Walnut Creek, CA: Left Coast Press.

Whitehall, Walter Muir

   1970   *Museum of Fine Arts Boston: A Centennial History.* Cambridge, MA: Belknap Press.

Whitehead, Alfred North

   1920   *The Concept of Nature.* Cambridge: Cambridge University Press.

Wiber, Melanie G.

   1997   *Erect Men/Undulating Women: The Visual Imagery of Gender, Race, and Progress in Reconstructive Illustrations of Human Evolution.* Waterloo: Wilfred Laurier Press.

Willey, Gordon R.

1972   *The Artifacts of Altar de Sacrificios.* Papers of the Peabody Museum of Archaeology and Ethnology, vol. 64, no. 1. Cambridge, MA: Harvard University.

1988   Portraits in American Archaeology: Remembrances of Some Distinguished Americanists. Albuquerque: University of New Mexico Press.

Willis, Robert

1868   The Architectural History of the Conventual Buildings of the Monastery of Christ Church in Canterbury. *Archaeologia Cantiana* 7: 1–206.

Wise, M. Norton (editor)

1995 *The Values of Precision.* Princeton, NJ: Princeton University Press.

Witmore, Christopher

2004a: On multiple fields: between the material world and media: two cases from the Peloponnesus, Greece. *Archaeological Dialogues* 11(2): 133–164.

2004b   Four Archaeological Engagements with Place: Mediating Bodily Experience through Peripatetic Video. *Visual Anthropology Review* 20(2): 157–172.

2006a   Vision, Media, Noise and the Percolation of Time: Symmetrical Approaches to the Mediation of the Material World. *Journal of Material Culture* 11: 267–292.

2006b   *Archaeology and Modernity,* Or Archaeology and a Modernist Amnesia? *Norwegian Archaeology Review* 39(1): 49–52.

Witmore, Christopher L. and T.V. Buttrey

2008   W.M. Leake: A Contemporary of P.O. Brøndsted in Greece and in London. In *Peter Oluf Brøndsted (1780–1842) A Danish Classicist in his European Context,* edited by Bodil Bundgaard Rasmussen, Jørgen Steetn Jensen, John Lund, and Michael Märcher, 15–34. Copenhagen: The Royal Danish Academy of Sciences and Letters.

Wolf, Josef, and Zdeněk Burian

1978   *The Dawn of Man.* London: Thames and Hudson.

Woodman, Francis

1992   The Waterworks Drawings of the Eadwine Psalter. In *The Eadwine Psalter: Text, Image, and Monastic Culture in Twelfth-Canterbury,* edited by Margaret Gibson, T. A. Heslop, and Richard W. Pfaff, 168–177. London: Modern Humanities Research Association.

Wylie, Alison

2002   *Thinking From Things: Essays in the Philosophy of Archaeology.* Berkeley: University of California Press.

2013   Alison Wylie, with William L. Rathje, Michael Shanks, Timothy Webmoor, and Christopher Witmore. In *Archaeology in the Making: Conversations Through a Discipline,* edited by William L. Rathje, Michael Shanks, and Christopher Witmore, 93–121. New York: Routledge.

Yegül, Fikret

1976   The Marble Court of Sardis and Historical Reconstruction. *Journal of Field Archaeology* 32: 169–194.

Yegül, Fikret, with T. Couch

2003   Building a Roman Bath for the Cameras. *Journal of Roman Archaeology* 16: 153–177.

Index